Valentine's Way

My Adventurous Life and Times

BOBBY VALENTINE
and Peter Golenbock

PERMUTED
PRESS

A PERMUTED PRESS BOOK
ISBN: 978-1-63758-094-3
ISBN (eBook): 978-1-63758-095-0

Valentine's Way:
My Adventurous Life and Times
© 2021 by Bobby Valentine and Peter Golenbock
All Rights Reserved

Permuted Press, LLC
New York • Nashville
permutedpress.com

Published in the United States of America
1 2 3 4 5 6 7 8 9 10

This book is dedicated to all the wonderful people and teachers who have made my life so exciting. My family and friends in Stamford. My teammates, coaches, players, and front office staff from all the teams that I had the opportunity to be with. To the late great Joe Romano and his family. To Paul Pupo, Frank Ramppen and his wife Michelle, Mike Allegra, Tom Kelley, Manganese Balthasar aka Max, and all the hard working people who kept the restaurants going for such a long time. Pete Moore and Paul Checkeye and many others who ran the Texas restaurant operation. A special thanks to Koji Takahashi and Shun Nakasone who made my years in Japan so exciting. My brother Joe, sister-in-law Patti, and their family, and, of course, Mary and Bobby Jr. A final dedication to a few who are no longer with us. Thank you to Chris Sabia, Ann and Ralph Branca, Mickey Lione, Tom Robson, Billy Buckner, my mom, Grace, my dad, Joe, and one last time to Tommy Lasorda.

UNIVERSITY OF SOUTHERN CALIFORNIA

DEPARTMENT OF INTERCOLLEGIATE ATHLETICS

UNIVERSITY PARK   •   LOS ANGELES, CALIFORNIA 90007

February 20, 1968

TELEPHONE: 746-2751
746-2754

Mr. Robert Valentine
735 Stillwater Road
Stamford, Connecticut

Dear Bob:

As I told you on the telephone, we are pleased to offer you a football scholarship to the University of Southern California. The scholarship is as follows:

(1)	Full tuition	$1800.00 per year
(2)	Room & Board	1100.00 per year
(3)	Health service fees	33.00 per year
(4)	Christmas vacation; period between semester, spring vacation employment on campus.	200.00 + per year
(5)	Tutoring upon request	

All our scholarships are for four years and naturally are not terminated because of injury. Also you would be able to participate in both football and baseball.

Our conference letter of intent is not issued until early May; the national letter comes out a short time later. You will receive both of these from us.

We only choose 24 men for our frosh squads-thus you are one of a very select group.

I'm planning on your visiting our campus March 8-9-10, as we discussed on the phone. You will hear from me soon regarding the particulars of this visit.

Bob, Coach McKay and our staff hope you will decide to wear the Cardinal and Gold of the Trojans.

Sincerely,

Phil Krueger

PHIL KRUEGER
Assistant Football Coach

PK/cn

CONTENTS

INTRODUCTION

I am a very lucky guy, and my luck began on October 10, 1910, when my grandfather, John Valentine, left Ellis Island and headed for Stamford, Connecticut. John was a mechanic from Naples, Italy, who had fifteen dollars in his pocket, according to the manifest I received from Governor George Pataki in 2001, when I was Grand Marshal of the Columbus Day parade in New York City.

Like many immigrants of that era, my family did not talk about the place they'd left because they were so excited about the new opportunities that lay ahead. My mom and dad met in the self-proclaimed "Baseball Capital of the World," and I am so fortunate they did. The wooden outfield wall at Cubeta Stadium, where I played many of my youth games, had this slogan plastered across center field: *Welcome to Stamford...The Baseball Capital of the World*. Baseball was played and enjoyed in Stamford from the early 1900s, and many of the early immigrants, especially after the war, used baseball as a rite of passage. I owe a debt of gratitude to those who came before me and to my friends and unbelievably supportive family that helped me along the way.

All four of my grandparents spoke Italian and very little English. They all passed away during my childhood. My dad's mom was the last to go. Her three-family house in the center of the town was the gathering place for Sunday dinner with most of the family. I remember watching the Beatles on *Ed Sullivan* there with many of my cousins. I also remember my grandma saying, with my Aunt Clemey translating, how proud she was to read a headline with Valentine in it that didn't involve the police. I had just thrown a no-hitter in the Little League All-Star Game, and it made the paper. I felt so happy that she was proud of me.

When I was a teenager, my sports schedule didn't allow time for the family dinners, so my mom took over the cooking. And take over she did. My mom always had a job. She worked a forty-hour week and, along with my dad, who worked at least eighty hours, did everything in her power to run our house well and care for her family. She belonged to all the school, church, and team groups, and was always generous with her time and expertise. Much of what she gave was love to my brother Joey and me. She always went out of her way to make everyone we came in contact with feel like they were part of our family. I said I was lucky, but I would need another entire book to explain just how wonderful my family and friends were to me my entire life.

CHAPTER 1

Growing Up

When my grandparents first arrived in America, Italians were as far down the totem pole as you could get. My uncles and aunts told me they were discriminated against, so they raised their kids *not* to be Italian. My folks were here to be *Americans*. My dad had three brothers and two sisters, while my mom had three brothers, and everyone lived in Stamford.

I was part of a great family unit. My dad Joseph, who did fine carpentry work, was a workaholic who toiled day and night. After working during the day, he went to his workstation in our basement after dinner and did more work!

My mother, Grace, was the greatest mom who ever lived. She cooked for everyone, volunteered in our schools and at church, as well as working a full-time office manager job. She smiled all the time and never missed a pitch, let alone a game.

I was born in Stamford Hospital on May 13, 1950. We lived at 39 Melrose Place, a small five-room house, consisting of my parents' bedroom, the bedroom for my brother and me, a living room with a couch and a TV, a bathroom, and a kitchen where we ate all our meals.

St. Clement's Church was right around the corner. One of the highlights of the summer was attending Stamford Twilight League baseball games after Mass, in which many of the stars of past championship Stamford teams played. There were many: Mickey Lione, Jr., Andy Wasil, Ron Parente, and my future agent, Tony Attanasio, to name a few. I cherish the memories of being at these games with my dad.

My dad was always working, even Sunday after the games, but somehow found the time to be at my games, and I mean every game. I was lucky to have him as a dad. Along with Joe and Mom, they were truly the best team in town.

The Twilight League was the best live baseball I got to see as a kid. I only went to a professional game twice as a youth. I have vague recollections of my first game. I was told it was Yankees–Red Sox, but the only thing I remember was we were behind a steel beam and couldn't see much from deep right field. Obstructed-view seats were sold in those days, and that's what we could afford! The other game came during my senior year in high school, also at Yankee Stadium. More about that later.

My brother Joe, a catcher, was a very good athlete, but his motivation was more about making money. When he was nineteen, he worked as a tool-and-die maker and was able to buy himself a very cool Chevy Chevelle.

Stamford's Waterside, where we grew up, was the perfect place in the 1950s and '60s. It had a Melfair Market, our church, and Southfield Park. There was also a small beach on the Long Island Sound. I never went to the beach. Summertime was for playing baseball. My brother always let me play with him and the older kids in the park, which became my second home once I was able to ride my bicycle there to play with whoever was there. The park's superintendent was Mr. Franchina, who made sure there wasn't too much fighting.

The kids of that era felt they had to have a fight every now and then. They'd meet behind the school or the church, and you would always get wind about who was fighting and where and when. My brother was with a group of guys who could handle themselves.

When I was in junior high school, in the mid-sixties, I snuck into Boyle Stadium to watch a Stamford High football game. After the game, different groups—gangs, you could say—would meet at different locations and duke it out. One of the toughest guys I ever walked past was Julo Jakuti. His German shepherd was even meaner than he was. Julo, who always wore black and had a black motorcycle that you could hear coming from around the corner, would always be in fights, and we'd go watch him fight, for entertainment.

My brother sang in one of those corner doo-wop groups. They cut a record at Playland, an old amusement park in Rye, New York. Jimmy Ienner, an idol of mine, had a group, the Barons. Their record, "Pledge of a Fool," became a hit. Jimmy, along with his brother Donnie, became big in the music industry, and their cousin Joey was the fullback on my high school team in 1967. Jimmy was also one of the toughest guys in town. He came from the Cove, not the West Side, and during one Stamford High game word got around that Jimmy and Julo were going to duke it out over by the oak tree in the parking lot. In front of a crowd of about seventy of us, Jimmy beat the shit out of Julo. *Wow*, I thought. *For a guy who didn't look that tough to be that tough—that is cool.*

Though I was only three years younger than my brother Joe, I was part of the next generation. In 1961, the film adaptation of *West Side Story* had just come out, and everyone decided they needed to form gangs. In Stamford we had a West Side, and many of the Italians lived there. I can't say that they were exactly gangs. The kids who lived in the High Ridge area, kids who were wealthier than we were, formed a club, and so we formed a group to compete with them. We called ourselves the *Gents*. The closest we ever came to a rumble was an egg fight. We stole eggs out of our parents' refrigerators and met up with the Swells at Chestnut Hill Park, and threw them at each other. Though not many landed, it was still fun.

My graduation from Ryle Elementary School ended with a parent conference. Mrs. Toner, the principal, told my mother and father I would never amount to anything because I fought too much, after which Mom decided I had to have more than sports and fights in my life, and convinced me to take ballroom dancing lessons. Nevertheless, junior high began with a fight in front of the school on day one. After that I stayed out of trouble and played sports in the seventh and eighth grades and on the Babe Ruth League teams in the summer.

John Esposito, my dad's cousin, along with Mike Mancini, coached the Visitations in the Mickey Lione Little League on the West Side of town. My dad would help out when he wasn't working. When I was eight, I was the batboy. If the game got out of hand or someone didn't show up, the coaches would let me play. It wasn't much playing time, but it was a start. I was always the young kid playing with the older kids. Being the youngest gives you an ability to figure out what the older ones are doing.

Little League was great fun. I made the All-Star team as both an eleven-year-old and twelve-year-old. I threw a no-hitter in All-Star play and won the city championship. Friends I made in Little League have lasted a lifetime: Frankie Abbott, Jim Zannino, Ken Dolan, Darrell Atterberry, and more. Crosstown rivals would become lifelong friends. Bobby Castrignano, Bennett Salvatore, and so many more of the friends I have today were guys I wanted to beat in these crosstown rivalries. One of my best friends today, Joe Chiappetta, played in the National Little League with the best player in town, Jimmy Sabia.

I think I was the first thirteen-year-old to make the All-Star team in the Babe Ruth League. I was in the ninth grade when I played for Rippowam High School. I was probably the only junior in high school to play in the Cape Cod League. I was a nineteen-year-old in the major leagues, and I was only thirty-five when I became a big-league manager.

Being younger than everyone else is a theme. It's also a badge of honor. Two of the other themes in this book are that I had mentors who helped me, and that I was really, really lucky. Serendipitous things happened in my life that I had no control over—I had *nothing* to do with them—but I was the benefactor.

When I was thirteen, I moved up to Babe Ruth, a league for thirteen-to fifteen-year-olds. The coach of my Holy Name team was Stanley Barosky. The All-Star coach was John "Sharkey" Laureno, a legendary figure in Stamford. Sharkey had coached the Stamford team that won the first three Babe Ruth League World Series in 1952, '53 and '54. When the team arrived in Austin, Texas, for the 1955 championship, Sharkey was told his two black players weren't allowed to stay at the same hotel as the white kids. Sharkey would always say with pride that he kept the team together and arranged to have them stay at Bergstrom Air Force Base.

We learned more baseball fundamentals from Sharkey and his two assistants, Al Judge and Stosh Barosky—my brother married his daughter—than most kids in the majors know today. We also learned from Sharkey that talent topped race. It was a very important lesson that has always stayed with me.

Sharkey Laureno graced my life by almost adopting me. He took me in as a player when I was thirteen. He was spectacular to me, and with him as my coach I somehow was able to make the Babe Ruth League All-Star team my first year, even though I had just moved from sixty-foot bases to ninety-foot bases. All of a sudden it was a whole different world.

The team got really hot when I was fourteen. We had Jimmy Sabia, the best pitcher in town. Jimmy and Joey Chiappetta had played on the best Little League team, but now we were teammates. I played center field and batted third. I stole bases, hit home runs, and racked up hits. I also pitched. At fourteen, I was coming into my own and had a really big year. I could run faster than everyone else, and I began to get a lot of publicity.

We beat Torrington, Connecticut, for the state championship, then went to Sanford, Maine, for the New England championships. We traveled on a school bus driven by Al Lopiano, who owned the greatest hot dog and hamburger joint in Stamford, called Al's Doghouse. For years, when a Babe Ruth team traveled out of the city, Al drove. We stopped at the best places: A&W had great root beer and hot dogs. It was a tremendous bonding experience. The bus rides were a prelude to my bus rides in the minor leagues. Our parents would follow the bus in a caravan of cars.

We won the regional championship in Maine, and then flew on United Airlines to Woodland, California, for the Babe Ruth League World Series. When we got there, we stayed in foster homes.

We lost by a close score in the first game, and then we played a team from Klamath Falls, Oregon. We'd never heard of Klamath Falls. *They must not play much baseball there*, we surmised.

We were wrong. I pitched, walked the ballpark, and gave up a couple of home runs. It was the only time in Sharkey Laureno's career that he was second-guessed, because he didn't pitch Jimmy Sabia. He was holding Jimmy back so he could pitch against Ken Brett's El Segundo, California, team, the favorite going in.

Ken Brett, George Brett's older brother, was a very mature fifteen-year-old who pitched a no-hitter and hit a couple of home runs to win the tournament.

The loss was heartbreaking, but the event was unforgettable. There was a parade. We sat in convertibles going down the main street. A couple of big-leaguers threw out the first pitch. And even though I blew that last game, I was named to the all-tournament team. After, we got to go to Disneyland and to Dodger Stadium, and over the years all the guys would comment and reflect that it was one of the greatest experiences of their lives. Mine, too. While in COVID lockdown, I located a box of old tapes with footage from the Babe Ruth League and dance clips which can be seen on YouTube. Ha!

Growing up, playing sports at school was what was most important to me. I was just a kid as events swirled around me, taking me on a path that, left to my own devices, I could never have imagined. My good luck continued in a big way when the city of Stamford closed my junior high the summer between eighth and ninth grades. Because of that, I went to high school as a ninth-grader, which wasn't as common then as it is now.

As an eighth-grader I played baseball for Cloonan, the most diverse junior high school in town. The kids from my side of town—working-class Italians, Polish kids, and African Americans—all went to Cloonan. Ordinarily, after graduating from the ninth grade we were scheduled to go to Stamford High School, but when Cloonan closed in 1964, the students were dispersed to other schools. The ninth-graders were split between two high schools: Stamford High and Rippowam. The other option was Stamford Catholic High, but the entrance test fell on the same day as the international ballroom dance championships in Miami, Florida. I chose to dance in the competition. The nun in charge of testing would not reschedule, thus making the decision for me to go to public high school.

My desire was to attend Rippowam High School and play baseball for Ron Parente. The problem was that I didn't live in the Rippowam district. It wasn't going to be easy for us to find a legal way for me to go there. My dad never, ever wanted to do anything wrong. He never drove over the speed limit and never did anything that could be considered unlawful by anyone. He was from that generation of Italians who were going to stay in line and always do the right thing. Looking back, I was in awe of him. He never smoked, never drank, and I hardly ever heard him curse until I was an adult. Even then it was limited. He adored my mom and really cared and lived for Joe and me.

Once Sharkey Laureno and Ron Parente convinced my dad and mom that it was important for me to go to Rippowam and play for Ron, my dad decided to sell our house and move into the Rippowam district.

My cousin Richie agreed to buy our house for $19,000. Richie, unfortunately, didn't have enough for the down payment, though he promised he would have it in a year. So in order to go to Rippowam legally, my freshman year I lived with my grandparents at 25 Irving Avenue in Southfield Village, a government housing project on the Rippowam side of the line. I gave my grandparents' address as my home, and I lived with them a lot that year.

Looking back at what was the nexus of my success, I still wonder, *How did that happen?* Because it turned out that Ron Parente was *absolutely the perfect person* for me to have as a coach and mentor. He was an Italian who had played Triple-A baseball and had a dignified and scholarly demeanor. He understood my situation better than I, and I thought it was cool that some of his friends were the Jewish teachers from the high school, one of whom was the football coach, Al Shanen.

Al and his wife Barbara, and Al's sister Sondra Melzer and her husband Frank, a local lawyer, pretty much adopted me. Sondra, just about the most spectacular woman who ever lived, was the head of the English department. Sondra convinced me to take Latin for four years so I could get good scores on the SAT tests. She convinced me to go out for the lead in the class play so I would have diversity in my life and be more than a jock. These wonderful people were more than part of my family. They cared for me as much as they cared for their own children. Their kids even resented me a little bit for it, as they should have.

They cared for me. They knew I had potential but needed their help to attain success, and they wanted me to be well-rounded, and I took their lead. Being a jock was easy for me. All that other stuff was hard. But I had goals I doubt I could have achieved without them. I wanted to score high on the SATs. I wanted to be recruited by Yale. I wanted to get into Dartmouth or the University of Pennsylvania. Not for me—I wasn't that excited about the Ivy League—but for *them*. *They* put in the time. *They* deserved the reward.

I tried to be as diverse as I could. There was a time when I thought I would be a lawyer, which was Sondra Melzer's vision for me. I also wanted to be a professional dancer. I started in Bill DeFormato's dance school in 1962. Bill paired me with an older girl, Pam Dempsey, and we started to win contests. We won a regional contest, went to the Nationals, and then the Internationals at the Fontainebleau hotel in Miami. We got to perform at the opening of the New York World's Fair in 1964. Six couples practiced for a month in synchronized fashion performing the Viennese waltz to "Moon River." We were outstanding and received a standing ovation. Pam and I talked of entering a contest at Coney Island, where the winning team received a fifty-dollar prize, until Parente interjected.

"You might not be able to play college sports if they consider dancing a sport and you get paid for it," he said. The risk was too great, he said. I didn't enter.

I had played very little competitive football before entering Rippowam. My football career was supposed to start in the Pop Warner League. I went through all the practices, and then the day before the first game, the coach demanded that everyone get a crewcut. I had a big wavy pompadour that I really liked, and I told my father I wasn't going to cut it or show up for the game. He didn't object, and I did not play.

The only football I played prior to high school was at Southfield Park with the older guys, mostly because they owned a football. Sandlot football is tackle without equipment, and it was nice that my brother and his friends let me play. I never got hurt badly because I was faster and quicker than just about anyone else there. I didn't get tackled very often.

Al Shanen convinced Ron and my dad that high school football was safe and I should play. He was a great coach and a better salesman. Most ninth-graders played on the JV team, but Parente, the varsity baseball coach, and Shanen, the varsity football coach, were close, and together they decided that to keep me from getting injured, I would not play on the JV team. Instead, I dressed for the varsity games so I could learn all of Al's plays. I played little, but the first time I got in a game, I returned a kickoff for a touchdown against Staples High School.

I started on the varsity baseball team at shortstop, which Ron felt was my best position. I became the first freshman ever selected as an all-county shortstop, so Ron's judgment was validated. I was playing with kids who were as much as three years older. I was so young and lucky, because the captains—Kip Atfield, a home-run hitter who later became a vice president in the Tandy Corporation, and Dennis Eveleigh, who became a Connecticut Supreme Court justice—were really good to me. They enjoyed my being part of the team when they easily could have been resentful, because it was their team and I was the new guy. It was okay for me to lead the baseball team in hitting.

I came into my own as a football player my sophomore year, playing with a great group of upperclassmen. In the first game, I scored four touchdowns. I scored twenty-four touchdowns that year and made first-team all-state. Our chief crosstown rival, Stamford Catholic, was also undefeated. This created an interesting dynamic in town. We hadn't played each other that year. Our last game that year was against Notre Dame of West Haven, which we won 50–16. I scored four touchdowns. I like to think that's why we were awarded the Waskowitz Trophy, given out by the *New Haven Register* to the best football team in the state.

Our baseball team continued to improve in my sophomore year. But more importantly, the stage was set for a football showdown in the fall. Rippowam and Stamford Catholic were undefeated again at the end of my junior season. The Fairfield County high schools were divided into two divisions, East and West. Rippowam won the West and Catholic High won the East. After we had each completed two undefeated seasons, we would now meet for the conference championship.

We played at Boyle Stadium in front of 12,000 people, the biggest crowd I'd ever played in front of. We could hardly get the team bus to the stadium. Playing Catholic High was like playing Notre Dame. They had a large squad of fifty. Their coaches, Bobby Horan and Lenny Rivers, were excellent. The legendary Mickey Lione, Jr. was on their sidelines. They had ponchos for the cold, in the colors of the Green Bay Packers, and the priests were there on the sidelines cheering them on.

We were a rather new school, started in 1961. The city was growing, and to meet the needs, Rippowam became the second public high school in town. We were only a six-year-old program.

In the first half, our quarterback, Johnny Baran, who was also a defensive back, broke his ankle but continued to play. Johnny was a good guy, someone who would do anything for the team. His primary target was Tom McCrocklin, a spectacular athlete who went on to play basketball at the University of Connecticut.

Darrell Atterberry was the heart of our defense. He also played offensive guard. Most of us played both offense and defense. Darrell was my close friend from Little League since age ten. He was the only black player on the All-Star team. At the beginning of the second half, he was knocked silly with a concussion, which impaired his life going forward. Darrell loved to stick his head into the runner, and on a screen pass with three blockers in front of the runner, Darrell broke up the lead blockers and made the tackle. The Catholic players had yellow helmets, and Darrell was hit helmet-to-helmet, ending up with the biggest paint mark on his helmet we had ever seen. He didn't play the second half; he was marching up and down the sideline wondering what day of the week it was. I wish we had known then what we know now about head injuries. Darrell was the co-captain and my best friend, and this was the first time we were not on the field together in over two seasons.

At the half we were winning 6–0. The only touchdown we scored was when a lineman recovered a fumble in the end zone. We almost scored a second touchdown when I fumbled and Joey Chiappetta recovered it in the end zone. It should have been a touchdown, but the referee ruled my knee was down before I fumbled.

In the second half, with our defense weakened, Stamford Catholic came out throwing screen passes over our linebackers, and we lost 32–6. They were state champs. The interesting thing about the game, when you looked at the total yardage, it was about the same. But the better team won. Guys that played in that game have had a lifelong bond. Some of my best friends today, including Rick Robustelli and Bennett Salvatore, played that day for Stamford Catholic.

My junior year for baseball was 1967. The other memorable activity that year for me was taking the advice of Sondra Melzer and winning the lead in the play *The Teahouse of the August Moon*. Marlon Brando was the lead in the film version. The role was that of a Japanese interpreter for the U.S. military during the American occupation of Okinawa after World War II. My name was Sakini, and some of my lines were spoken in Japanese. How ironic it was that I later would spend seven years in Japan with a Japanese interpreter at my side while I was trying to occupy the world of Japanese baseball.

I was planning on spending the summer playing in the newly formed Senior Babe Ruth League. Instead, my lucky star was shining bright, and I spent that summer playing in the prestigious Cape Cod Baseball League, a summer league for the best college players in the country. I might not have been the *only* high school kid to play in the history of the league—Tom Grieve may have as well—but there weren't many of us.

Billy O'Connor, a great basketball player from Stamford and, at the time, an assistant basketball coach at Providence College, was home for Easter break. Billy was the nephew of Andy Robustelli, the All-Pro and Hall of Fame defensive end and later general manager of the New York Giants, who lived in Stamford. Every Italian and most Stamfordites worshiped the ground he walked on. Billy invited the assistant baseball coach at Providence, Lou Lamoriello, to come to dinner at Andy's house. Lou went on to have a Hall of Fame career in hockey, winning three Stanley Cup championships as general manager of the New Jersey Devils. Today he is GM of the New York Islanders. Anyway, during dinner Andy convinced Lou to stay an extra day to watch Bennett Salvatore, who would later marry one of Andy's daughters, play a baseball game. I was on the other team.

Lou, who was twenty-four, was going to be the first-year manager of the South Yarmouth Indians team in Cape Cod. I had one of those days, hitting and running and making plays. At game's end, Lou found my mom and dad, and he proposed that I play for him that summer. I'm sure my dad had no idea where Cape Cod was. My mom might have had an idea, only because my Aunt Doris might have mentioned it once or twice.

We didn't give him an immediate answer. Ron Parente had to give his blessing, but before I knew it, my dad was dropping me off to play baseball with college stars in Yarmouth, Massachusetts.

It was a glorious summer. I hung around with the college guys, though I hardly did anything they did. They took care of me. Buddy Pepin, our second baseman from UConn, made sure if I was making a road trip in the trunk of a car that I wasn't left there during batting practice. I lived with a family for two months and roomed with Dan DeMichele, the first baseman from Harvard who also played hockey. Dan had a car, so I could get to practice.

One of the memorable people I played against was Thurman Munson. He was with Chatham, a team that also featured UConn pitcher Ed

Baird. In one of my first games, Baird was pitching and Thurman was catching. Their center fielder was George Greer, an All-American, also from UConn, who had an illustrious college coaching career at Wake Forest and then went on to become the hitting coach for the St. Louis Cardinals. George was batting third, and I was in center field, and I made a good running catch in left-center, right against the fence, to end the inning.

I was leading off the next inning and standing beside the batter's box, timing Baird as he was warming up, just as we did in high school. As Thurman threw a ball back, he said, "Don't stand there and time the pitcher, because this pitcher might hit you in the head if you keep timing him like that."

"Yes, sir," I said.

Baird threw six or seven warm-up pitches. While Thurman was throwing them back, he never shut up.

"Hey," he said, "I hear you're a high school kid, and that was a really good catch you made, and hey, you know what I want you to do?"

"What?" I said.

"Next inning when I get up, go stand where you made that catch. I'm going to hit one over your head."

As he's talking to me, I'm thinking, *Catchers aren't supposed to talk to me. He's on the other team.*

I grounded out, and when I came back to the bench, I said to Buddy Pepin, "Who's the catcher? God, he talks a lot."

Buddy told me his name, but it was such a foreign-sounding name I paid no attention.

I took the field the next inning. The first hitter hit the first pitch deep into left-center. I ran to make the catch but soon realized that it was going out of the park. I slowed down and looked back at the infield. The batter was rounding second base looking out at me. I caught his eye and realized it was the catcher. When I got back to the bench, I asked Buddy again what the guy's name was. "Thurman Munson," he repeated. I never forgot his name again.

I didn't write many letters that summer, but I wrote one to one of my best friends and high school teammate, Joe Chiappetta, and I told him about this player who called his shot. Fast-forward to the early 2000s, when I was awarded the Thurman Munson Award at the Waldorf Astoria Hotel. I told the story, and Thurman's wife Diana was in tears. Diana told me later that Thurman often told that story, though few believed him and thought he was making it up. Thirty years later I was telling the world it was true.

The next time I heard his name was in June the following year. We turned on the news late at night on Channel 11, WPIX, and that's when I heard the Yankees had drafted Thurman Munson.

"Dad," I said, "that's the catcher from Cape Cod who said he would hit a home run over my head, and then did."

The night before I played my last football game against Stamford High, Darrell Atterberry, our co-captain, and I took my brother's car and went to the pep rally in their auditorium. We looked through the doors, and my likeness, complete with uniform, was being hanged on the stage. Everyone was cheering as the Stamford players each punched the Valentine dummy. I was infuriated, and as I drove Darrell to his home, we vowed to each other that they were going to pay a price.

To prevent injury, Coach Shanen had limited how many times I was allowed to carry the ball. As we were leaving Rippowam to get on the bus to go to Stamford High, I said to Al, "Coach, please, let me carry the ball thirty times today. I want to score six touchdowns." As it turned out, I scored six touchdowns, every way you could score one—ran back a kickoff, returned a punt, caught a pass, ran through the line of scrimmage—and the first time I touched the ball was an intercepted pass that I ran in for a touchdown.

With five minutes elapsed in the third quarter, I came out of the game. The more important game, however, was a rematch against Stamford Catholic. We were ahead 12–0, and in the last five minutes they scored two touchdowns on Bennett Salvatore passes. We lost 16–12. I rushed for over 200 yards and left it all on the field, but it wasn't enough.

My senior year I was getting a lot of attention with scholarship offers, and with my flying around the country to visit colleges, I was the target of criticism the second half of the season. I was accused of being selfish. The publicity was getting to be too much. I didn't like the feeling. I was getting too much attention, so during the last three or four games when Coach Shanen would call my number near the goal line, I would switch positions with the other halfback and let him go in for the touchdown. Bruce Alter, our quarterback, would give the ball to Anthony Zezima or Bob Palo. After we scored, Coach Shanen would take us aside, ask us what we were doing, and scream at us for changing the play, even though our intentions were good.

For three years I was inundated with college scholarship offers. They didn't come to me. Al Shanen conducted all of the college recruitment that I went through, talked to the college coaches, planned the trips, and booked me on flights so I could visit and get back in time for the game. Al, his sister Sondra, and my mom were secretaries bringing order to my life for almost two years. Al read every letter, and there were hundreds of them. He weeded out the weak and presented me with those he felt were important. Notre Dame, Miami, Nebraska, and USC, along with many of the Ivy and ACC schools, were given high priority.

As though my life wasn't busy enough with sports, AP courses, ballroom dancing, and learning lines for school plays, I also had the interests normal to most teenagers. My first girlfriend was an Italian girl, Ana Romano. She was a spectacular person who was ready to give up her life to be my sidekick. Ana lived in one of the government projects in Stamford. Her dad was a police officer. Her mom was a wonderful stay-at-home mom, a great cook, and a great person. Ana invited me to the Sadie Hawkins dance, but a girl asking a boy on a date was not something my mom approved of. As a result, our relationship was always a bit secretive. We dated until I was twenty and I then had to make a decision between her and my other high school sweetheart, Roxana Sisson. But Ana shines brightly in my heart to this day.

Roxy was the head cheerleader. She was slender, attractive, and lived in a world that was foreign to me. Her dad was a Dartmouth grad who worked in corporate America. Her mom was an elementary school teacher in Stamford. Her grandmother was an amazing woman from the other side of the tracks. Roxy was Protestant, and her family did not have the same immigrant background as mine. Nonetheless, we both respected each other's backgrounds and were excited by the mix of our differences. Her family's biggest holiday was Thanksgiving. Their house was one hundred years old, and there was heirloomed silverware on the table and books all over the place. They recognized the authors and quoted some poetry, and it was a world I wanted to understand with her, so she was my conduit. Roxy was such an absolutely amazingly smart gal, and she was intrigued by the side of the tracks I came from. She embraced my ethnicity, and she and her parents loved my mom and dad, even though my mom and dad didn't totally understand their world.

There was actually a third girl in my young dating life: Diane Martino, whom I took to the junior prom. She was the daughter of a bank president. Amazingly, many decades later I connected with her daughter, who coaches basketball at Sacred Heart University. Diane and I are friends to this day.

Roxy and I married, then divorced, but Roxy has always been in my life. Even after our divorce, she was loyal and supportive during the difficult period of my shattered leg and medical malpractice situation, but more about that later.

I graduated from Rippowam in June of 1968. My parents threw me the party of the decade, with a big white sheet cake large enough to feed a couple hundred guests. They wrapped hundreds of sandwiches and hired a live band, making it a night to remember for me and all my friends.

It was the Sixties. I was doing a lot, and it was all turning out very, very well.

CHAPTER 2

College Bound

'd been accepted to every university I applied to, and now it was decision time. In addition to my athletics, I was in the Key Club, the Junior Kiwanis Club doing good things in and for the community, and I was president of the student body. I was the lead in the class play, and I was the only three-time all-state football player and four-time all-county baseball player in Connecticut history. I also set state records in the 60- and 300-yard dashes in indoor track. My College Boards were 1260. It was four years of Latin along with college-prep math that earned me the good scores on the Boards. During my junior and senior years, I was always scouted during my baseball games. I think my last baseball game was about a week before the 1968 professional draft.

I visited three Ivy League schools: Dartmouth, Penn, and Yale. I met with Dartmouth head football coach Bob Blackman primarily because I was dating Roxy, and her dad, Dale, had gone there. I was also recruited by Bobby Odell, the University of Pennsylvania coach. Penn had a really good football team, and Franklin Field was one of those stadiums that stuck out in my mind as a cool place, cooler than the Yale Bowl. *Two* owners of major league baseball teams recommended that I go to Penn. Each said I should go to college rather than sign professionally—that I should get my education first. One was Dodger owner Walter O'Malley, who went to Penn and was doing his alumni duty, and the other was Michael Burke, the president of the Yankees.

Mr. Burke invited me to come to Yankee Stadium to watch a game. He said he had heard I was a Yankee fan, and he wanted to treat me to a Yankee game and try to convince me to go to the University of Pennsylvania, even though my dream was to play for the Yankees. Stamford wasn't far from New York, and the Yankee scouts had been all over me, as had been the Mets scouts.

When Mr. Burke and I talked on the phone, he said, "Tell me who your favorite Yankee is."

"Of course it's Mickey Mantle," I said.

"I will arrange for a photograph of you and Mickey," he said.

My Uncle John was so excited he drove down to Canal Street in the city to buy me a sport coat to wear to Yankee Stadium. It became family legend that he came home with two sport coats for seven dollars. They wanted five dollars for one, and he got two for seven. So, for the first time, I wore a sport coat when I got into the town car that Mr. Burke sent for me, and I wore that sport coat while I stood behind the batting cage with the president of the team and watched the Yankees take batting practice.

Mr. Burke brought players over. I got to meet Bobby Richardson, the Yankees second baseman, and shortstop Tony Kubek. He brought over Joe Pepitone, the first baseman, as well.

Finally, Mickey came out of the dugout. It was a day game, and Mickey wasn't at his best late in his career during day games. He wasn't going to stand out in the sun for an hour before the game, that's for sure. He took a little batting practice, and when Mike called him over, Mickey ignored him and walked toward the dugout.

"Mickey, Mickey, Mickey," Mike was saying. The photographer, who was also waiting for Mickey so he could take our picture, ran and caught

Mickey before he entered the dugout, tugged on Mickey's sleeve, and brought him over to me. Mickey put his arm around my shoulder, and just as the photographer snapped the picture, he bent over and whispered in my ear, "I hope you have to go through this shit someday, kid."

Later we became friends. This photo of Mickey whispering in my ear sat at center stage in my uncle's gas station and in my folks' home.

Calvin Hill was the star running back when I visited Yale. Joe Chiappetta came with me, and as we drove to New Haven, I asked him what the big to-do was about going to an Ivy League school. I was getting a great education about higher ed, but I did not quite understand the difference between Ivy and all the others. Joe's sister was older and went to college and was valedictorian of her class and only hung out with kids who were thinking of going to college, so Joe got it, and he kept telling me why college was so important, trying to convince me to go to Yale.

We were sitting in the stands during the game against Harvard, and I said to Joe, "What do you think?"

"What do you mean, 'What do I think?'" he said.

"Do you think I should go to Yale?"

"I wouldn't hesitate," Joe said. "Are you nuts? This is *Yale*. Do you see this stadium? You're going to be playing football in this league, which is the Ivy League, and you're going to break every record there is. You're going to start as a freshman and you're going to play four years, and everyone in this stadium is going to know who you are. Plus, you're going to get a great education."

After the game, we were taken into the locker room to meet Carmen Cozza, the Yale football coach. He introduced me to the admissions director, who said to me, "We really want you here. There's a seat in the class if you want it." Coach Cozza also brought over their star running back, Calvin Hill. He looked at me and said that Yale was the greatest place to go to school. We were very impressed.

On my way to South Bend, Indiana, to visit Notre Dame, I made a stop at the University of Michigan, where I was greeted by head baseball coach Moby Benedict. In all, I made about twenty different college visits, and each time I was greeted by the head coach, including Bear Bryant at Alabama, which was like going to the president's office. I went because Al Shanen told me to go, and when I got to Tuscaloosa, I was surprised to find that Alabama was, well, Alabama. Coach Bryant wasn't wearing his houndstooth hat that I later saw him wear at games, but he was smoking a cigar. I had never seen Alabama play on television prior to my visit. I hadn't seen most of the colleges, because on Saturday afternoons I was playing football.

In Alabama, I felt like I was in a foreign country. The players' accents were really thick, as were the accents of Bear and his coaches. I don't think I understood one thing anybody said to me the entire weekend. I just did a lot of nodding.

I'll translate what I think Bear said. "We don't have many guys from the North playing on our team, but you could be one of them." When I arrived in South Bend for a Saturday-and-Sunday quick trip, I got off the bus and was met by a group of players. I was surprised that Ara Parseghian, the Notre Dame head coach, wasn't there. The guys who met me took me to a cool bar, all hardwood. Joe Theismann, their future star quarterback, sat across from me having a beer.

On Sunday I went to Mass and then went back to the student union to have breakfast. Ara walked in, came over and introduced himself, welcoming me and thanking me for coming. He praised my football ability and told me if I came to Notre Dame, I could start as a sophomore.

"You probably wonder why I didn't meet you the first day you were here," he said.

"I was wondering about that," I said, "because my Aunt Angie is a really big fan, and she really wants your autograph."

I was holding a napkin I wanted him to sign, but he pulled out a small photograph of himself, signed it for Aunt Angie, and handed it to me.

"Bob," he said, "I want you to understand why I didn't meet you yesterday, and why I didn't pamper you the way the other coaches I'm sure did."

I sat there enthralled.

"Because we believe here at Notre Dame that you don't have to sell a Cadillac, and we *are* the Cadillac."

It was very impactful.

It was a snow-covered morning when Ara and I walked out of the student union to meet the man who was going to drive me to the airport. The snow was piled high on each side of the walkway, and as we walked down the stairs, I saw two lines of students standing there. There were six on one side and six on the other. When I walked among these students, I could see that they were among the biggest people I had ever seen in my life.

As I stood amidst this mass of humanity, Ara said to me, "Other than us being the Cadillac, there is another reason for you to come to Notre Dame. Because when you're here"—on cue, the players on the left side of the sidewalk turned so that I was looking at their backs—"if you come to play at Notre Dame, you'll be looking at the backs of these guys. They are our offensive line." I couldn't see over them. Each looked to be over nine hundred pounds. Ara said, "And remember, if you decide to go to that school behind the highway on the West Coast"—he knew I was considering USC—"you'll be looking at the front of these guys. They are our defensive line." The players on the opposite side were just as big, if not bigger.

Ara shook my hand and hugged me. "I'll see you at the Waldorf for our alumni event," he said.

I was interested in going to the University of Southern California because Rod Dedeaux, the head baseball coach, had reached out to Ron Parente, my high school baseball coach, and told him he had a great relationship with John McKay, the USC football coach. Rod said they had decided that if I came to USC, I would be allowed to play freshman baseball and would not have to attend spring football practice. The coming season in 1968 was the first year that NCAA Division I freshman would be allowed to play varsity sports. John McKay wrote me to say I was the first high school football player east of the Mississippi that he was recruiting.

Wow, I thought, *this seems to fit.* And when I got out there, it fit. USC was different from any other college I had visited. After landing at LAX, I was driven to campus, and on the way, I noticed that USC was adjacent to Watts, where there had been riots the year before. I was surprised, because in my mind I saw USC as being the most glorious place in the world. There were burned-down buildings a couple of blocks from campus. On the other side of campus was fraternity row, with the beautiful fraternity and sorority houses that glittered and looked ritzy, like homes in New Canaan. I saw the magnificent Coliseum, which fed my dreams of running in the Olympics, and I saw the football players playing choose-up basketball games and having great fun.

When I went to football practice, I was given USC shorts and track shoes my size. SC was the only place that I was asked to show my ability. I went to the track and got to hand off a baton to Earl McCullouch, lead-leg runner on USC's world record-setting 4 X 110-yard relay team, and later a star for the Detroit Lions in the NFL. I went to a game and got to watch O. J. Simpson play. I knew who O. J. Simpson was. He had just scored three TDs against Notre Dame on national TV, and Howard Cosell mentioned him as a Heisman candidate. I sat in the USC student section of the Coliseum, and O. J. had a hell of a game. Afterward, Coach McKay promised me that if I came to SC, he would give me O. J.'s number and position. I am sure, now, that he told that to all the recruits. I met O. J., and we walked around campus together. For a high school senior, this felt like I had come to heaven.

I was dropped off at a fall baseball game and was introduced to USC catcher Steve Sogge, who also was a quarterback on the football team. He was playing two sports, which I was hoping to do.

While I was sitting in the stands waiting for the game to end, an older, round-faced man came over and tapped me on the shoulder. He said, "Hey, are you Bobby Valentine?"

"Yeah, I am."

"Good," he said. "Take my card and take this."

He handed me a little transistor radio with the word "Dodgers" inscribed on the front of it.

"Don't tell anyone where you got this," he said, "but the Dodgers really like you."

"Thanks a lot," I said.

When I went home, I gave the transistor radio to my Aunt Doris, who lived across the street from us and was a big Dodger fan. I hated the Dodgers. I was a Yankee fan. The first bet I ever made was when I was a seventh-grader at Cloonan Junior High School. The Dodgers were playing the Yankees in the 1963 World Series. During recess, a big-mouthed kid was running around the gym yelling, "The Dodgers are going to sweep the Yankees! The Dodgers are going to sweep the Yankees!"

My cousin Donnie, who knew I, too, had a big mouth, said to me, "Tell him they won't sweep the Yankees, Bobby."

I told him that, and he said to me, "I'll tell you what. I'll bet you five dollars that the Dodgers sweep the Yankees."

I had never had five dollars on my person in my life. I had coins to buy a quart of milk and a pack of cigarettes for my mom, but five dollars wasn't happening. Even so, I stuck out my chest and stuck out my hand, not really knowing what a handshake and a bet meant, and shook his hand.

I watched with trepidation the final two games of the 1963 World Series in our little living room, with our little rabbit-eared black-and-white TV with the aluminum foil on the ends, which my father could masterfully point in the right directions to get the picture. As the twenty-seventh out of the fourth and final game was made, the phone rang. Before I could get to it, my father answered, and he said, "I can't believe what you are saying. But you will get your money." He hung up.

That was the first and last time that my dad had to explain to me there were consequences for actions. I can feel the impact of his belt on my butt right now! Every Monday, I took fifty cents to school to give to that kid, and I had him sign a piece of paper that he had received it. After ten weeks the debt was paid off, and from that day on I hated the

Dodgers. This kid, Joey Ienner, later became my friend and fullback on the Rip football team.

Not long after returning from my trip to California, I signed a letter of intent to go to USC. I was sitting with Al Shanen. Out of respect, he had me call Ara Parseghian. I didn't have the money to make long-distance calls. I don't know who paid for them, the school or Al. Either way, the adventure was over, and I was going to USC! The world was spinning fast.

CHAPTER 3

I'm a Dodger

I signed the letter of intent on February 20 and was given a full scholarship to play football and baseball at the University of Southern California. The scholarship included $1,800 per year for tuition, $1,100 for room and board, $33 health services fee, and $200-plus per year for "spring semester employment," whatever that was. I was taking it all in. It was very exciting, and I tried to share the excitement with as many of my friends and family as possible.

During this time, America was in turmoil. Martin Luther King was murdered on April 4, and Robert Kennedy assassinated on June 5. I was infatuated with the speaking ability of these great leaders, having watched their speeches on television with my family.

On June 7, 1968, Major League Baseball held its amateur draft. I was three weeks into my eighteenth year. We were told the draft began at 6:00 p.m. and to be home that night in case the phone call came. There was no media coverage. We just sat and waited. At about 8:30 the phone rang, and I answered. The voice on the other end introduced himself as Fresco

Thompson, vice president of the Los Angeles Dodgers. He said the hated Dodgers had just drafted me in the first round. "The scouting director will contact you tomorrow," he said. Then he hung up.

WOW! That was it!

I learned that the New York Mets had picked first, taking Tim Foli. Oakland then took Dartmouth pitcher Pete Broberg. Houston took high school catcher Marty Cott third. The Yankees, the team I desperately wanted to play for, were next. To my disappointment, they also took a catcher, the chatterbox college kid out of Kent State whom I knew from the Cape Cod League—Thurman Munson. I was chosen fifth.

Al Campanis, the newly appointed Dodgers general manager, flew to Connecticut the next day. Campanis had been scouting director before his promotion. The Stamford community was really excited for me, including Andy Robustelli, who was a few years away from his induction into the Pro Football Hall of Fame. My dad reached out to Andy to help us with the negotiations. On June 17 I signed a contract for $65,000. To put things in perspective, my dad had bought his dream home two years prior for $29,000.

I signed ten days after I was drafted, and the next day I flew from New York to Salt Lake City. I got off the plane, and a stocky, round-faced man who was vaguely familiar was there to greet me.

"Remember me?" he said. "I'm the guy who gave you the transistor radio. I'm Tommy Lasorda, and I'm going to be your manager."

I arrived in Ogden at night, and Tommy drove me to the Ben Lomond Hotel. I went to my room, all excited that I would have a roommate. I opened the door and said, "Hey, I'm your roommate."

He was in bed, and I woke him up.

"Who gives a shit?" he said. "I'll talk to you in the morning."

Tom Paciorek had just played in the College World Series for the University of Houston, was an All-American football and baseball player in college, and the Dodgers' fifth-round pick in the draft.

In the morning, I went to see Lasorda, who had me call both Rod Dedeaux, the USC baseball coach, and John McKay, the football coach. Tommy was close friends with Rod.

The conversation started with Tommy saying, "Rod, I got your boy." There was laughter, and then he put me on the phone. The next day Tommy called Rod Dedeaux back to tell him the Dodgers had drafted another highly rated USC prospect, Bill Buckner, in the second round. Buck, like me, was just out of high school. He was a little older than me, but not by much. He had been really upset he wasn't the number-one pick, and rightly so. He held out until I signed, to make sure he got every penny he could.

My next calls were to my girlfriends, Roxy and Ana. I had to go to a phone booth with my coins, putting five quarters in the slot for the first three minutes. I would make a lot of phone calls to Ana and Roxy.

Over the next few days, more Ogden players arrived. One of them was Steve Garvey, who was from Michigan State University. Steve showed up with all his shirts monogrammed SPG (Steven Patrick Garvey), either on the cuff or on the breast pocket. I had never seen a monogrammed shirt before. His shoes were always shined. My roomie, Tom Paciorek, had also gone to college, but I doubt if he had *one pair* of dress pants. He had shorts and t-shirts and a pair of running shoes that he wore every day. Garvey wore pressed and starched dress shirts when he traveled on the team bus. I don't think he ever slept on the bus, because he didn't want to wrinkle any of his shirts. I loved Garv. It was just who Garv was. I think of him as a friend today, but he sure was different. Garv had his act together, while the rest of us were trying to create our acts.

There's a backstory that is important for you to understand. The backstory is that the 1968 draft was being acclaimed as the greatest Dodger draft ever. In addition to Garvey (who had been the first pick in the supplemental draft), Buck, and me, we also had a high-draft-choice pitcher, Sandy Vance—a real hard thrower out of Stanford—and we had Paciorek, a hitting machine who left us halfway through the season for the A-League Dodger team in Bakersfield. This remarkable draft also included Ron Cey, Joe Ferguson, Geoff Zahn, Doyle Alexander, and Davey Lopes. Most believe this was the best draft in the history of MLB.

The scouting director and the man who had orchestrated most of the 1968 draft was Al Campanis, and Al's guy was Tommy Lasorda. Al had campaigned for Tommy to go from a Dodger scout to getting him the manager's job in rookie ball with Ogden, even though a lot of the other members of the organization felt that Tommy's persona wasn't one the Dodgers wanted to emulate. Tommy wasn't as flamboyant as Leo Durocher, but he was certainly as loud and provocative. Tommy was a loyal company guy, but he didn't play by *all* the company rules.

In contrast, the type of manager the stiff-collared, always-serious Dodger management seemed to prefer was the incumbent, Walter Alston. Owner Walter O'Malley believed in loyalty, and he gave Alston twenty-three consecutive one-year contracts. The prior manager, the feisty Charlie Dressen, was sick of being a lame duck with one-year deals, and after the 1953 season he demanded a three-year deal. O'Malley fired him and hired Alston. Alston was going to last forever on one-year contracts, because the Dodgers put trust in their people who were loyal. Alston signing a one-year contract was a sign of loyalty to O'Malley.

The major players from the '68 draft that Al Campanis oversaw were given over to Tommy, as manager of Ogden in the Pioneer League. Fresco Thompson, Campanis's boss, was the man who had called to tell me I'd been drafted, but he'd since been diagnosed with cancer. Campanis, who went to college, took over, and he threatened the conservative nature of the Dodger brass that included O'Malley, Thompson, and Walter Alston. The reason: Campanis was putting his faith in wild child Tommy Lasorda to lead the charge with the new players from the draft.

Tommy was involved with his team 24/7. At home we'd have early practice. Tommy would take a few of us out early—usually me, Buck, Paciorek, and Garvey, along with a few others mixed in every once in a while. In the morning, he'd throw batting practice for an hour. Then we'd go back and get lunch, maybe take a nap before going back to take batting practice and play a game at night.

Tommy was something of a perfectionist. Our record was 39–25 in '68. We won the Pioneer League championship on the last day of the season. During the season we lost three games in a row, and Tommy called a team meeting in the clubhouse.

"Valentine," he said, "if you don't steal more bases, we're not going to score more runs. Go out there, go on the first pitch, for Christmas sake. What the fuck are you waiting for? When someone's on, drive in the goddamn run. How can you not?"

He went around from player to player. We had a player by the name of Gary Pullins, who had just gotten back from a Mormon mission where he spent two years spreading the word of God. Pullins didn't drink, smoke, or curse. He was the cleanest, coolest kid on the team. Tommy was screaming at each of his players, telling them what they weren't doing right, what they should do or might do, and Pullins was the last player he addressed. Tommy hesitated for a second, then pointed, and he said, "And you, Pullins, I was just like you when I was your age."

We knew that wasn't true, and we cracked up. No one cussed like Tommy—it just broke us all up. It was his way to go from being tense and everyone being yelled at and having your tail between your legs, to laughing and running out with your tail wagging.

After that meeting, we went on a ten-game winning streak. That year Buck, Garv, and I played in nearly every game. Garvey hit .338 with 20 home runs, 59 RBIs, and 9 stolen bases. Buck hit .344 with 4 home runs, 41 RBIs, and 15 stolen bases. I hit .281 with 6 home runs, 26 RBIs, and 20 stolen bases. Tommy Paciorek hit .386, which is why he moved up to A-ball so quickly. Sandy Vance had the perfect Dodger name—part Sandy Koufax, part Dazzy Vance—and in '68, pitching for Ogden, he won 14 games. He would have been a star for the Dodgers, but arm injuries ended his career too soon. All the while, we were being cheer-led by Lasorda.

About halfway through the '68 season, Tommy did something that shook the entire Dodger organization. At night Tommy would have dinner with his flock: Bill Buckner, Tom Paciorek, me, Steve Garvey often, and one or two other top players on the team. Buck and I were mainstays almost every night, and Paciorek was a regular until he was promoted to A-ball. At one of these dinners Tommy said to us, "Okay, you guys, here's a homework assignment. When you go back to the hotel, I want you to write a letter to the major-leaguer who is at your position, and tell him to get ready to retire or play with another team, because you are on your way."

Billy Buckner and I were eighteen years old. The older guys were twenty-one, and our forty-one-year-old manager was telling us to write these inflammatory letters. Not for a second did we consider the consequences. We were just as brash as Tommy. Billy Buck dutifully wrote to Wes Parker, and believe it or not, that was as much a reason as any that Parker retired prematurely at age thirty. I wrote to center fielder Willie Davis. Steve Garvey's father drove the Dodger bus in spring training and knew many of the Dodgers, so Steve decided against sending his letter. These letters would come back to haunt Buck, Paciorek, and, especially, me.

We had no off-days. This is true in all the minor leagues. You play three games, get on the bus, and drive for hours to get to the next town. A lot of times we'd get there in the middle of the night, check into a hotel, try to get some sleep, and go to the ballpark. If you couldn't sleep on the bus, you couldn't play in the minor leagues. Often, I would sleep in the overhead luggage rack.

During these trips Tommy began to create his reputation for getting free meals. He taught us the life lesson of using leverage. The bus would pull into a truck stop. Zack Minasian, our sixteen-year-old traveling secretary, trainer, and clubhouse boy, would enter the restaurant. He informed the restaurant manager that twenty-five hungry young men were ready to enter and have dinner. However, for that to happen, Zack would explain, he and the team manager would have to eat for free! It almost always worked.

One night in rookie ball we were playing in Caldwell, Idaho, and a player on the Caldwell team was all over me, calling me every name in the book.

"You're not good enough to be the number-one draft choice," he kept shouting.

We were playing a doubleheader, and from the beginning of the first game through the end of the second game, as soon as I left the dugout, this guy started yelling.

I was on third base, and Tommy was the third-base coach. This guy was screaming at me, and I said to Tommy, "I have to go get him."

"No, you can't," Tommy said. "You have to stay in the game."

We swept the double-dip, and I was out on the field shaking hands with my teammates. As I headed to the dugout, Tommy grabbed me by the shoulder and said, "You still want to go?"

"Yeah," I said. "I want him."

"Good," he said. "Go out on the mound."

Tommy walked across the field, yelled to my tormentor and told him to go out on the mound. He lined our team along the first-base line. He lined their team along the third-base line.

"You get over there. You get over here. No one is to step over the line," Tommy said. Then he yelled, "You two guys, any time you're ready, go at it."

This guy jumped into a karate stance, which I had never seen before. Immediately I bull-rushed him, tackled him, and got him on the ground. I was whacking him as Tommy yelled in my ear, "Hit him again! Hit him again!"

Their manager, who had been in the locker room, came out, saw us fighting, and started yelling, "What's going on?"

"I'll tell you what's going on," Tommy said to him. "My guy is kicking the shit out of your guy, and if you don't get inside, I'm going to kick the shit out of you."

This was right after the game, while fans were still in the stands of this rickety Caldwell ball field at the fairgrounds. It became quite raucous, and we needed a police escort to get out of town.

It's the way baseball squabbles ought to be handled, Tommy and I agreed. *Kind of like hockey.*

That season was just eating, sleeping, and playing baseball, and being entertained by Tommy—whether he was telling us the history of the game while we sat around, or while we were walking the streets of Ogden until the town's curfew, as he told stories of good players and bad and entertained us with Dodger history. Tommy was totally captivating, and we were really lucky he was so engaged. He was totally into being our manager, mentor, and friend.

Under Tommy we won the Pioneer League championship in 1968. I played center field and was named the MVP of the league.

When the season ended, Buck and I enrolled at USC. I had to get there by the third of September to register myself. I had to sign my own checks in the presence of the registrar, because students were dodging the military draft. Buck and I flew to L.A. together and went to the campus. The admissions papers said we were to live in Trojan Hall, the dorm for the SC athletes. We went into the Trojan Hall lobby carrying our suitcases, walked up to the table where they were checking people in, and waited. The girl at the desk couldn't find our names.

"Are you on scholarship here at SC?" she asked.

I was the one who did the talking because Billy Buck, a country boy from the wine country of Vallejo, California, was very shy.

"We were on scholarship, but we signed professionally with the Los Angeles Dodgers," I said.

She wasn't impressed at all.

"If that's the case," she said, "you're not staying in this dorm. Let me find out where you are." After a half-hour wait, she said, "You're at Tutten Hall." She told Buck he was assigned to another off-campus dorm.

My dorm was for international students, where almost no one spoke English, and it was off campus, as I discovered when I checked in. I had a

Japanese roommate. Buck's dorm also had a lot of foreign students. They had dumped us wherever they could find a bed. After a night in our new digs, we were both miserable. We were in the worst dorms on campus, and we had to make a move. I went to see Rod Dedeaux's son Justin, an assistant coach on the baseball team.

"The only option you have is to join a fraternity," he said.

Neither Buck nor I knew what a fraternity was. "Really?" I said. "Where are the fraternities?"

"Go over to Twenty-Eighth Street and you'll find them there," he said. "It's rush week. Good luck."

Buck and I went right over. The first house on the corner was the Sigma Chi house. Lunch was getting out, and the fraternity brothers were hanging out on the front stairs.

"Hi guys," I said. "We are here to join your fraternity."

We had no idea what it took to join a fraternity. We didn't know about rushing and pledging and having all the brothers vote on you. We figured it was like a drinking club, where you just go down and join. They laughed at us.

"You want to join somewhere," one said, "go across the street and join there."

Across the street was a fraternity that had been suspended and kicked off campus. They had rooms for rent, and so we said, "The heck with it," and rented a room.

The entire time of rush we were living across the street from Sigma Chi, when an article came out in the *Los Angeles Times* that talked about the rookie seasons of Garvey, Buck, and me. We were the stars of the Dodger rookie Class of '68, and the article touted this great Dodger draft. Someone from Sigma Chi read it and put the names and faces in the newspaper with the faces of the two guys living across the street, and the next day, as Buck and I were returning from class, we were met by four of the Sigma Chi brothers who asked us, "Why don't you come for lunch?"

We got to pledge and went through hell week. Some of the things I saw were hard to imagine. I saw Tim Rossovich, who had a ten-year career in the NFL and then became a movie actor, break the glass of a fire box, take the ax, and throw it from a second-floor window clean across the parking lot until it stuck in a palm tree, thirty feet up. Thirty years later the ax was still there. Mike Battle, who ran back punts for USC and later played for the New York Jets, ate glass. He took bites of glassware, chewing it in front of horrified onlookers. He slept on the floor next to Rossovich.

Did you ever see the movie *Animal House*, where one of the brothers of the Delta house went into a dumpster to steal the purple mimeograph sheets used to print the final exam? The guy who did that first was in our fraternity, and he dropped out of school to start a printing business. His hell week nickname was Kinko. He was Greek. He had that black, wild, kinky hair. I never met him, but he turned out to be Paul Orfalea, who founded Kinko's in 1970.

I studied and played and had the good fortune of meeting Skip Farina, my lifelong fraternity big brother, and his good friend Mike Holmgren. The Sigma Chi fraternity also had four or five sons of the President's Men, Nixon's henchmen. Kurt Kalmbach, Herb Kalmbach's son, was there, along with three or four others.

I'll never forget hell night. We were blindfolded, put in a car, driven a long way out into Topanga Canyon, and were told we had to get out of the car and "find the white cross of Sigma Chi." What we were actually supposed to do was sit in solitude and understand the teachings of Sigma Chi.

That wasn't for me. I decided that I was going to find the white cross. I figured it was at the top of the mountain. Buck went one way, and I went another. In my loafers and slacks I climbed and climbed, until I found a helicopter pad with a huge wooden white cross on it. I was elated but stumped. *How do I prove I found it?* I thought. I found a rock and chipped off a piece of the wood. I then went running down the mountain to show the guys. I was sure my big brother Skip was going to be mightily impressed. Buck was in the car waiting.

I opened the car door and said, "I found it." I wish I had had a photograph of their faces when I said that.

We drove back in silence and I wondered why I wasn't being congratulated. Then my big brother turned around and said, "You weren't supposed to find any fucking white cross, you moron."

"Oh," I said. Finally, I got it.

My first year at USC, I was like a duck out of water. When I arrived on campus and went to take my physical, I found out that the students whose names began with V weren't scheduled until the second day. While I was hanging around, I poked my head in to where they were giving physicals, and one of the nurses said to me, "Are you free?"

"Sure," I said. "What is it?"

"Can you run into the student union and get us a couple of cups of coffee?"

"Sure," I said, although I had no idea where the student union was. Quickly, though, I found it, and I brought back the coffee to the nurses.

When I returned the next day, I got in line to take my physical. The same two nurses were there, and one said, "I'm happy you came back."

"Why?" I asked. "Do you need some more coffee?"

"No," she said. "My son was supposed to audition for a spot on *The Dating Game,* and he can't make it. You seem like a nice young man. Would you like to go in his place?"

I wasn't a fan of *The Dating Game*, but it sounded like fun, so I agreed. I made a phone call and went down to interview for the show. Two other guys were also trying out. They played a fake game with a real audience, and I was thrown hypothetical questions about love and romance. I answered them, and the judges judged them, and I was told I had to wait and see whether I'd be called back.

The call came into the pay phone of the fraternity house. One of the brothers, Mike Draculich, another friend of mine today, answered the phone. "You made *The Dating Game*," he yelled down the hallway. "Put on a jacket and tie. You're on next Tuesday."

My big brother, Skip Farina, drove me down to the studio in Burbank. There were three of us answering questions, and one girl asking them from behind the curtain. After answering four questions each, Jim Lange, the host, asked her, "Okay, who did you pick?" I was contestant number one, and she picked contestant number three, even though she cited my answer as the reason she picked him.

I was backstage after the game, and one of the producers said to me, "You should have won. We're going to have you back." A couple days later they called and said, "We're going to film the nighttime version, and you're going to be one of the contestants."

The Dating Game aired several times during the day and once a week at night. Had I won the afternoon contest, my prize would have been a trip to Laguna Beach. I wound up winning the night contest, and my prize was a trip to Amsterdam, Rotterdam, and The Hague.

This was a big deal with Roxy and Ana. They were terrified I was going to go on a trip to Europe with this beautiful girl. I won that night, but you can't see the reruns of the show because Chuck Barris bought all the shows and he's refused to release them. You cannot find *The Dating Game* on YouTube.

I had to make the trip to Europe within a certain time limit, but during that short window I was studying at school and going to spring training. I had no chance to take it, so the girl ended up going with her boyfriend.

During spring break, I went to spring training with the Dodgers, and then I went back to school to make sure I didn't miss any classes. Billy Buckner was doing the same thing. We were two outliers, because he knew as little about college as I did, but we got good grades. I never got a grade lower than an A-minus. We knew we had to get good grades and stay in school to keep from going to Vietnam.

CHAPTER 4

A Lucky Break

In 1969 I was slated to go to the Bakersfield A-league team in the California League, and I was changing positions. I had played center field in youth All-Star competition, in Cape Cod, my senior year of high school, and my rookie year of pro baseball, but Tommy Lasorda felt the quickest way for me to get to Dodger Stadium was to become a shortstop.

After I took my finals, I went to a game at Dodger Stadium with Zack Minasian, the clubhouse boy from Ogden who was the son of Tommy's close friend Eddie. Eddie was the catering manager of the Cocoanut Grove, a great entertainment space in the Ambassador Hotel off Sunset Boulevard. I saw the Supremes there when I was being recruited at USC, and it was where Bobby Kennedy was killed. Because I was with the Dodgers, I was able to park in the players' parking lot. If I had parked with the paying customers, what happened next never would have happened.

Zack and I were leaving the game to walk to the car, and the route took us past the executive offices. I looked through the glass windows and saw Al Campanis, the newly appointed general manager, at his desk. He was on the phone, and when he looked up, he waved for me to come in.

My heart started pounding, because I had only talked to Al Campanis in my parents' dining room, and once in spring training. This was only the third time. I went in figuring he was going to wish me luck at Bakersfield. Al was smoking a cigarette, talking on the phone, and he pointed to a chair for me to sit down in front of him as he was talking.

"So, who do you have to replace him?" I heard him say.

I didn't know what that meant, but I knew he was talking with Tommy Lasorda, who had been promoted to Triple-A Spokane from the Pioneer Rookie League after leading Ogden to three championships in a row. He was asking Tommy how he was going to replace Tommy Dean, a second baseman who had been injured in the game that evening. Al needed Tommy to send someone up from Spokane. I couldn't hear what Tommy said, but over the years Tommy told the story a million times, when he said to Al, "I will give you a player by the name of Billy Grabarkewitz. Billy is a better player than Tommy Dean. You're going to love him when you get him. Pound for pound he's one of the best hitters in the league."

"Well, that's great," said Campanis. "Who do you want to replace Grabarkewitz on your team?" There was a long silence, and the next thing out of Campanis's mouth was, "What? Are you crazy? They'll run both of you out of town in a month."

I came to find out that Tommy's answer was "Bobby Valentine."

The year before, I was a center fielder in Rookie ball, and now Tommy was going to bring me to Triple-A to play shortstop. It was a giant leap for any player, never mind a nineteen-year-old who was supposed to be going to A-ball!

"That's a crazy idea," said Campanis.

Tommy was nothing if not insistent, and Al said, "Where do you think Valentine is now?"

"I have no idea."

"He's right here," Al said.

He hands me the phone. Tommy says, "Bobby, we're in Hawaii right now. We're going to be home in Spokane on Monday. Can you make it to Spokane by Monday?"

I had no idea where Spokane was. My car was packed, because I was going to leave for Bakersfield the next morning, a Friday.

"Monday?" I said. "That will be easy. I'll see you on Monday. What should I do?"

"Go to the ballpark," Tommy said, "and Elten Schiller, the general manager, will be waiting for you whenever you arrive."

"Great," I said.

Roxy was staying with me, so I drove home and told her, "This is crazy, but I'm going to Spokane. I'll see you there before the summer is over."

The next morning, I left the fraternity house, drove to Burroughs High School in Burbank, and picked up Zack for the drive to Spokane. We drove through California, Oregon, and into Washington. The twenty-hour trip was not without situations. I got pulled over three times for speeding before I got out of California. I was out of cash when I was stopped for the third time. In those days when you got a ticket, you handed the cop the cash, or you went to the constable's house and you gave him the cash. Or you spent the night in jail before the constable could give you a hearing the next morning.

I had a Connecticut license, and I was driving in California, and this cop decided I had to spend the night in jail for not having a California license. While waiting in the lobby of the jail house, Zack talked to the gal who was working the midnight shift, and she found an ordinance that said if you were a college student from out of state, you didn't need a California license. Zack talked the girl into persuading somebody to let me out of jail, and we were off and running to Spokane.

CHAPTER 5

Spokane

O nce again I was playing with the older kids. I would turn twenty in a few days. The next-youngest player was twenty-five. My primary job was to make the switch from center field to shortstop. I was scared, out of my league, and from the start of the season I played terribly. Charlie Hough, one of our pitchers, yelled at me one time to boot the ball, because I was throwing the ball into the stands more often than not. One time I hit a lady in the face and broke her cheekbone. It was starting to look like Al Campanis was right when he told Tommy that they were going to run both of us out of town before the first month was over.

Tommy was the greatest promoter that ever lived. He was always at an affair talking up the Dodgers, getting a free meal, and selling tickets. He was speaking at the Kiwanis Club breakfast one morning while we were taking batting practice before a Sunday day game. Before he got there, he had Dick McLaughlin, our left fielder and a player/coach, pitch batting practice while the pitchers were supposed to shag and throw the balls in from the outfield.

On this day, Tommy arrived during practice to see that the pitchers were not out shagging. Tommy was in street clothes, and he said to Dick, "Where are the pitchers?"

"They're up in the clubhouse, Tommy," Dick said. "They want to meet with you, because they don't want to pitch if Valentine is at shortstop."

These were mostly thirty-year-old guys who had their cup of coffee in the big leagues, and were now in Triple-A hoping for the phone to ring, thinking they were going back to the majors someday. Quite candidly, I was costing them wins, which was their ultimate statistic. Nothing else really mattered. No one looked at walks and hits per nine innings, or strikeouts.

Tommy stopped practice and called everyone up into the clubhouse. When we got there, he began marching up and down between the lockers. He said, "I just got the news that some of you guys don't like what's going on around here. Sit at your locker and think about it for a second. I'm going to come right out."

He went into his office and put on his uniform. He reappeared to his twenty-two players and started marching again. Then he said, "Okay, so what I hear is that pitchers don't want to pitch"—Tommy was standing right in front of my locker, and he points to me—"when this kid is playing shortstop."

He marched back and forth a few more times. Meanwhile, I'm looking down at the floor. I didn't want to look up to see anyone's facial expression. I figured that this was the day I was being sent down to Bakersfield, where I was supposed to be playing. If I go to Bakersfield, the pitchers will live happily ever after.

Tommy walked a little more before he said, "Well, I'm going to tell you what we're going to do. Not only is this kid going to play shortstop, but everybody in this room, right now, when I go back to my office, is going to stand in front of this fuckin' guy's locker, and you're going to have a pencil and paper in your hand, and you're going to get his fuckin' autograph, because when you're all home carrying a lunch bucket, he's going to be playing in the big leagues, and you're going to tell your friends that you played with him. And the only proof you're going to have is the autograph you're going to get today."

Tommy went into his office and slammed the door. I was still looking down at the top of my shoes, and the next thing I knew, I could see the spikes of the players in front of me. I looked up, and the whole team was lined up for my autograph. I signed them all.

I was probably hitting .210 at the time and had probably made thirty errors. From that day on I hit .300 and don't think I made ten errors the rest of the way. I was the most improved player on the team, and the next year I came back as a twenty-year-old to lead the league in seven different categories.

That was Tommy Lasorda, putting it all on the line.

Tommy did something else. After he preened at my improvement, he was so impressed with my play that he said to me, "You're going to write that letter to Maury Wills now, because you're going to be the next Dodger shortstop."

I knew someone on the Dodgers wasn't going to like it, and yet Tommy told me to do it, so I wrote that letter to Maury Wills telling him I was gunning for his job, and that he better get out of the way.

The season ended September 1, and I enrolled again at USC. At the same time, the major league rosters were expanded for the month of September, and Billy Buckner and I got to suit up for nine home games with the Dodgers. We were college students by day, Dodgers by night.

The first major league game I appeared in, I was inserted as a pinch-runner against the New York Mets, who were fighting for the pennant. I went from first to third. Jerry Koosman was pitching for the Mets, and Danny Ozark, our third-base coach, told me to steal home. I got a late start, then stopped and went back to third.

"I got the timing," I said to Danny. "I'll get it this pitch."

I didn't get the chance to steal because the hitter lined out to the shortstop to end the inning. As I arrived in that pinch-running role, I started my relationship with Walter Alston. I came to find out many years later that because I was Tommy Lasorda's number-one guy, Walt was *never* going to look in my direction. After years of seeing the politics that play out in baseball, when I saw who Walt was and Walt understood who I was, I totally understand it. In a book he wrote in 1971, Alston mentioned that I was a guy who should be captain of the team, but that was the only compliment I ever got from him.

I wasn't expecting to play. I was a nineteen-year-old going to see what Major League Baseball was like, so Walt really didn't have to decide what to do with me. But for two years Walter Alston showed his indifference, or perhaps his disdain for me, by calling me Billy Valentine. At the Welcome Home banquet, he introduced me as Billy Valentine. When he was corrected by Danny Ozark or one of the other coaches, he just shrugged it off.

"We've got a lot of Billys," Walt said. "What's one more?"

There were Billy Grabarkewitz, Billy Buckner, Billy Sudakis, and Bill Russell. Why not have one more?

At the time I arrived in L.A. in 1969, Walter Alston was well established. He had been managing in the big leagues since 1954, and this was after spending years in the minors. Young players didn't mean anything to him. I was the neophyte. I was a pledge. For Walt, I had to earn my stripes. I understood that, because being the youngest wherever I went, all my life, earning my stripes was all I did.

CHAPTER 6

MVP

The 1970 season was a magical one for Tommy, me, and the Spokane Indians. We finished the season with a 94–52 record, and I was named the Most Valuable Player of the Pacific Coast League. The second-place team in our division, Portland, was 26 games behind us. I hit .340, with 211 hits, 122 runs scored, 39 doubles, 16 triples, 14 home runs, 80 RBIs, and 29 stolen bases. I was Ichiro before there was an Ichiro.

This was a team for the ages. Steve Garvey was at third, I played short, Davey Lopes was at second, and Tommy Hutton was the best-fielding first baseman I ever played with. Von Joshua, Billy Buckner, and Tom Paciorek played the outfield, as well as catchers Bob Stinson and USC quarterback Steve Sogge. Our pitchers included Charlie Hough and Doyle Alexander, to mention just two.

During the season we played ten games in Hawaii. We had to play each team ten times and could only afford one trip to Hawaii, so we stayed for all ten days. The Hawaiian Islanders was a team made up of half California Angels minor league players and half free agents. The owners of the Islanders knew their fans never got to watch major league ballplayers, so they signed veterans with real names like Bo Belinsky, Juan Pizarro, and Jim Coates.

For all away games we had a little ritual. I batted first, Billy Buck batted second, and Tommy Lasorda was our manager and third-base coach, so while the national anthem was playing, all three of us would stand together in the on-deck circle. When the anthem was over, Tommy would sprint to the third-base box, I would walk up to the plate, and Buck would start swinging the weighted bat to get ready to hit.

On this day, the anthem was playing, and Buck started mumbling. Buck was the greatest mumbler who ever lived. He could speak underneath his breath and would mumble sometimes even when he wanted to be articulate, drowning himself out with a little murmur behind his words. He was mumbling things like, "I hate that motherfucker. I'd like to kill that cocksucker." By 1970 we were around Tommy Lasorda enough to be able to speak his lingo.

Lloyd Allen, the pitcher on the mound, had just been called up to Triple-A. I would find out later he was a high school player from Buck's area whom the Angels had signed as their number-one draft choice out of high school. This was three seasons later, and Buck was seeing him for the first time since high school. He could throw ninety-five and was a great prospect.

Tommy and I looked at Buck. "Son, what are you talking about?" Tommy wanted to know.

"I'm going to hit him in the forehead with a line drive and kill him," Buck said.

The national anthem ended, and Tommy ran out to third base. I still wasn't sure what Buck was talking about. I was getting ready to go up and hit. I didn't know it was Lloyd Allen, didn't know he had been drafted number one. I had heard of him because Buck and I had been roommates for three years, and we talked about everything. But Allen had just been called up, so for me he was just another pitcher. He was pitching. I was hitting, and I got a hit.

Buck came to the plate, and Lloyd threw him a first-pitch fastball. Buck hit a line drive that hit Lloyd square in the forehead and knocked him to the ground. The ball hit him so squarely that it caromed off his forehead and landed behind the catcher. Buck got a double, and I wound up on third. The catcher didn't know whether to run for the ball or to the mound. Lloyd got up with a knot on his forehead that was protruding as though two golf balls had been implanted in his forehead. Incredibly, Chuck Tanner, the Islanders manager, left him in to pitch. He threw eight straight balls before Tanner took him out.

Our players were amazed when Tommy said to Buck the next inning, "You said you were going to hit him in the forehead and kill him."

"He didn't say that," said our teammates.

"I was in the on-deck circle," I said, "and he actually said he was going to do that. And he almost did it."

The incident became more than legendary. It was Buck 101 as a hitter. Buck was an amazing hitter.

In 1970, I played every inning of every game for Spokane—146 games in just five months. I don't think we had two days off the whole season. I won the batting championship with a .340 average on the last day of the season. I had to go 3 for 3, and I did that. Winston Llenas, the player I beat out by one percentage point, was playing for the Islanders. He played a doubleheader his last day, in Salt Lake in the afternoon. Our game was in the evening. It came over the ticker tape from our press box that Llenas had gone 1 for 2 in the first game and come out of the game. He'd moved his average up from .337 to .338 and a half. In the next game he went 1 for 2, raising it to .339, and came out of the game. Because I had had so many at-bats, I needed to go 3 for 3 to beat him. When you have so many at-bats, the needle doesn't move very much. I hit a ball off the glove of the third baseman that could have been called a hit or an error, but we were playing at home, so it was ruled a hit. My next at-bat I got another hit, and at the end of the game I was 3 for 3, raising my average to .340.

The press box notified Tommy that I was a half point ahead of Winston Llenas. Tommy came over to me and said, "You're coming out of the game."

"Are you crazy?" I said. I had played every inning of every game. "Why would I come out of the game?"

"Because you have just won the batting championship," Tommy said.

"So what?" I said. "I'll win it anyway. I have a couple more at-bats. I'll get a couple more hits."

"We're not going to take that chance," Tommy said. "You might never have another chance to win a batting title. You're coming out of the game."

While we were arguing, he sent in another player in my stead. I won the batting championship, and Spokane won the Eastern Division championship. This set up a best-of-seven series with the winners of the West, the Hawaii Islanders.

Over in Hawaii, they got wind of the fact that there was a controversial call that gave me the hit to win the championship. The radio broadcaster for the Islanders was Al Michaels (yes, *that* Al Michaels, the Hall of Fame broadcaster who went on to call the "Miracle on Ice" and so many years of *Monday Night Football*). Al, who is now a good friend, was adamantly anti-Bobby Valentine. We played the first two playoff games in Spokane and won them both. We then went to Hawaii to play the middle three games. Every time I stepped foot on the field, I was booed. A lot of people were in the stands, and in those days the fans brought transistor radios with them so they could hear Michaels explain the nuances of the game and to hear what he had to say about me. What he was saying was that I had stolen the batting championship from their own Winston Llenas. We were up 3–0 in games, and I had nine hits in those three games, and when I came to bat leading off game number four, I got a standing ovation.

Michaels wrote about this in his book. He said it was the greatest lesson he ever learned, because on the first pitch of the fourth playoff game,

I was beaned intentionally by pitcher Greg Washburn. I was supposed to get called up to the Dodgers and the big leagues, but instead I ended up in the hospital for a week with my head bandaged.

The pitch hit me in the face and pushed my cheekbone down three and a half inches. After I was hit, I got up, and I was deformed. Everyone looked at me in horror. Tommy Paciorek became so ill he threw up when he saw what I looked like. My cheekbone was protruding down at the bottom of my face. The trainer applied a towel above my eye to stop the bleeding, and I walked to the clubhouse in center field. They were calling for a stretcher, but I was not going to let them carry me out.

Meanwhile, fights were breaking out all over the field. Their third baseman and our third basemen were rolling on the ground. Tommy was screaming at Chuck Tanner as I was walking with our trainer. Eddie Minasian, Zack's father, jumped out of the stands and walked with us. Also walking with us was an unassuming Japanese man.

When I got to the clubhouse, I looked in the mirror and threw up. I soon was in an ambulance on the way to the emergency room. Little did I know that the unassuming man who walked to the clubhouse with us was a renowned plastic surgeon from Japan and an incredible Dodger fan. He went into the emergency room with me. I didn't know it, but he had called the Dodgers and Dr. Bob Kerlan, the Dodgers' doctor, and got permission to operate on me.

Instead of cutting my face open and pulling up the bone, which was the norm and which resulted in a large scar across your face, he went into my skull with a little stainless-steel crowbar, figured out where the bone was, took the bone, and pulled it back up in place. He then maneuvered it in place properly with his hands. He made an incision under my eye along the crack, where he pulled out some bone spurs, and when I woke up the next day, my left eye and skull were wrapped in a white bandage. The doctors and nurses were saying how successful the operation had been, but they also said, "We'll know in a few days whether you will be able to see."

The Spokane season over, I was scheduled to go to L.A. and become the Dodger shortstop. As I lay in the hospital bed, I wondered whether I would ever play again.

Tommy Lasorda came to the hospital to see me. He told me we'd won that game 16–1, giving us the series, and letting me know the team was flying back home. He said the player who took my place, Marv Galliher, had hit a home run, a triple, and two singles. He asked to see my surgeon, but my surgeon had left. As it turned out, the surgeon had been in Los Angeles for a plastic surgeons' convention. On his way home to Japan, he had stopped in Hawaii, as all flights did, to refuel. But he also decided to stay to see the Dodgers' Triple-A team play in the championship series.

I never saw him, never got to meet him, and the crazy thing was for many years when I was managing in Japan, I asked about him. This started in the 1980s, the first time I was in Japan, and I returned in the 1990s and was back in the 2000s, and there were articles in the Japanese papers that talked about my career and the Japanese doctor who had operated on me after I was hit in the face.

Thirty-seven years later, while I was managing in Japan, my interpreter came over during batting practice and handed me the business card of someone who was standing back of the dugout. The card was in Japanese, and I couldn't read it.

"Who is this?" I asked.

"It's a plastic surgeon. He wants to talk to you."

My heart started pounding, thinking this had to be the guy. I ran back, and there was a man standing there in a dark suit. He had dark hair, and he was younger than me, so I knew he couldn't have been the guy. I introduced myself, went through all the proper formalities, and he then introduced himself as the son of the surgeon who had performed my operation but who had died the year before.

"Why didn't I ever get to meet him?" I asked.

"He never wanted to get in the papers and get his name out," the son said.

"Why is that?"

"Because my mom didn't know he had stayed an extra three days in Hawaii to watch those games, and he didn't want to get in trouble at home," he said.

⤳

From the hospital in Hawaii, I returned to USC and completed the first semester. My face seemed to heal quickly. At the end of the semester, the Dodgers had me transfer to Arizona State so that I could participate in the Arizona Instructional League. The Dodgers and I needed to see if I could still hit and play the game. I proved that I could and was excited. I was lucky when my draft lottery number came out at 295. I no longer had to be concerned with the military draft, so baseball could be my number-one focus.

In Triple-A I was making $1,200 a month, but only during the season. I was hoping to get a major league contract in the mail any day, and after playing well at Triple-A I was hoping to get a good raise, so I could tell Mom and Dad and Roxy and Ana that I was making a lot of money.

A week before spring training began was the last flag football game of the Sigma Chi fraternity championship season at ASU. We had one hell of a team. Undefeated. Most guys on the team were scholarship football players who didn't want to play for Frank Kush, who was a pretty severe taskmaster, and had quit the Arizona State team. It was hard-hitting flag football, and after the games we would go to Freddy's Tavern, which was the Mexican-run bar next to the train tracks that allowed everyone to drink without IDs and had really cheap pitchers of beer. This was going to be my send-off. We were going to win the championship and party hearty, and Sigma Chi was going to be the reigning champions when I checked out of school.

The first kickoff I received, I ran back for a touchdown. The Law School team scored, and when they kicked off, we ran a fake reverse. The other back got the ball, and I came around as though he was going to hand it to me and he was going to run up the sideline. As I faked getting the ball, I was watching him, when I got hit from the blind side.

The hit totally destroyed my knee.

Instead of being the starting shortstop for the Dodgers, I arrived at spring training with my entire right leg in a cast. At their organizational meeting, the Dodgers had to decide whether to ask Maury Wills to retire, even though he had had a good year, or whether they keep him so he could mentor me for shortstop. When I arrived for spring training with my leg in a cast, Maury Wills referred to the letter I had written telling him I was taking his job. He told me his job was to mentor me, and every day during spring training my job was to get in line at the Morrison's Cafeteria, where everyone at Dodgertown ate, and I was to fetch breakfast for him.

When the cast came off, I got a couple of at-bats at the end of spring training. I was fitted with a very cumbersome knee brace, the type that was designed for Joe Namath by Dr. James Nicholas in New York. For the first year and a half in the big leagues, I wore that brace under my very baggy uniform.

The Dodger brass were more than upset. I told them I had stepped on a sprinkler head chasing a fly ball in practice, because that was how Mickey Mantle had hurt his knee in the '51 World Series. They weren't buying it, and they flew me to L.A. to see Dr. Frank Jobe, who was the protégé of Dr. Bob Kerlan, the renowned orthopedic surgeon. Dr. Jobe was the surgeon who operated on Tommy John's arm. He repaired my knee as best he could, putting in a staple to hold the ligament together. It was a total reconstruction.

That's how I limped around the first year and a half in the big leagues. When I finally rid myself of the brace, I tried to run the way I was used to running, and I fell maybe a half-step short. Because of that half-step, Al Campanis and Walt Alston decided that I no longer had the ability to play shortstop.

Nevertheless, I was determined to prove them wrong, and slowly worked my way back to being fully functional at shortstop. In the middle of May, Walt Alston called me into his office and said I was getting sent back to Triple-A.

I felt I was running fine, even though I wore a brace and wasn't as fast as I once was, so I asked him why.

"You have to work on your underhand feed to the second baseman," Walt said. "Your defense isn't polished enough for a major-leaguer."

You can't imagine the disdain I had for that man.

In 1971 Alston sent me down to learn who knows what, and I spent ten days playing with Tommy. I was upset and discouraged, but since the Triple-A team was playing in Hawaii, I put on a happy face.

Al Campanis flew to Hawaii to watch me play. I played in seven games at shortstop and was called back up to the Dodgers. Alston put me in the starting lineup. I had to face Bob Gibson, one of the toughest pitchers in the game, and was inserted at third base.

This situation was very confusing because I had been sent back to Triple-A for polishing at shortstop, and when I came back, I was put at a position I had never played. I hated third base. I *hated* it. The good news is I got the game-winning hit off Gibson.

I was caught up in the middle of a tornado of Dodger politics. Al Campanis was the general manager. Walter O'Malley, who had owned the Dodgers since the 1940s, was turning over the reins to his son Peter, and Peter had taken a real liking to Tommy. Tommy was also Al Campanis's boy, but even after Tommy won championship after championship in the minor leagues, he still wasn't given the Dodger manager's job. They made him a coach under Alston in 1973.

I was being groomed away from shortstop. Billy Russell was Walt's choice for shortstop. Billy was from Pittsburg, Kansas. Walt, too, was from the Midwest—Darrtown, Ohio.

I was the Italian kid who didn't hunt and fish. I was from the Northeast, and I was championed by the Italian guy who openly wanted Walt's job. Tommy was always the loyal soldier. He did everything Walt asked him to do, but if he was out to dinner with his friends, he didn't have a lot of nice words to say about Walt. When Walt went out to dinner, I'm just as sure there weren't many nice words about Tommy.

In 1971, Maury played in 144 games at shortstop. I played 21 games at second base, 24 games at third, 36 games at short, having started 10 of them, 9 games in right field, and 2 in center field.

Alston saw that Tommy had taken me from center field and groomed me as a shortstop, and the next season he decided he would do the same thing with Bill Russell. I would bet that Walt said to himself, *If Tommy can do that with Valentine, I can do that with Russell.* Only when I got older did it make sense. At the time, I knew nothing of the politics of it. I knew Alston liked Russell a lot and didn't like me, but I didn't know all the backstage workings until I was backstage. People would say to me, "Remember when you were with the Dodgers?" "Oh," I'd say, "so that's how it worked." Eventually, Russell got the shortstop's job, and he stayed there forever.

In 1971, as the world was changing, I was a young man trying to adapt to the change. My hair was growing longer, and my ideas on life were expanding. During the '71 season I became very close to Richie Allen, who the Dodgers got in a trade from St. Louis for Ted Sizemore. This opened up the second-base job with the Dodgers. Richie taught me that our careers were short and that life was not always fair.

In June of '71, the Dodgers made an East Coast swing. Many of my family and friends, including Mickey Lione, drove to Montreal to see our series against the Expos. Richie treated Mickey and my friends like family, and they remembered that. I hit my first home run in the last game of that series, and went 4 for 4, to everyone's delight. The next day we traveled to New York, and I got the game-winning hit off Tom Seaver. I doubled off Nolan Ryan the next day and finished the series going 2 for 3 against Jerry Koosman. In seven days I played third base, shortstop, left field, and right field. I was 7 for 23, with 3 doubles, 3 RBIs, and 2 runs scored; but after going 0 for 3 against Bob Gibson, I found myself back on the bench.

When the '71 season ended, I was still wearing the cumbersome brace on my right knee and looking forward to a chance at being the everyday shortstop.

During the winter, I had the opportunity to go with Tommy to Venezuela and play for the Caracas Leones. The military draft was replaced by a lottery system, and Billy Buck and I got really high numbers. We were no longer full-time students and were now enrolled officially in Lasorda U. Vic Davalillo was a Dodger player at the time, and his brother Pompeyo was the winter league manager. Tommy would be a coach on the team, and Buck and I, along with Billy Russell and Charlie Hough, would get more experience against very good competition. Americans had to be invited to play, and there was a limit on the number of foreign players per team.

The day the big-league season ended, I needed to drive across the country—Los Angeles to New York—to get my visa. I was in the Dodger clubhouse after the last game, telling everyone my plans, when our assistant trainer introduced me to amphetamines. "Any time you get tired, take one of these," he said.

I was able to drive my 1968 Camaro, which I bought with my signing bonus, the entire 3,000 miles without stopping. I picked up hitchhikers along the way and had a good time driving.

I barely got to New York in time to get the visa and make the plane, but I did. After Roxy finished her semester at Denison University, she met me in Venezuela, and we rented an apartment in downtown Caracas. It was a spectacular location, except that the flower salesman under my third-floor window began business at 5:30 a.m. As the sun came up every morning, I could hear, "Flores. Flores."

The last two months of the season with the Dodgers, I had decided I wasn't going to cut my hair or shave my mustache. I wanted to look like so many of the twenty-one-year-olds outside of baseball. I arrived in Caracas with my hair flowing down my neck and a thick mustache. The local press named me "El Loco."

Caracas was an amazing town. Some of the players stayed at the Hotel Tamanaco, which was on a hill overlooking the city. It had a spectacular pool. I have great memories there, but not great baseball memories.

I'm not sure why, but Tommy was miserable in Venezuela. Bill Russell was miserable, too, and decided to leave early, as did a couple other players. We were allowed to go home for Christmas for a few days, and I did that and never went back. It wasn't right, but I was engaged and had to get home to plan the wedding. Roxy and I were married and took off in our car to spring training. That was our honeymoon. We stopped in D.C., had a nice dinner, and made another stop before we arrived in Vero Beach, Florida, home of Dodgertown.

I would return to winter ball, and the next time I'd be the star of the league.

ॐ

I began my second season with the Dodgers in 1972. I was hoping and praying and waiting for Tommy Lasorda to become the manager, but Alston was there for another year, and he played Bill Russell at shortstop. Bill hit .272. I played almost as much, but not at shortstop, and hit .274.

I was seen as something of a young radical and wasn't fitting the Dodger mold. I was getting involved in anti-war politics. When I arrived at Dodger Stadium, I found a pair of scissors and a razor on my stool. The previous year, I'd spent a lot of time hanging out with Richie Allen, who was African American and the player I admired most on the team. I thought the way he was treated by management was improper, and I even said that sometimes. In those days you didn't say things like that. You just didn't. I more than loved Richie. He called me Little Bro. On flights I would sit with him at the back of the Dodger planes.

"We're going to be here a long time," I said to him at the beginning of the season. "I can't wait to play my career with you."

"I've been here a month," Richie said, "and I can tell you, I'm only going to be here a year. I will lead the team in all the offensive categories, but these guys aren't keeping me."

In 1971, Richie hit 23 home runs at Dodger Stadium, and back then that was like hitting 50. I have to say that Richie Allen was as good a player as I have ever seen. He ran the bases better than Maury Wills. He used a 42-ounce bat. He could hit-and-run to right field. His batting practice was exemplary. He'd get eight swings, and he'd hit two to right field, two to center field, two to left field, and two over the fence. It was ridiculous how spectacular he was.

Richie had the most impeccable physique that was ever created. He was Bo Jackson, Rickey Hendersonesque. His waist was 19 inches, his chest was 46, and his custom-made suits fit him like he was just off a Hollywood runway.

Richie had morals. He didn't like the fact that some of the Dodger pitchers were creating unfair advantages when they were pitching. If he ever saw a ball that was scuffed, he'd throw it out of the game. Don Sutton was scuffing the ball, and so was Bill Singer, though Bill used a little more Vaseline than scuff. Bill was the master of the Vaseline ball. Claude Osteen scuffed some, but Don Sutton was the master, and Richie didn't like that. When Richie moved to first base, the Dodgers threw it around the infield, but they didn't throw it to Richie.

Richie loved his scotch, and he smoked a little pot, but he was never boisterous. He was never aggressively vocal. He would talk about his mom and his horses, and once in a while about Arkansas in the minor leagues, and the racial taunts and insults he'd had to endure. He said he thought it would be different in the major leagues but found out for him it wasn't.

Richie was black. He was real black. He had a real blackness to him, especially in the summertime, and some of the white players were fearful of him. He also had a stare, a way of looking at people that intimidated them, especially if he took off his glasses.

But that wasn't why I liked him. I liked him because not many other white players were hanging with him. Or with Maury. Or Willie Davis, who was black and unto himself. I hung with Willie a bit, too, and I liked Willie a lot.

Looking back at it, I don't think my hanging around with the black guys on the team created a favorable impression with Walter Alston. Call it a hunch. I'm not making an accusation, I'm just telling you my feeling. Walter was good racially, but Walt and I didn't have much of a relationship. He favored Bill Russell, and when I started playing second base, I had competition from Jimmy Lefebvre, because Jimmy was another favorite of Alston's. He brought the apple to the teacher, and Walt liked that.

So did Steve Garvey, who took it to another level. He played Walt like a drum. After games, he was usually with his girlfriend Cindy, who understood Walt perfectly. We'd come back from little day trips during spring training, the bus would pull into Vero Beach, and Cindy would be waiting with Walt's favorite cookies that she had baked at home. She'd blatantly stand there as Walt got off the bus and bring them over to him. It was stunning the way she manipulated him, and it drove Roxy crazy. Roxy was trying to compete with Cindy, but that was like trying to run a marathon without sneakers. Cindy had custom-made Nikes. One day when Garv and I were playing winter ball in the Dominican Republic, Cindy and Roxy locked the door of Tommy's suite and had a screaming match. It had to be the only time in Roxy's life that she ever yelled or thought about pulling out someone's hair.

Soon after the All-Star break, the doctors gave me the go-ahead to play without my leg brace. It was a monumental day. I can't tell you how much I hated that brace. Every day when I put it on for practice, I felt less than the athlete I wanted to be.

My strong motivation was that I felt Tommy was getting close to replacing Alston as manager. For much of the season, that's what I was playing for. I was thinking things would be very different under Tommy.

When the 1972 season began, Richie Allen was no longer with us, as he had predicted. In December 1971, Al Campanis traded Richie for Tommy John and also traded to get Frank Robinson from Baltimore.

Frank was mean when I played against him in spring training. He was a hard, hard dude, and you better get out of his way when he slid into second base. When he came to the Dodgers, there were rumors that he was in line to become the first black manager, and so he was putting on the face he would put on if he became a manager. Also, he was older, and everyone lightens up when they get older. Frank was thirty-six, and back then that was a lot of age. I'm sure Frank would have loved to replace Walt Alston, but that was not in the Dodgers' plans. We found out why in April 1987, when Al Campanis went on television and told Ted Koppel on *Nightline* that blacks "may not have some of the necessities to be a field manager or a general manager." Al was asked to resign the next day. The Dodgers had Major League Baseball's first black player in 1947, and they had other plans for the successor to the managerial throne.

I didn't hang around with Frank, but I did hang around with Willie Davis, who was trying to convert me to Buddhism. I'd go with Willie to these meetings where we'd chant our mornings away: *Nam Myoho Renge Kyo…Nam Myoho Renge Kyo.* His interest in the Buddhist religion became public when he began to chant in his locker before the game. Willie had this amazingly deep baritone voice, and his chanting would resonate throughout the entire clubhouse. As you can imagine, it was frowned upon by Alston and company, to say the least. Every time I watch the movie *Major League* and see Dennis Haysbert as Pedro Cerrano chanting to Jobu in front of his locker, I think of Willie. I know that's where they got it. Without a doubt.

Like I say, I was different. I was radical. Regardless of what Walt thought of me, I was a Dodger, and if I was in trouble, he knew it was his job to help. We were in Chicago, and I was having dinner with my good friend Zack Minasian, who lived there. After dinner, I returned to the hotel. Billy Buck was my roommate.

"Bobby," he said, "Walt just called."

Let it be said that Walt Alston never called me or any other young player. Immediately I thought that I had been traded, but it was pretty late, around eleven-thirty. Buck was already in bed.

I called down to the hotel operator and asked for Walt's room. Walt answered and sounded like he had just taken a hit on a cigarette. Walt was never without a cigarette. He smoked during every game. He had the ability to take a tremendous hit on the cigarette and talk without the smoke ever coming out.

There was a long pause before he said, "Hello."

"Walt," I said. "This is Bobby Valentine."

"Are you in your room?"

"Yes, sir," I said.

"I'll be right up. Colleen and the police will be here soon." He hung up.

Colleen and the police? I thought. *Who is Colleen? Why are the police coming?*

Buck and I were scared to death. I went to my shaving kit and flushed two joints I had down the toilet.

Walt knocked on the door, and I let him in. He walked in slowly and half-sat on the little desk in the room.

Buck was in bed, and I was sitting in the one available chair.

"Colleen is underage," Walt said. She's on her way here with her parents and the police. Tell me what happened."

I looked at him and said, "Who's Colleen?"

"I told you I was here to help you," he said. "If you don't want my help, I will leave right now."

"Just tell me what you're talking about, Skip," I said.

"The girl you were out with tonight is only seventeen," Walt said.

"Skip," I said, "I was with Zack Minasian," thinking he might have known Zack's dad. "I have his telephone number right here. You want to call him?"

Walt obviously didn't believe me.

"I told you I'm here to help," he said. "If you don't want my help, you're on your own."

With that, Billy Buck put the covers over his head and began laughing. I don't know why he was laughing. Maybe it was because of what we had flushed down the toilet, or that I hadn't been traded, or that this old fuck didn't know what he was talking about.

Who was this Colleen, anyway?

Walt took a big, long hit on his cigarette, turned, walked out of the room, closed the door, and was gone. About five minutes later there was a knock on the door. I looked through the little peephole in the door, and sure enough, looking right back at me was a Chicago policeman with some people behind him.

I opened the door.

"We're here to see Bobby Valentine," the policeman said.

"I'm Bobby Valentine."

The girl standing behind him and in front of her parents said, "No, you're not."

I looked at her, and I said, "Oh yes, I am."

"That's not the guy," she said.

I opened my wallet and got my Social Security card and my driver's license. I had one of my baseball cards on the desk that Zack had given me. This year's cards had just come out. The baseball card had my picture in uniform. I brought these items over and gave them to the officer.

He looked at them, and he said, "Well, I guess you *are* Bobby Valentine."

He closed the door and left.

Oh my gosh, I was wondering. *What was that all about?* It haunted me. For years.

Later, after I had been traded to the Angels, I was at a bar with a group of players, one of whom was Billy Grabarkewitz, who had been traded with me, and Joe Lahoud, who said to Billy, "Isn't it crazy that you guys got traded together? Didn't you always go out on dates and pretend that you were Bobby Valentine?"

"No, that wasn't me. That was the other infielder," Gabby said.

60

He never mentioned Jim Lefebvre's name, but none of the other infielders on the Dodgers would have done that. I guess this was commonplace, because the games weren't on TV. They only carried the Saturday *Game of the Week*. You'd come into a town, and the married guys would assume the alias of a young player, in case the girl he was out with decided to call the police for whatever reason. It was the perfect way to keep a cover and not have to make up the entire story. All a player had to do was change his name, and no one would be wiser. Walt Alston went to his grave thinking that I didn't trust him enough to have him help me in a situation that was about to get me arrested.

The next day, I went to the ballpark. Walt never asked me what happened. Clearly, he didn't care. Not one coach came over and asked me anything. Lee Scott, the traveling secretary, a man in the know, never asked. I was waiting to tell the story to clear my name, but no one ever asked me the question.

The worst insult Walt Alston paid me that year occurred on Bobby Valentine Day at Shea Stadium. The Stamford sports community had a major fundraiser, and they were presenting me with a new car. In between batting practice and the game, the mayor of Stamford, Julius Wilensky, came out onto the field, and with other proud members of the Stamford community, presented me with the keys.

There were perhaps a hundred Stamfordites who had come to see me play, including my folks and my grandmother, the only time she ever went to a game. The night before, I had gotten the winning hit against Nolan Ryan, and on this day a left-hander was starting, and normally I played against left-handers. Sometimes, Alston played Jimmy Lefebvre, because even though he batted left-handed, he hit left-handers better than right-handers. Anyway, on this day, Bobby Valentine Day, Alston played Lefebvre, and I only got to pinch-hit. After the game, Danny Ozark—who was the one to soften the blow when Alston criticized me in the newspapers—was good enough to come over and explain to me that Walt thought I might be too nervous because of the circumstances, so he took me out of the lineup, which I didn't believe for a second. There was no love lost at all between Walt and me.

Another time, the Dodgers were playing Philadelphia, and we were staying at the Bellevue-Stratford Hotel, a grand old hotel. My Uncle Mike had driven my parents to Philly to see the game, and they were waiting in the lobby for the bus. They quickly greeted me, and we got into the elevator. Walt entered the elevator last. As he pushed the button, I was standing behind him, and said, "Hey, Skip, I'd like to introduce you to my parents." Walt just stood there looking forward. The door opened on the third floor, and he got out, and didn't acknowledge my mom or dad. My dad, who was five feet seven and 135 pounds, was a very soft-spoken man and very polite, but this was not right, and he was tempted to get off the elevator and say something.

I wanted to show Dad what a big-league hotel room looked like, but my dad said to me, "No, I think I'd better go. I'm not in the mood to talk right now, but good luck today. You know I'm always pulling for you." With his veins popping out of his neck, my dad went to his room. He was so humiliated he couldn't even speak. I had never told him over the past year and a half what was going on between Walt and me. I never wanted to get them involved, never wanted them to think anything but that the manager loved me. What the hell? Every team I ever played on, the manager totally loved me. Why would it be any different in the big leagues?

That was one of the most humiliating moments. It was similar to when Walt introduced me at boosters dinners as Billy Valentine. I'll never forget the time all the Billys on the team raised their hands and laughed. Players used to say that I ignored Walt when he spoke to me, but when he'd call me Billy, I didn't think he was talking to me. By the end of the second year, when he did it, I wouldn't acknowledge him on purpose, and toward the end of the season he called me Valentine. "Hey, Valentine."

Late in the season, after Alston refused to acknowledge my parents, he didn't play me at shortstop, and I went to see Danny Ozark. I had been told I would play shortstop at the end of the season for so many games because I was fully healthy and the Dodgers wanted a good look.

But when that wasn't happening, I asked Danny what I was to do, and Danny said, "You'll just have to talk to Walt." Having a meeting with the manager, unless he called it, did not happen.

"Where do I go to talk to Walt?" I asked him.

"He's always sitting in the corner of the lobby," Danny said. Walt would sit there and smoke and check curfew to see who was coming in late.

"Get a little bit to eat," Danny said. "You know where to find him."

I went over and stood as Walt was sitting down, not paying attention and smoking a cigarette.

"Skip," I said, "I was supposed to play shortstop at the end of the season, and it doesn't look like I'm going to get much playing time."

"Yeah," Alston said. "You're not a shortstop. You can be a second baseman if you're better than the Lopes kid."

Lopes was three years older than I was, a tremendous guy and a fine player. My head was telling me that Davey should be the second baseman, and I should be the shortstop.

"I'm not a second baseman, Skip," I said. "I'm a shortstop."

"Well," Alston said, "You can be a shortstop on another team. Not on this one."

That shook me up. I had gotten drafted number one, and I had been sure I was going to be a Dodger all my life and that I'd go into the Hall of Fame. I realized then if Tommy wasn't going to be the manager of the Dodgers, my future was with another team. I thought, *I'm going to get traded*, and so I called Tommy the next day and asked if I could play for him in the Dominican Republic after the season.

"Hell yeah," Tommy said.

"Tommy," I said, "if you know anyone who is looking for a shortstop, all I want to do is play shortstop. I want to show people I can do it. And I want to go to their team."

"You're not going to get traded," Tommy said. "We're going to keep you. You're going to be a Dodger. Don't worry. It's all going to work out. Don't worry."

Tommy was still managing Spokane. He so badly wanted to manage the Dodgers he took the job in the Dominican for additional experience. I went with him, though I had my reservations after my poor experience in Caracas.

The team was the Licey Tigres, in the capital city of Santo Domingo. Most of the players were veteran major-leaguers from the Dominican. I had to get acclimated to this entirely different world. The owner of the team, Monchín Pichardo, owned a successful concrete company. More important, he thought Tommy Lasorda hung the moon. Pichardo embraced all the American players, and Tommy brought down his entire group—Garvey, Buck, Hough, and Von Joshua. It was a great group of guys. We named the team Lasorda U., because Buck and I were choosing to play for Tommy rather than finish our college studies.

Every morning when we played at home, we would pile into the 1971 Chevy station wagon owned by Señor Pichardo and drive from our hotel out to the stadium. Tommy threw batting practice for an hour and a half every morning. Then we'd go back to the hotel and shower, and Tommy would fall asleep on the balcony. We'd go sit by the pool, and then we'd pile into the station wagon again and go to Estadio Quisqueya for the game.

It was glorious. The stands were full of fanatical baseball fans, and as the game went on, they would become even more fanatical, because everyone was betting and everyone was drinking and getting a little higher. They were so into their team that they couldn't see straight by the time the game had ended.

It was a four-team league, and our biggest rival was the Aguilas Cibaeñas, who were from Santiago. We also played the Estrellas from San Pedro de Macorís, and we shared a stadium with the fourth team, the Leones del Escogido.

The player I edged out for the batting title, Winston Llenas, was one of the star players on the Aguilas. We had quite a rivalry. When we'd ride into town on our bus, the streets would be lined with the Estrellas fans waving banners and yelling at us. The games were standing room only, and there were cheerleaders on top of the dugouts. We had some amazing homegrown players, like Rico Carty, who was in the Orlando Cepeda mold. Rico was larger than life. He had hands that could open a coconut by squeezing it. He was a great hitter and a wonderful human being.

Manny Mota played for Licey and was as fine a hitter as I ever played with. Manny hit the ball on the barrel of the bat as consistently as anyone I had ever seen, until I managed Julio Franco. He had been traded to the Dodgers in the Richie Allen trade. We also had a pitcher by the name of Pedro Borbón, who was a member of the Cincinnati Reds relief staff. Pedro was as crazy as anyone I had ever met. The crowd could ignite him. He would throw at a hitter without a blink of the eye, and he could argue with the fans at the drop of a hat. One time he came out of the game after giving up a home run, and the fans were yelling everything you could imagine at him. One fan in particular was all over him. Pedro headed for the clubhouse as the other pitcher was warming up, and he came running back out onto the field carrying his pearl-handled six-shooter. He jumped into the stands and went running after the man who had been abusing him. It was real-life drama, even though no shots were fired.

Guns were ever-present. The police were military police, so they all had long guns, and they stood guard all around the stadium.

The owners of the teams would bet. To get the most out of players, the owners offered prize money for each game. The bigger the game, the more the prize money. The owner would designate which game, and he'd say how much a hit was worth, how much a run was worth, how much a win was worth, how much a home run was worth, and at the end of the game Tommy would be handed an envelope full of cash to distribute. The distribution always brought lively discussions, especially with the Dominican players, but he was great at distributing the money, which increased as we went into the playoffs. There were a lot of walking-around pesos to be made, and I made more money there in a month than I had made in any month previously. My second year with the Dodgers I made $6,500.

Tommy had an eleventh-grade education. While playing winter ball in Cuba, he taught himself Spanish. Tommy spoke four languages: English, Italian, Spanish, and the language he spoke to umpires. He was our interpreter, and he would be the one to speak to the umpires, to the other team, and the press in Spanish.

Tommy let me play shortstop every day, and I was happy again. Tommy was managing and I was playing, and we had a really fine team with César Gerónimo, Manny Mota, and Rico Carty in the outfield; Steve Garvey at first base; me at shortstop; Eduardo Diaz, a Dominican, at second; and our catcher, Frederico Valdez, who had been the bodyguard for Rafael Trujillo, the Dominican dictator. Frederico had a legendary reputation for the many men he killed in his lifetime, a couple with his hands. Frederico had amazingly long, strong fingers. We also had Jesús Alou, the youngest of the Alou boys, who was spectacularly educated and led all the players in our trivia games on the bus. He knew all the world capitals. He knew a lot more about a lot more than any of us did. Charlie Hough, who was becoming a world-class crossword puzzler, always was amazed at Alou's breadth of knowledge.

At Lasorda U., every day was an education. I would get up early and take the car. I was the designated driver, the chauffeur, because I drove the players to the morning practices and to the games. I knew my way around Santo Domingo quite well. In the morning I would often drive down to the marketplace. I loved the way they slaughtered their chickens and the way they marketed their food, barking out whatever they were selling. I'd take a book and sit over in the park and read as all that commotion was going on. It was very stimulating.

One time, driving to a night game in San Pedro, we were stuck in traffic, and I decided to take a shortcut. The street that I thought would be better was totally backed up with rush-hour traffic. We were dressed in our uniforms. Tommy had been second-guessing my choice of route until I finally said, "Tommy, I'm tired of your screaming at me, and I'm tired of your cursing me. Here are the keys. You drive." I got out of the car and started walking toward the other end of the street, in an attempt to stop the traffic so we could advance.

Tommy jumped out of the car. Around us were colorful one-story buildings on the street where *The Godfather* filmed its scenes depicting Cuba. I was walking, and people were hanging out their windows in the heat as Tommy walked after me, cursing at the top of his lungs and screaming, "Get in the car, Bobby! Get back in the fuckin' car!"

All of a sudden the people in the street began whistling and yelling, "Hey, Lasorda, Lasorda! Valentine, Valentine!" It became a scene, and then Lasorda said to somebody, "We're going to be late for our game." After he said that, a whole crew of people ran down the street and moved off to the side the cars that were blocking us. We had to drive down the sidewalk to get around the traffic jam. Once free, I drove ninety miles an hour down the highway to get to the game on time.

In the back, I could hear Von Joshua yelling, "You're going ninety miles an hour! Are you crazy?" Tommy said it was ninety kilometers, since we were in a foreign country. Ha! It was an American car. With that, Von threw up in the car. I did a great job of dodging the cattle and other animals along the unlit highway to get us there safely.

It was close to game time when I pulled into the stadium lot. The stadium lights had not been turned on, so we knew the game hadn't yet started. Tommy rushed to home plate with the lineup card, and only then did they turn on the lights. In the Dominican, there wasn't always enough electricity to go around. As they were playing the national anthems, we arrived, tucking in our uniforms and tying our shoes.

I was leading off. We had taken no batting practice, no sprints, hadn't even warmed up. We were going from the car to the ball game. I walked up to the batter's box swinging my weighted bat, and when I looked out to the mound, J. R. Richard, who was six foot five, 260 pounds, was staring at me. He threw about 97 miles per hour, with a slider from hell. He wound up to throw the first pitch, and as he let go, the lights blew out in the stadium. Luckily the ball went to the backstop as the umpire, catcher, and I all hit the deck.

A generator at the hospital had blown, and it blew out all the electricity in the area. We had to sit around for an hour and a half, but were able to get loose before we finally started the game.

We beat San Pedro de Macorís that day, and after we won the Dominican playoff series, we headed to Caracas to play for the Caribbean championship. It was a media event when we arrived, in part because I had bailed on the Caracas team the winter before. The fans recognized me, and they were all over me, calling me "Loco" and any number of names they could think of. But by the end of the series, they changed their tune when I was named the MVP of the series and awarded a wonderful plaque.

One night while in the Dominican Republic, I was in Tommy's suite. The phone rang, and Tommy handed it to me. Al Campanis was on the line, and he told me that I'd been traded to the California Angels.

I was relieved. I didn't want to go through another year of not being excited about going to the baseball field, thinking my manager was hoping I didn't do well. I was happy to get away from Walt Alston, and Tommy was happy for me because he knew the situation. We always thought Tommy would get to be the Dodger manager. We just didn't know when.

Maybe I'm not being fair to Walt, who knew I was loyal to Tommy and not to him. But what happened to me also happened to Tom Paciorek and to Buck. Billy Buck's story with the Dodgers is even more tragic than his story with the Boston Red Sox. Tom Paciorek, another of Tommy's boys, didn't fare much better. Tom arrived in 1973 after spending three years in the minors hitting .300 and driving in 100 runs, and when he got to the Dodgers, Alston used him as a pinch-hitter.

Billy Buck's story is that he wrote that letter to first baseman Wes Parker, who was the Dodger player rep at the time. I was his alternate. Wes was wonderfully educated, really talented, and very sensitive. He was a switch-hitter, the best first baseman I ever played with, and he hit .300 with 12 home runs and 100 RBIs in 1971. He was spectacular, but from the time he got Billy's letter, he was looking over his shoulder. When Billy came to spring training and people got to see the way he played, it was apparent he was a born hitter and that his fire burned brighter than most. Billy Buck was the best competitor I ever played with or against—to a fault. Buck enjoyed hitting, but he hated making outs, hated a pitcher getting the best of him. We all did. I didn't like making an out, but Buck took it to a whole new level. Anyone who played with him would tell you that if he ever struck out, don't be near him in the dugout because he couldn't even see straight.

Wes Parker was as talented a player as I've seen, but he basically retired prematurely so Buck could have that job. Wes was fearful that he'd lose the job to Buck, and that's not how he wanted to go out.

Buck started as the opening-day first baseman in 1973, while at the same time the Dodgers were trying to find a position for Steve Garvey. They tried Garv at third, and they finally said, "No, you will never play third base again." They tried him in left field, but he couldn't throw well enough to play the outfield. Garv was only five foot nine, so they didn't think first base was right for him either, though when he took ground balls, he had pretty good hands. Garv had real thick Irish mason's hands.

Wes Parker had retired early so Buck could have first base, but on June 23, Alston put Buck in left and Garvey at first. After that, Buck hardly ever played first again. The scuttlebutt was that Garvey was going to get traded, but he didn't. Once Garvey got in the lineup and played first, Alston and then Lasorda rarely took him out, and he played well for a decade. But it had been Buck's position.

Many times, Buck complained to me about not playing first, even though it took Garvey a while to solidify his hold on the position. Garv couldn't throw well, and he'd have strike-out days, and he rarely threw the ball to second base. Maybe never. His arm was his bête noire when he was playing third, and he sure couldn't throw from left, but he always could hit. The pregame talk was that he would have fit better with an American League team, because it was the first year of the DH. If Garvey ever had a better day than Buck at the plate, it would kill Buck.

In '76, Buck went into Al Campanis's office after getting his contract offer for the next year. In front of Al, he ripped it up. "I will play for this money as a first baseman, but I'm not going to do it as an outfielder." The next day Buck was a Chicago Cub. And he got to play first base.

Why wasn't Bill Buckner a lifetime Dodger? It could very well have been because Buck was one of Tommy's boys. It may have also been because Buck was a hard-headed guy who didn't like it when batting coach Dixie Walker tried to change him, tried to make him do things differently. If Buck made an out, it was as though the world was coming to an end, he was that demonstrative, and that was not Walter Alston. Tommy didn't mind it at all, but Alston did. Tommy had that emotional side, and Walt had no emotion. He wanted the guys to play like Bill Russell, who played without emotion, like Steve Garvey. That's understandable. That's what you do. Buck wasn't that way.

Tommy knew I was miserable in Los Angeles. He knew I wasn't going to get a shot at shortstop. He had been to all the organizational meetings and knew the way the tide was going. He was happy that I was staying in Southern California. He thought it better that I was going to the American League, so I wouldn't be playing against the Dodgers. As much as Tommy desired Alston's job, and deserved it, he was true blue. When he said he bled Dodger blue, he meant it. He would do anything for the Dodgers, and he'd also do anything for me and for some of his guys. He was glad when Buck got traded to the Cubs, because Garvey had established himself at first base. And he knew I wasn't going to play shortstop. He got that. Tommy wanted what was best for us.

I was traded on November 28, 1972—along with Frank Robinson, Bill Singer, Billy Grabarkewitz, and pitcher Mike Strahler—to the Angels for Andy Messersmith and Ken McMullen. Tom Paciorek was traded on November 17, 1975, along with Lee Lacy and Jim Wynn, to the Atlanta Braves for Dusty Baker and Ed Goodson. Tom played another twelve years, mostly in the American League. Wherever he went, he hit. The Dodgers traded Billy Buck on January 11, 1977, along with Iván de Jesus, to the Cubs for Rick Monday and Mike Garman. He played thirteen more seasons, winning the batting title in 1980 and becoming the scapegoat for the Red Sox loss to the Mets in the 1986 World Series. Billy died, too soon, in May 2019 at age 69. I miss him every day. Steve Garvey played for the Los Angeles Dodgers from 1969 to 1982.

Tommy Lasorda finally took over for Walt Alston at the end of 1976. He managed the Dodgers until 1996, winning four pennants and two World Series championships. All too late for me.

I could have played for the Dodgers for the next twenty years. I was still developing. I needed to get over the fact that I had a great arm. It didn't suit me well, because I always wanted to show it off. I would watch the other shortstops get the ball and throw over to first and just beat the runner by half a step. I wanted to get that runner by five steps. I threw ninety-five, and it was hard to control. It's why Wes Parker was so great. He saved me so many errors, as did Tommy Hutton, who was the second-best first baseman I ever saw.

But I always felt bad for Buck, even before a lot of other people felt bad for Buck.

CHAPTER 7

I'm an Angel

Harry Dalton was in his second year as general manager of the Angels. He had come from Baltimore, and one of the reasons he got Frank Robinson in the trade that brought me to California was that Harry wanted Frank to be the Angels manager. But the cowboy who owned the Angels, Gene Autry, didn't think his club was the right place for the first black manager. In that the designated hitter had come into the league, Frank didn't cry bloody murder. He became the Angels' DH and was a regular. After the '74 season, Frank was traded to Cleveland, where he became the first black manager in the history of baseball.

In 1972 Harry Dalton wanted to change the identity of his team. Jim Fregosi was the shortstop and the face of the team. Harry traded Jim to the Mets for Nolan Ryan, in what turned out to be one of the best trades in Angels history. He also brought in Zoilo Versalles, who had been an All-Star, to replace Fregosi at shortstop.

Nolan Ryan was an up-and-coming star who had control problems. He helped the Mets win the 1969 World Series but was still struggling with his control three years later. He'd been with the Mets for several years but never developed into the pitcher they were hoping for. It wasn't until he got to the Angels that he finally hit his stride.

I knew about Nolan, because I had played against him when I was with the Dodgers. I knew about his fastball and his curveball, and knew he was really wild. In those days, pitchers in the beginning of their careers would start in the bullpen and only start games once in a while. It's what Nolan did with the Mets. When he came to the Angels, manager Del Rice didn't have the arms the Mets did, and he gave Nolan the opportunity to start as much as he could. It was amazing how many pitches Nolan could throw in a game. As a manager you have to have *a lot* of patience. When Nolan pitched early in his career, a manager was always on the edge of his seat as to whether he would walk six batters and we'd be behind 2–0 before he found the strike zone. Nolan always wanted the ball. He never wanted to come out of the game. Most of the time his stuff was unhittable. He had seven no-hitters. He also had twelve one-hitters, tied for the most with Bob Feller, and eighteen two-hitters.

One day when I was playing shortstop for the Angels, Al Kaline walked and went to second on a wild pitch. I went over to say hi.

"How's he throwing today, Al?" I asked.

"If you don't make one of those pitches illegal," said Kaline, "he's going to throw a no-hitter."

That day Nolan threw a one-hitter. Eddie Brinkman got the one hit.

Nolan had days when mere mortals weren't going to hit him. The other team was just hoping he'd run out of gas and someone else would come into the game. He brought intimidation into the game. He was Big Tex, and the first thing he'd do would be to walk down toward the first hitter before the game began and check out the ground in front of home plate. As he was looking around at the ground, as though he was looking for a four-leaf clover, he would look up and catch the eye of the leadoff hitter. It was always a cool sight to see.

You had to watch yourself with Nolan. One day in Boston, Doug Griffin was going to bunt against him. Nolan dropped his right foot back, leaned his head toward the plate, and threw a fastball that hit Griffin in the head. Griffin was never the same player again.

Nolan pitched for twenty-seven seasons, from 1966 until 1993, winning 324 games and losing 292. He finished with 5,714 strikeouts, the most ever. Behind him are Randy Johnson with 4,875, and Roger Clemens with 4,672.

Nolan and I would reunite in Texas.

During the winter of 1972, a short time before concluding the trade with the Dodgers that brought me to the Angels, Harry made a very bold statement by hiring the first collegiate head coach to manage his team. Bobby Winkles had an outstanding record while coaching the Arizona State Sun Devils, where he nurtured such star players as Reggie Jackson, Rick Monday, and Sal Bando.

At the beginning of spring training in 1973, Bobby, who had a strong Southern accent, made it clear that what he wanted more than anything else was to speed up the game. He believed there was too much dead time. We weren't allowed to step out of the batter's box. Relief pitchers were told to run in from the bullpen and sprint off the field. Mickey Rivers was the backup center fielder to Ken Berry, but Mickey was always so slow in everything he did that it made Bobby's stomach turn, because Mickey just would not speed up the game.

Bobby Winkles told me in spring training that if I could beat out Leo Cardenas, the shortstop job would be mine. Winkles played us every other game, about ten games each, and he decided I had won the position. I became the regular shortstop, and they traded Cardenas to Cleveland.

I played shortstop almost every game when the season began. I batted third in Bobby Winkles's lineup, and I was becoming the force everyone expected me to be. What I needed was the good fortune to pursue my dreams without getting injured again. It's the part of the game you can't prepare for or guard against.

On May 13, 1973, while I was leading the Angels in hitting, Bobby came to me and said, "Listen, Kenny [Berry] needs a day off. I don't want to put Mickey Rivers out there. I want you to play center field. When we get back home, you'll be the shortstop. I'll get [Rudy] Meoli to play short today, and if he does good, I'll insert him at second base when we get home."

On May 15, Nolan Ryan threw his first no-hitter. I was in center field and made a couple of good plays, and Bobby Winkles, like every other baseball person, was superstitious. We returned home after winning that final game in Kansas City and Bobby said to me, "I can't change the lineup. We just broke a losing streak, and Nolan threw a no-hitter." Bobby Winkles and I had a great relationship. I loved his style.

"Anything you want, Bobby," I said.

"I guarantee you," said Winkles, "tomorrow you'll be back at shortstop."

May 17 was just a regular day. One of my good friends on the team, Rudy May, was pitching. Rudy was an African-American guy with a big smile and a good change-up. He had a consecutive scoreless streak going, and we were playing Oakland, who were just beginning to become the powerful Oakland A's.

"Don't worry, Rudy," I said, "you're covered in the outfield."

I was peaking. I had a rich career ahead of me. My manager was in my corner, the wind was at my back, and fortune was smiling. I couldn't wait every day to get out of bed and head to the ballpark. In the 32 games I had played in '73, I was batting .302 with 12 runs scored, 13 RBIs, and 6 stolen bases.

I singled off Catfish Hunter my first at-bat. In the third inning, Dick Green came up to bat. I was playing over in shallow right-center field, and Green hit the ball to deep left-center. I leapt to climb the fence to catch the ball. A green plastic tarp was stretched across the chain-link fence at the Big A, and though I have never watched video of what happened, apparently my spike lodged in the canvas. Instead of my foot sliding down the canvas and my body taking the force of the collision, my leg and foot took the force of the collision, and, halfway between my leg and my foot, my tibia and fibula snapped. It felt as though the upper and lower parts of my leg were not connected.

Vada Pinson, who was playing left field, came over to see if I was okay.

"I broke my leg," I said. "Shoot me."

They loaded me on a stretcher and carried me off. Some players couldn't watch, because my foot was flopping from side to side uncontrollably. It didn't feel attached to my leg. Billy Grabarkewitz, who ran out to me as fast as anyone, was holding my toe up to keep my foot from jiggling.

When I got to the clubhouse, the trainer gave me a tranquilizer. I woke up in the hospital with a nurse telling me they were waiting for the swelling to go down so they could set my leg.

I had just turned twenty-three a few days earlier.

My doctor was the Angels' orthopedic surgeon, Donald Ball. Prior to 1973 the Angels' doctor had been Robert Kerlan, the father of sports orthopedic medicine. Dr. Kerlan took care of all the Los Angeles teams: the Rams, Dodgers, Angels, and Lakers. But this year there was a break between the Angels and the Kerlan group, and they hired Dr. Ball, whose father and grandfather were both prominent citizens. In fact, Ball Street, which was adjacent to the stadium, was named after his family. This young Donald Ball came in to see me as I was lying in the hospital bed.

"I saw the x-rays," he said, "and the bones are both broken," meaning the tibia and the fibula. "But the tibia is broken in a way that I feel I can put it back together without surgery."

He wanted to perform what was called a closed reduction, since the skin had not been broken. What he had to do was manipulate the pieces that were broken back together again, using x-ray imagery to guide his hands. The other option was to surgically open the skin, manipulate bones into place, and secure them with a metal insert. He told me this was the conventional practice, but he didn't think it was necessary. If all the fragments could be put back together again, it would heal just fine, he was sure.

His concern was with the tibia. Since the fibula wasn't weight-bearing, he said, he wasn't going to worry about it. And because the operation was not invasive, the healing time would be shorter. I'd be out of the cast and back onto the field sooner, he said.

As I waited for the swelling to go down, I got a phone call. On the other end of the line was a baritone voice introducing himself as Dr. Robert Kerlan. When I had hurt my knee playing flag football, his protégé, Frank Jobe, had done the operation, and he had done a perfect job. It took a while for me to rehab the knee, but today the only problem I have is when the metal detector goes off because I have a staple holding some of the ligaments together.

"Bob," Dr. Kerlan said, "I just want you to understand I am available if you need me to do the procedure."

These are the key moments in one's life. I needed Tommy Lasorda or Bobby Winkles or my father or someone to say to me, "Let Dr. Kerlan do this operation."

Instead, I said, "Thank you very much, but it seems as though I am in good hands with Dr. Ball."

Dr. Kerlan wished me luck and said if I needed him to please call.

Dr. Ball put my tibia, the shinbone, back together perfectly. But the fibula, the smaller of the two bones in the lower leg, was initially not connected. A complicating factor was that that I was pigeon-toed, and because I was pigeon-toed, I could run faster than just about anyone on the planet. I was so pigeon-toed that I would occasionally kick my ankle and I'd bleed. In setting my leg, it was never taken into consideration that I was pigeon-toed. Who were the fastest runners of the day? Mickey Rivers. Richie Allen. Ricky Henderson. Carl Lewis. They all had a pigeon-toed walk, and I walked like them and I could run like them.

It was only a couple months later that I realized I wasn't pigeon-toed anymore. I had a hard plaster cast, and after a few months when I went to the doctor to change it, I could see my leg had atrophied. My leg inside the cast had become smaller, and the tibia had started to bend. When the doctor said he was going to have to put on a new cast, I asked him, "What is that bump on the middle of my shin?"

"Oh, that's just calcification," he said. "That's normal. It's a good thing you're getting that much calcium there for the healing process."

He wasn't giving me all the information. My shin was starting to bend, and the protrusion of calcium on the front of my shin made my leg look abnormal. It was disgusting. As he put on the new cast, his intern was pushing down on my leg at the point of the break and causing me tremendous pain. I didn't cry, but I made noise because of the pain, and when he was finished putting on the new cast, he said, "The atrophy probably has finished its course, and this cast will be very tight on your leg. If you feel discomfort, please let me know."

The new cast was fiberglass instead of plaster. It was lighter, and I was supposed to be able to get around better on crutches. But the atrophy continued, and about two weeks later I felt a burning sensation and could see blood coming through the cast at the break.

When I called, I was told, "If you come in two weeks, Dr. Ball should be back from vacation."

Meanwhile, I went to all the Angels games. I would walk into the clubhouse on my crutches, wish them all luck, and then go sit in the stands, watch the game, and put my leg up on the seat in front of me. When the Angels went on the road, I stayed home and watched the games on TV.

One morning I went to speak at the local Anaheim Kiwanis Club breakfast. I was an ex-Key Club member, and so I went to the basement of a church in one of the neighboring towns of Anaheim and talked about rooting for the home team for about an hour, and then I opened it up for questions. There were thirty older Angels fans there, and one of them asked me how Frank Robinson was using his leadership abilities to help first-year manager Bobby Winkles.

"Help him?" I said.

And then I said something negative about Frank. I was telling the truth, because every time Bobby Winkles called a meeting, as soon as

Bobby walked out, Frank said something like, "That's a bunch of bull-shit," or "Who's he trying to kid?" When Frank came to the Angels, he thought he was going to be the manager, and even though Harry Dalton was his guy, he didn't get the job. Bobby was different, and many of the players resisted his new ideas. Whenever Bobby wanted his players to do something unorthodox, Frank would say, "Oh bullshit."

The next day there was a headline in the local paper which read, "Valentine: Robinson Isn't on Board." I never saw the newspaper, so when I was called into Bobby Winkles's office, I had no idea what the meeting was about. When I walked in on my crutches, Harry Dalton and Frank Robinson were there, too. On Bobby's desk was the newspaper.

Harry picked it up and said, "Bobby, were you at the Kiwanis Club breakfast yesterday?"

"Yeah, Harry," I said, thinking he was going to say, "You did a great job promoting the team."

He just asked me why I said what I said about Frank.

"Because it's the truth," I said. "At every clubhouse meeting there is this growing group of dissenters, led by Frank."

I was Bobby's lead disciple. I carried the flag for him. I had seen this deterioration of teamwork, and Frank was one of the ringleaders. I probably should have told Bobby and Harry about it, but instead I told the Kiwanis Club members. I was scolded. I apologized for it getting out and for handling it the wrong way. I didn't apologize for what I said, and on my way out of the office Frank walked by me, muttered something unpleasant, and bumped me. I gave him a push, and in a mega-second we were on the floor of the clubhouse, with my cast draping over his leg as I tried to get him in the upper wrestling position. Harry Dalton and Bobby Winkles broke it up.

C'est la vie.

(Later on, Frank, Nolan, and I were teammates on the quiz show *Sports Challenge*. We won for six weeks in a row, beating the likes of Frank Gifford, Muhammad Ali, Charlie Conerly, Dick Williams, and a couple of his A's. We retired as undefeated champions.)

79

CHAPTER 8

Agony

When the time came to take off my cast, I was taken aback by how the leg looked. I had a large protrusion on the front of my shin, and my calf and thigh had no muscle. My leg looked like I had had polio, with a big bump on it.

I called Bobby Winkles, who had coached the Arizona State baseball team, and asked him if he would set up a rehabilitation program for me at Arizona State.

"Sure," he said, "just go and meet Frank Kush," the ASU football coach. "His trainer will set you up with a rehab program."

I flew to Tempe, Arizona, that night, had some beers with the boys in the fraternity house, and went to see Coach Kush the next day. He was waiting for me on the sideline during football practice. I pulled up my pant leg to show him how ugly the leg looked, and he said, "What? Are you crazy? You can't rehab that leg. It's crooked, and you'll never be able to run again."

Walking was no problem, and I had tried to jog a little. I figured all I would have to do was a little rehab, until Coach Kush's reaction sent me running to the nearest phone booth. I called Dr. Ball in a panic and started screaming and yelling at him.

"Is this true? What does Coach Kush mean, it's deformed and crooked, and I'll never be able to run again?"

Dr. Ball told me to get on a plane and fly back to L.A. He would meet with me and Bobby Winkles.

Roxy was in a panic and so was I.

"Before I suggest that I re-break your leg," Dr. Ball said, "I want you to do rehab and see what you can do."

That's what I did. I went back to the gym at Arizona State, started working out, and tried to take batting practice. For a couple of months, I had no strength or flexibility, but then it started to get better, and I kept at it.

I went to other doctors and to chiropractors, and when they measured my leg, they found one leg was shorter than the other because of the curvature. I was given lifts. I got a custom-made shoe, a baseball spike with a heel. It's ridiculous when you think about it, but it allowed my two legs to be the same length and gave me a little better balance. I could play with it, even though I found myself tripping over things, including the bases.

I was miserable because of my leg, but also because Roxy and I were going in different directions. I liked my guy friends, and they were always around. She liked private time and she had interests other than baseball, but she bit the bullet and sacrificed and changed so she could be my partner.

Roxy had tried to be a baseball wife, but most of the baseball players weren't cut from the same cloth as the men she wanted to be with. When we got to the big leagues and were married, my high school football team captain and good friend, Darrell Atterberry, who had strayed from the athletic field and descended into drugs, lived with us the first year we were married, if you can imagine that for Roxy. There were hair follicles in the sink every day, and boys were being boys; and as hard as she tried, it was an amazing world she was trying to adjust to. It wasn't fair to her. I was trying to pound that round peg into a square hole, and there were times I was totally in her world, but those times were too few and far between. I was looking for her to make the adjustments, and that's not what marriage is all about.

At the end of the summer of 1973, I was rehabilitating my leg, and I was trying to do a lot of bike riding to get my thigh back in shape. I was riding thirty to forty miles a day from Irvine, California, where we lived. Irvine was just being developed, and there were orange groves all around. Our home was right off McArthur Boulevard on the 405 Freeway.

I came back from a long bike ride, and who was there but a male friend whom Roxy had dated at Denison University. Andy was there having coffee with Roxy, and I was a little surprised at first. Then my surprise morphed into being wary and upset. Andy left, Roxy and I talked, and soon after that the season ended, I was going to Arizona State to rehab my leg. We decided that she should go home to Stamford and we should think about getting a divorce.

We had two cars. One was given to me by the Stamford residents, and the other I bought in California, and Roxy took the one given to me. We went to Tommy Lasorda's garage, where we stored a lot of our belongings, and packed her car. That was where we kissed and said goodbye.

There was no anger, no bitterness. We had a meeting of the minds that it wasn't going to work out the way we had hoped. We had the teenage dream of the football captain and the cheerleader captain/homecoming queen living happily ever after. I went to Arizona by myself, and she went home to Stamford and soon married Andy.

CHAPTER 9

Trying to Come Back

On opening day of 1974, I started in left field for the Angels. I was no longer considered a shortstop, which was heartbreaking, because most of my quickness and balance had been left at the hospital, or really against the left-field wall in Anaheim.

Opening weekend was at Comiskey Park (named White Sox Park at the time) in Chicago. For the third game of the series, it was snowing and the wind was howling, blowing straight in from left. Game time temperature was thirty-eight degrees. The place was packed, and we were going to get this one in.

Bill Singer was pitching for us, and Richie Allen, now playing for the White Sox, hit the ball to left. He could hit towering fly balls for home runs. Richie swung and hit a monster shot that was clearly a home run. I made a courtesy run to the fence and watched the ball disappear over the protruding second deck, when the infamous Chicago wind stopped his home run from leaving the stadium and pushed it back toward the infield. It was the only ball I ever caught as an outfielder running *toward* the infield, with the ball over my shoulder coming from the outfield stands. It was one of the best catches I ever made. The game ended in a 4–4 tie after ten innings due to the weather.

Bobby Winkles and I were connected at the hip. He was for me, and I was for him, and when I came back, he tried to do everything he could to keep me in the lineup. I was always telling Winkles, "Look, I will do anything to play. Whatever I can do." I was given a cortisone shot every three weeks for my ankle, and I'd get a day off to get it.

I was adjusting to a new sense of balance provided by the special shoes I was wearing. I felt, finally, that I was hitting my stride.

During the off-season I had been a guest on a local radio show in San Bernardino, California. I was picking up a car from a dealer who was letting me use the car for the season, which was always a big deal. While I was out there, I was sitting in the dealership, signing autographs, and the local radio host came over for an interview.

"How much is the team going to miss Clyde Wright?" he asked me.

The Angels had just made a wintertime trade, sending Clyde Wright, a thirty-two-year-old star pitcher, to Milwaukee. The trade was part of Bobby Winkles's policy of playing younger players. I was supporting Bobby when I answered: "Oh, it was the right thing to do. We won't miss Clyde at all."

I didn't know it, but Clyde Wright lived in San Bernardino, and he was either listening to me on the radio or someone told him what I said. On a day in May, we were playing the Brewers, and Clyde was pitching. Before the game, the trainer for the Brewers went over to the trainer for the Angels, and said, "Give the word to Valentine that Clyde is going to hit him in the head the first time he comes up to bat."

After I got the word, I tried going over to the Brewers' dugout to smooth things over with Clyde. I asked their trainer if he'd bring Clyde to see me. The trainer came back.

"Clyde said you can go fuck yourself," he said. "He'll see you during the game."

Oh well, I thought, *why didn't I listen to my mom when she told me to keep my mouth shut?*

My brother and his wife Pat were at the game. My brother Joe had never gone on the road to see me play. I went over to him and asked him if the tickets were okay.

"Everything's great," he said. "We're excited."

"Good," I said, "because I'm going to get hit the first time up, and I'm not going to charge the mound. I'm going to take first base and then try to steal second, but fasten your seat belt."

I was the third batter in the bottom of the first. Clyde was on the mound, and the first pitch was aimed right at my head. The ball came so close to my face that I don't know how it missed me. I figured I was going to get hit, and I'd run down to first, but the ball came directly at my noggin, and I went down in a heap on my back, my heart pounding. I had flashbacks of getting beaned in Hawaii. As I lay there, I thought to myself, *I can't let this happen again.* I got up and grabbed my bat, and I flipped it to Ron Luciano, the umpire.

"Here, hold this," I said. I turned to run out to the mound, but after taking one step, standing there was Clyde Wright. He had thrown his glove down and was intent on meeting me at the batter's box. I hit him with a good right cross just below his left eye, but he didn't go down. The next thing I knew he picked me up as though I were a rag doll. Clyde outweighed me by twenty pounds and was strong as an ox. He threw me over his leg, as you would do with a wrestling move, and as I went down, my left shoulder hit the ground and separated.

I was at the bottom of a pile holding onto his head with all my might, and when the pile was unpacked, I walked off holding my arm at my side. I was replaced by Winston Llenas. Clyde Wright was thrown out of the game.

I rehabbed my shoulder for two weeks. I felt I had let Bobby Winkles down terribly, because once again, I was on the DL. His style was getting push-back from our veterans, and the day I got off the disabled list and

85

took batting practice, I could hardly swing, but I told him I was okay because I wanted to be activated.

In that game, Nolan Ryan struck out 19 Boston Red Sox and threw 235 pitches. He came out of the game after completing 13 innings with a no-decision. Late in the game, I pinch-hit against Luis Tiant and popped out to second with the winning run on base. I swung at a breaking ball, using only my left arm, and re-injured my shoulder. Tiant was the losing pitcher after tossing $14^1/_3$ innings.

I was hitting about .280, but my shoulder was not healed. I continued to play, but went 0 for 20 before Bobby Winkles was fired twelve days after the Ryan/Tiant game, on June 26. Winkles had had a 30–44 record, and he was replaced for four days by Whitey Herzog, our third-base coach.

"Whitey," I said, "I feel real bad about Bobby. It's terrible, but I want you to know I'm with you all the way. If you need anything, I can be as loyal to you as I was to Bobby."

"Ah, kid," Whitey said, "I'm not going to last in this job. They're going to hire someone else. He's going to come in and clean house and get rid of all the old players, like Bobby wanted to do, and they're going to rebuild the team."

That's just what happened. Whitey was a young, enthusiastic guy on the fast track to be a manager, but he wasn't quite there yet, and the Angels hired Dick Williams. The next year, Whitey was hired to manage the Royals.

Dick had begun his managerial career with the Red Sox, leading them to a pennant in 1967. When the players rebelled at his discipline, he was fired. He spent three years with the Oakland A's, leading them to three pennants and two World Series championships. But Dick was abrasive and again wore out his welcome. Now he was the manager of the Angels.

Dick came in, and I didn't welcome him. When asked about his hiring, I repeated what Whitey had said to me.

"Now that Dick's here and Bobby Winkles is gone," I said, "they will probably do what Bobby wanted to do. They didn't let Bobby have the young team he wanted."

My problem was that I liked Bobby's style, and I didn't like Dick's. Dick was old school, like Billy Martin and Earl Weaver. I felt their time had passed. I much preferred the way Tommy Lasorda and Bobby Winkles ran things.

Two weeks into his tenure, an angry Dick Williams tipped over the clubhouse spread, the hamburgers and the hot dogs, after the game. He shouted we weren't deserving of having a meal, because big-leaguers get meals after the game, and this was a minor league team. The next day we came to the ballpark, and there was a blackboard pushed out into the middle of the room, and it had a cover over it. Dick called the meeting, and he pulled off the cover.

"Everyone look at this," he demanded.

On the right side of the blackboard were fifteen names. On the left side were ten, including Nolan, Frank Tanana, and me.

"Take a look at this blackboard," he said. "If you are on the right side of this blackboard, this is the only major league team you can play for in the major leagues."

I was disgusted. *I can't believe this is what we're in for,* I thought.

Williams was saying we all stank, and what he was going to do was get rid of as many players as he could and rebuild the team, because this team had been built by someone else, and *he* knew how to build a winner. I didn't like him at all, but part of it was because of me. I had thought that in Bobby Winkles I'd found a manager who was most like Tommy Lasorda, in caring for me and having energy and thinking about the young guys succeeding. Instead, I had somebody else.

There was also another issue at the time that affected my situation with the Angels. While at Arizona State, I'd become friends with Pete Serino, an ASU graduate who was practicing law. On a visit to L.A., Pete saw my crooked leg and convinced me to sue Dr. Ball for malpractice. My intent in the lawsuit was not a monetary windfall, but to have enough funds to cover future medical costs.

I was convinced this was the thing to do, but when the Angels got wind of it, I became *persona non grata* during the winter of 1974–75.

The season ended, and I had a lackluster year, playing many positions and hitting .261. I asked Tommy Lasorda if I could come and play with his team in the Dominican Republic. It was lucky for me that he said yes. It was another of life's wonderful occurrences that changed my life for the better. That wonderful happenstance was Ralph Branca vacationing in the Dominican with his family, at Tommy's suggestion.

"La Romana is one of the great vacation spots in the world," Tommy had told Ralph. "Why don't you think about taking a family trip, and when you're here, you can come and watch some of the young Dodger players."

I knew of Ralph Branca because he'd thrown the famous pitch to Bobby Thomson in 1951 that led to the Shot Heard 'Round the World. He was married to the daughter of Jim Mulvey, a part owner of the Dodgers. Every spring he came to Dodgertown in Vero Beach. The only other thing I knew about Ralph was that he had worn number 13, because when the Dodgers drafted me and asked me what number I wanted to wear, I said "thirteen," and they said, "No. We don't give out thirteen. That's Ralph Branca's number." After Ralph came to the ballpark and threw batting practice to us, he went and sat with the owner of the Dominican team to watch the game.

I was playing shortstop, and in the middle of the second inning Ralph's wife Ann walked into the park with their two college-aged daughters. Patty, the older sister, had dark hair, and Mary, the younger one, had blonde hair, like her mother. Not only were Patty, Mary, and Ann beautiful, but they stood out among all the dark-haired Dominicans. They might as well have had haloes around their heads, like Glenn Close in *The Natural*. When I saw them take their seats, I called time out and went to the mound to talk with Charlie Hough. Steve Yeager, our catcher, joined us.

"Did you see what just came into the stadium?" I said.

Ann was in her forties and beautiful, as were her two daughters. They richly deserved a time-out and a trip to the mound. They were sitting right behind the on-deck circle in the front row.

"Charlie," said Yeager, "throw one of your knuckleballs, and I'll let it get away so I can get a close-up."

It was our turn to bat. I was the leadoff hitter, and while I was in the on-deck circle, I playfully flirted with the three stunning women.

"Where are you staying?" I asked.

"We're staying at the Embajador," Ann said.

El Embajador was an upscale hotel in Santo Domingo. Our team was staying at the Jaragua Hotel, the same hotel where the Dodgers stayed in 1947, because the citizens of Vero Beach wouldn't allow Jackie Robinson to stay with his white Dodger teammates during spring training in Florida.

I knew where the Embajador Hotel was, and after the game, I and a few of the boys—Tom Paciorek, our batboy John Boggs (who would become the agent for Robin Ventura, Tony Gwynn, and many others), and a couple others—drove over there. We wanted to meet these American gals, not knowing who they were. When we arrived, we opened the hotel's front door and there they were, standing in the lobby with former Brooklyn Dodger pitcher Ralph Branca.

Holy shit, I thought. *They're with Ralph.*

After talking awhile in the lobby, I said, "Why don't we all go to the discotheque?" It wasn't one of the sharpest lines in opening lines history.

Ralph and Ann excused themselves, and Patty, Mary, Tom Paciorek, John Boggs, and I went to the discotheque.

That's how I met Mary Branca and started a wonderful new chapter in my life. She was only in the Dominican for a week, on her Christmas break from college. We had instant synergy. She had an irresistible smile, and her eyes were like beacons in the night. We danced that night, and after I learned she was attending the University of North Carolina, I started making trips to see her. We had many great times together in Chapel Hill.

After winter ball came spring training with the Angels. Spring training in 1975 with Dick Williams was a nightmare. In camp, Dick fed me some BS as to why he wasn't going to play me. He said, "Listen, Bobby, we know what you can do. What we need to do is see as many of the young players as we can, so stay ready. You're not going to get many at-bats, but don't worry about that, because we know what you can do."

All through spring training I was running the stadium stairs, doing what I could to strengthen my leg. I was in a lot of pain and taking a lot of shots of cortisone and Novocain. My goal was to gain enough strength in the leg and flexibility in my ankle so I could stop taking these shots that were necessary to get on the field.

At the end of spring training, we played a three-game Freeway Series against the Dodgers. I batted a couple times in the second game, and then Dick Williams called me into his office.

"We need more time to look at the younger players," he said.

Mike Miley was twenty-two, Dave Collins was twenty-two, Jerry Remy was twenty-two. I was a not-so-young anymore, approaching twenty-five in May.

My reaction was that either Dick needed to look more closely at Miley, or it was bullshit. It didn't really matter. My attitude was, *Okay, you need to see him. I'll play every day at Salt Lake City,* the Angels' Triple-A club.

It's what I was expecting Dick to say. Instead, he said, "Harry is coming in. He wants to explain this to you."

Dick left the office, and Harry Dalton, our general manager, sat down.

"Geez, Bobby, we weren't planning on this. We didn't think this was going to happen. It's such a late date that there's no room at Salt Lake City for you."

I gulped.

"But I found a place where you can play every day. It's the Pittsburgh Pirates' Triple-A team in Charlestown, West Virginia. We're going to loan you to them."

I was shell-shocked. We were playing the Dodgers, so I left Dick's office and ran across the field into the other dugout, to see Tommy in the Dodger clubhouse. In '75, Tommy was still a coach.

I was really upset and said to Tommy, "Have you ever heard of anything like this? They are sending me to Charleston. They say I'm not traded. They are sending me there on loan. What can I do? What should I do? What do you think? They didn't let me play all spring. They are fucking me, Tommy. They're fucking me."

"Yeah," Tommy said upon reflection. "They are fucking you, all right."

"What should I do?"

"Don't worry about it," Tommy said. "A buddy of mine is managing Charleston. He'll take care of you."

Steve Demeter, the brother of Don Demeter, an ex-Dodger, was the Charleston manager. He was the best of a bad situation. The Pirates were always seen as one of the cheapest organizations in baseball, going back to when Branch Rickey ran the franchise. This is not a scoop. As a result, Charleston always had the worst playing conditions. The general manager there, it turned out, had been the minor league general manager for Harry Dalton in Baltimore.

My problem: this was Charleston, West Virginia, for crying out loud. This was coal country, and the coal freight trains, which had at least a million cars connected to each other, passed by Watt Powell Park behind the left-field fence every night, for what seemed like an eternity. For innings upon innings, these coal trains would chug by.

Additionally, Charleston was the only team in Triple-A that didn't fly for road trips. They rode a bus many hundreds of miles, to places like Pawtucket, Rhode Island, and Columbus, Ohio. Some of the rides were fourteen hours. On the plus side, we had a wonderful group of guys, a whole team of Pirates of the future, with players like John Candelaria,

Craig Reynolds, Eddie Ott, Kurt Bevacqua, Doug Bair, Omar Moreno, Kent Tekulve, Miguel Diloné, Tony Armas, and Willie Randolph.

It was a spectacular team, and when I arrived in Charleston, I lightened my load by trying to be a good camper. I didn't bitch or moan. I did free clinics for the kids, and I played pretty well. I played third base, and what lit my fire was that I was told by Steve Demeter, and also by scouts, that what the Angels were doing was trying to get me to quit. They couldn't trade me. No one wanted me. I was damaged goods. The Angels said they were still hoping maybe I could come back and maybe even play shortstop again. Maybe this. Maybe that. Maybe they were hoping I would quit.

I decided I would do some PR for myself to let the Angels know how well I was doing. You will see later this wasn't the smartest thing I ever did in my life. A reporter from *Sports Illustrated* came to see me, and I lied a little bit when I told him, "Yeah, I'm running good." I didn't mention that I didn't have the grace and balance I once had, or that my leg really looked ugly.

In Charleston, I found a small place with a little kitchenette to live over a garage. I was only going to be there a month, the Angels said, so I paid the owner, whose name was Beulah, a month's rent. When the month was up, I was hitting over .300, doing well, and I talked to the Angels' farm director. I said, "Listen, I gotta know now about the rent for next month. We're through with this home stand, and we go on a really long road trip." It was that road trip from hell where we went to Pawtucket, Columbus, Rochester, and then home, all in an un-air-conditioned bus.

"We'll have something done by the end of the home stand," he promised.

I told that to Charleston general manager Carl Steinfeldt. "That's what I've been told, too," he said, which is why the team held a day for me right after the last game of the home stand. The booster club thanked me and, in a presentation at home plate, gave me a blender.

After the game, I was sitting in the clubhouse waiting for the general manager to come and tell me which flight I was going to take, when he said to me, "Bobby, they have changed their mind in California. You better get on the bus, because you're staying with us."

I hadn't segregated my belongings for what I would need for this fourteen-day road trip. Everything I owned was stuffed in two large suitcases, and I stuck one underneath the bus. There was barely enough room for the other piece of luggage on the bus, and it sat there in the aisle taunting me and making everyone else step over it.

I was upset. I was incredibly embarrassed. I had said my goodbyes to everyone in the expectation that I would be leaving this hellhole, and here I was stuck on that bus for the next fourteen hours, and who knows how much longer.

Steve Demeter, who was a really good guy, had me sit up front next to him for the rest of the trip as he tried to calm me down. He said he'd make a phone call and straighten it all out. He didn't play me the next day. He wanted me to cool my heels. No one from the Angels returned phone calls from Steve or me.

I stuck with the Charleston team for the next two weeks, then word finally came down from the minor league director that the Angels were trying to clear a roster spot for me in Salt Lake City. I don't want to say I wasn't trying on that road trip, but I wasn't concentrating the way I should have been. I had a lot of angry at-bats. After you go around to all your teammates and they say, "Good luck. Great being with you. See you in the big leagues," and then you wind up sitting with them in an un-air-conditioned bus for two weeks, I was miserable. I wasn't a spoiled brat. For five years in the big leagues, I had flown from city to city, and here I was kicked back to that old bus-centric lifestyle. I tried hard to put it all in perspective, but I have to admit, I pouted awhile.

The saving grace of my playing in Charleston was that I was in love. I was dating Mary Branca, and she was living with me in Charleston. Because Mary was the daughter of a major league baseball player, unlike Roxy, Mary was well aware of the vagaries of the baseball life. When I found out I wasn't going to leave Charleston, she canceled her plane ticket and made other arrangements. She liked everything to be planned and organized, but when it wasn't, she managed, because she knew my lifestyle was not the easiest in the world.

During the road trip, I would get phone calls from the Angels' minor league director. "You'll be out of Charleston in a day." And so I would go to the ballpark, whether it was Rochester or Syracuse, and I'd go by Steve Demeter's hotel room to give him an update so he could prepare a lineup, with me or without me. Many days, after lunch I'd knock on his door and find him in his room, and I'd say, "Well, it's not today."

A couple times I told him, "It is today," because they told me I would hear from them the next day, but I never did. I spent the entire road trip with the team. We got back to Charleston at four in the morning, and I went to the general manager's office. Carl Steinfeldt was there waiting for me at Watt Powell Park at four in the morning.

Carl called me inside and said he was told to buy me a ticket, not to Anaheim but to Salt Lake City. He thanked me for my services, and the next morning I flew out of Charleston.

I was met at the Salt Lake City airport by manager Norm Sherry, the former Dodger catcher and another of Lasorda's posse. His brother was Larry Sherry, who pitched for the Dodgers. Tommy and Norm once had ridden buses and played winter ball together.

I drove with Norm to the hotel. He expected me to be outraged and cursing, but I told him, "I'm here to play, man. I'm glad I'm with the Triple-A team of the Angels." I asked, "We do fly, don't we?"

"We do," he said.

"Listen," I said. "This is all great. I'm glad to be here."

We had a really great group of guys, but I wasn't with the Gulls long. I hit .306 with 17 RBIs and 13 stolen bases in 46 games. Once again I could run, though not the way I once could fly. What I didn't know was that my ankle couldn't bend enough to allow me to bend forward. After twenty degrees, my heel would have to come off the ground. I couldn't do a deep knee bend. When players saw my leg, they were amazed I could even walk.

I was sure I'd be in Salt Lake City for the long haul. I paid the whole summer's rent to get the apartment I wanted. Mary was coming, and I didn't want to live in a hotel.

The Gulls were trying to win the division, which was a lot of fun, and I was contributing, but then came a rash of injuries on the major league team. In August, Norm called me into his office and said, "You're going up to the big leagues."

I arrived in Anaheim the first week of August 1975. I played in a couple games, pinch-hit a couple times, but with Dick Williams still the manager, I always had an uneasy feeling. The Angels were in need of someone who could play the infield and bat right-handed and perhaps even play shortstop. They were overrun with second basemen. Denny Doyle, Sandy Alomar Jr., Rudy Meoli, and Jerry Remy had come up to become their regular second baseman. When Jerry came up, they moved Sandy to short. Sandy had been my second baseman when I was the shortstop, before I broke my leg. I wasn't part of their equation.

I played a few games, but I didn't do much. We were in Minnesota, and a friend of Bruce Bochte was having a birthday. We went to a restaurant to celebrate. Bruce and his friend, and Nolan Ryan, Dave Chalk, and I were there. There was a bar side to the restaurant, and we didn't see who was there—Dick Miller, a reporter from the *Santa Ana Register*, and Jerry Adair, a coach on the Angels.

When I was playing in Charleston, Dick Miller had called me to ask how I was doing. I said I was hitting over .300, playing third base, playing pretty well, but I criticized Adair, because Dick had told me that Adair was the one who decided I should be sent down to the minors.

Dick would say to the reporters, "Jerry doesn't think Valentine has the quality to be a major league infielder." The reporters would go from Dick's office to Jerry's locker to ask, "What kind of evaluation was that? Valentine didn't even play in spring training for you."

I guess Adair got caught between a rock and a hard spot, because he was being blamed for my not being in the big leagues.

I had to go to the bathroom, and so I left the table and walked to the bar side. I was walking past Adair, whom I hadn't seen. Adair swung around on his bar stool and put his foot out as though it was a toll gate. He wouldn't let me pass. He was in the middle of a conversation with Miller, when he said, "And this fucker has caused me more misery than anybody I've ever been around."

"Hi, Coach," I said. "How are you doing? I have to go to the bathroom."

"Why don't you just piss your pants, you little prick," he said. I can hear his words echo in my memory.

"Yeah, well," I said, "It's good talking to you, Coach."

I pushed his leg down, and as I did, he jumped off the bar stool. It propelled him like a seesaw into the aisle, and with it he swung his right hand and aimed it at my nose. I ducked, and he hit me in the forehead. I came back with a punch underneath his jaw that stood him up, and I then put my shoulder into his chest to send us over the railing that separated the bar from the restaurant. When we landed, chairs and glass bottles broke, and in a mega-second the bouncer/doorman, who was an oversized weightlifter type, came over and picked me up by my belt and the back of my shirt, ran me out the side door, and threw me out, like you see in the movies. As the door swung open, I went crashing into the parking lot.

It was a scene, very emotional, with bar patrons screaming. I tried to go back inside to finish what Adair had started, thinking that as long as my career was over, I might as well get in a couple more good licks. The back door was locked, so I went around to the front. Bruce Bochte and his friend were there to hold me back, calm me down, and walk me back to the hotel. I was bleeding behind my ear. My head must have hit something when we landed. I had a little knot on my forehead, and I was talking about getting arrested. This was one of the more stupid things I've done in my life. Jerry Adair was a coach. A reporter was there, and I was sure that as soon as this hit the wire, no other team would touch me with a ten-foot pole.

I'll be disgraced and run out of baseball, was what was running through my mind.

I was sitting in my hotel room stewing with Bochte and my roommate when Nolan Ryan knocked on the door.

"Don't worry about Dick Miller," he said. "He's not going to say or print a word."

"And what about Jerry?" I asked.

"He's not going to say anything, either," Nolan said.

I was relieved and thanked Nolan. I made a few phone calls and slept. When I went to the ballpark the next day, Jerry Adair wasn't there, and nothing was said about it. I figured we were going to pretend this never happened, and maybe it would go away.

The next morning, I was having breakfast. The Angels were staying at this cool, old hotel in Minneapolis. I was sitting in the big dining area, when the waiter came over and said, "The gentleman in the corner would like to talk with you." The gentleman in the corner, sitting by himself, was Dick Williams.

I'm going before the judge, I thought.

I had my story. I had witnesses. Adair had started it. He threw the first punch.

As I got to Dick's table, he said, "You don't have to sit down. We just traded you to the San Diego Padres. They want you in San Diego tonight."

I went and found the Angels' traveling secretary, who gave me the money for the ticket. At the airport I bought a ticket and flew to San Diego. Waiting for me was Buzzie Bavasi, who had been the general manager of the Dodgers before I got drafted. He went from the Dodgers to the expansion Padres, and he welcomed me and gave me a contract to sign.

I didn't play much. There was no plan for me to be there. It must have been a friendship trade. Buzzie must have owed Harry Dalton a favor. Harry wanted to get Jerry Adair back in uniform, and he couldn't do that unless I was gone.

Johnny McNamara was the Padres' manager, and I was with Johnny for seven games. I had 20 at-bats and hit a solid .133 when the 1975 season ended.

⸙

I was thinking of retiring. But first I wanted to know for sure whether I had anything left. I decided I would go play winter ball for Tommy again in the Dominican. He would know what I should do.

I was still a young player, only twenty-five. I had overcome every injury I ever had, so even though my leg didn't look good, I thought, *All I need is the opportunity. If I have an opportunity with a manager who likes me, maybe I can still play.*

I played some shortstop for Tommy, and after a game we went to have dinner at the Vesuvio, our favorite Santo Domingo restaurant. We were having pizza, drinking a beer, and I said to him, "Well, Tommy, you have seen me at my best, and I'm rehabbing and trying to get back, and people are saying I can't play shortstop any more. Have you seen enough to make an evaluation?"

He looked at me and said, "Yeah, I have."

"So, what do you think?"

"No," Tommy said, "you're not that kind of player anymore. I think you should start thinking about becoming a coach."

It was a crying moment. I felt so much emotion, because you never really know. It's like when an older player reaches that time in his career when everyone else knows he's not the player he once was. He's the last one to know. It's similar with an injury. You don't think you're done when you are.

That was the low point.

CHAPTER 10

I Manage

During spring training of 1976, I had a talk with Padres general manager Buzzie Bavasi, and maybe Tommy Lasorda had talked to him, too. Buzzie told me the Padres had two young draft choices: shortstop Billy Almon, the number-one draft choice out of Brown University, and Mike Champion, a second baseman projected highly in the organization.

"Would you go down to Triple-A to make sure these guys get developed properly?" Buzzie wanted to know.

He wanted me to go play for the Hawaii Islanders, managed by Roy Hartsfield, who had been the third-base coach when I was with the Dodgers. While I was there, I would work with the Padres' up-and-comers.

"Roy is having a very difficult time with the health of his wife," Buzzie said. "She's had six cancer operations, and he's not the guy to get the kids out there early and work them out and practice with them and teach them the game. Can you do that?"

"Am I going to play?" I asked. If not, I was considering retirement.

"There's an opening at first base," he said.

"Hell, I can play first base," I said, even though I had never played it before.

I went to Honolulu to play for the Islanders, which ran as a stand-alone team but was in fact a co-op operation. Half the players on the team were owned by the Hawaiian team, and half were owned by the Padres. The Hawaiian team paid all the salaries of the non-Padres players.

I wasn't going to play first base in the major leagues, but the Islanders' home field was Astroturf, so it was easy to move around and catch ground balls and errant throws. I was there with the kids at all times, and I took Billy and Mike under my wing. They were only a few years younger than me. I had had a little big-league experience, so I had a little cachet with them. I loved the work, and I took them and a young third baseman, Dave Hilton, and another number-one draft choice, Dave Roberts, to workouts. I also threw a lot of batting practice. Every time we could, I took them out early and hit them ground balls.

It was a relaxed situation. I played a lot, knowing it was probably my last hurrah. Roy Hartsfield knew me from the Dodgers and was a good baseball guy. He was into the game all his life, and he kind of liked me. He was one of Walt Alston's guys. Roy had been a minor league manager moving up from A-ball, and I'm sure he was hoping someone would tap him to manage in the big leagues. Roy was cool with me. He let me do everything with the kids.

We had some older players, as well. Diego Seguí was our ace. Pitcher Eddie Watt was on the team. One reason the veterans were playing on the Islanders was that there was to be an expansion draft for two new teams, the Seattle Mariners and the Toronto Blue Jays. The Mariners would draft Diego, a fine fastball pitcher, first. Roy Hartsfield would manage the Blue Jays.

It was fun to play on the Islanders. I wasn't thinking anyone would draft me. I wasn't thinking I was going to have a great major league career, but I was thinking, *I'm having a really good time, and this is cool.* It became cooler when Mary came to live with me. Mary was close in age to

Bill Almon, Mike Champion, Dave Hilton, Dave Roberts, and a number of others, and to their wives. It was a good group to hang out with.

We were treated to the appearance of Joe Pepitone, who had signed to play in Japan at the end of his career. Joe was anything but what Japan could handle. Japan was organized. It was on time. It was everyone doing the same thing. Joe was the antithesis of their culture, and he lasted maybe into the second week of the season. He was released, or he quit, or he took the money and ran. On the way home from Japan, Joe stopped off in Hawaii and had a tryout with the Islanders. Not the Padres, the Islanders, who considered Joe to be a big box-office draw. Before Joe, the Islanders had featured Bo Belinsky, a sensation in Hawaii. Bo was a playboy. He had famous Playboy girlfriends. He was everything a tabloid would want, plus he was a good player. Bo helped make the franchise, and the Islanders hoped that Pepi could do the same for them.

Joe could still hit a low fastball, but he was in the midst of his sex, drugs, and rock-and-roll lifestyle. His extracurricular activities distracted him and everyone else, and Joe didn't last very long.

I was his roommate on the last road trip. We were in Eugene, Oregon, and we were having a beer after a game at one of the only places open. The bar had a couple of pool tables and a long bar, hot dogs spinning behind the counter, and peanut shells on the floor. There were a couple of motorcycles outside and a couple girls from the town hanging out. Over on the shuffleboard table, Joe was playing partners with someone, and we thought the powder on the edge of the table was the silicone beads you used to make the puck go faster, but it was actually stuff you put up your nose so you could stay up late at night. A couple of patrons saw it and said something, and there was a fight, and that might well have been the event to bring about Joe's swan song. Joe took his hair dryer and went home.

I loved every minute of being with Pepi. I was the other Italian guy on the team, and my job was to make sure that whatever he was doing didn't affect the young players on the team. I tried to be the buffer between the big-league world and the naïve. I tried to be a fish one day and a fowl the other. I liked it, even though it was a little hard on me, but then Joe was gone.

It was August, and we'd won a lot of games and were fighting for the pennant. We had just finished batting practice when Roy called me into his little office. It's not fair to call it an office. It had a table and a chair, and it was separated from the players. It was more like a closet. Roy called me in and said, "I just got a call. Alice has to go in for another cancer operation. It might be the last one, and I'm leaving. I'm going to stay with her until she gets better or until it's all over." He handed me the lineup card and said, "I want you to take over the team and do the best job you can."

"Roy," I said, "I'm so sorry that Alice is sick." I had known her when we were with the Dodgers. She didn't come to Hawaii. Roy was going back to the States, and who knew if I was ever going to see him again.

Roy called a team meeting and told everyone that he was leaving. "I want you to treat Bobby as though it was me," he said to the team. "And good luck." Then he left.

A lot of players on the Islanders were older than I. I had no experience managing. I didn't feel prepared. I was always thinking strategically. When I didn't play, I always thought about moves to make. I second-guessed every manager I ever played for, as often as I could, except for maybe Tommy Lasorda. I even second-guessed him once in a while.

To celebrate, Mary and I got engaged.

It was my time, and so I didn't do anything different from what Roy did, except I moved myself to the third spot in the lineup. Rod Gaspar, our center fielder, hit second, and Gene Richards led off. Rod walked 133 times that year. He was a walking machine, though the walk wasn't appreciated. Gene and Rod were always on base ahead of me, and I finished the season with 89 RBIs.

Winning the season's last game on the road, we tied for the lead in our division. We won the coin flip for home-field advantage, and we flew back to Honolulu for a three-game playoff series with Tacoma. When we got back to Hawaii, we went to the stadium to drop off our gear, only to find a big chain and a padlock on the gates. There was a note about all possessions being under the ownership of the State of Hawaii. Islanders owner Jack Quinn hadn't paid his taxes.

We were standing outside looking in. We couldn't go inside.

"Now what do we do?" we asked.

"Throw your stuff in a car," I said, "and we'll meet back here in the morning."

Someone in an official capacity told us we could play at the stadium in Maui. The three-game series against Tacoma was to start the next day, and we were to be at the airport ready to fly to Maui.

The last paychecks for the players were in their mailboxes inside the stadium clubhouse. These players were thinking, *Tax liens? We're not going to get paid. So, screw it. We're not going to play.* We couldn't field a team without them, so the Padres said they would pay everyone's expenses, and the players were allowed to bring their wives. Many of us had never been to Maui. With a little cajoling, everyone agreed to play the three games except Diego Seguí, our ace. He didn't want to pitch. Word got out he was going to get drafted by the Mariners, and he wasn't going to risk being hit by a line drive.

We won one and lost one, and a lot of players were thinking, *Screw this. Let's lose this game and go on home.*

In the eighth inning of Game 3, I hit a three-run home run to put us ahead, and when I returned to the dugout I got the silent treatment, as bad as the rookie who hits his first home run in the major leagues. There was no excitement at all.

We won our division, but there was no celebration. We were scheduled to play the Pacific Coast League Championship against the Gulls in Salt Lake City in two days. We were not coming back to Hawaii. We were told plane tickets would be ready for us. Pack up all your stuff. We're going to the mainland. We were to play all five games in Salt Lake City, and then we'd fly home.

The Padres made good on everyone's checks except for our backup catcher, Kala Kaaihue, who was Hawaiian. All Kala wanted was to be with the team when we won the championship. He didn't have a pot to piss in, and he had no paycheck, and yet there was a plane ticket for him to fly to Salt Lake City—but no ticket for him to fly back.

I convinced him to come and that we'd take up a collection to pay for his ticket back. The ticket was about $150.

It was a complete shit show. When we got to Salt Lake City, the hotel we usually stayed at wouldn't let us in, because there was a prior unpaid bill. I was given the money to pay for our stay, but I didn't have the money to pay past debts. We had to go to a different hotel. We went to another fleabag and set up the rooms.

After our final win in Game 5, we had to drink Salt Lake City's champagne. The day we won, as a sign of gratitude, I was called up to the Padres to finish out the season, as were Billy Almon, Mike Champion, and several of the other young up-and-comers I was coaching.

Our reward was a call-up to the major league team for a few weeks in September. I continued to hit well, batting .367 in 49 at-bats. No big deal. I had bigger fish to fry. I had to buy a house, go to court, get back to the East Coast, and get married!

CHAPTER 11

The Trial

My trial before the Superior Court of the State of California, to prove that Dr. Ball had screwed up my leg with his negligence, occurred in the fall of 1976. Phil Hersh, one of my buddies from Arizona State, introduced me to Pete Serino, who had been practicing law in Phoenix. At the end of '75, Pete started hinting to me that I really should sue the doctor. At the time, people weren't suing doctors, and the doctor was the team orthopedist. To sue the doctor meant I was suing the Angels. Was that a good thing to do? It all hinged on the verdict.

Pete did some research and found a group of lawyers in downtown L.A. who supposedly never lost. They never accepted a case that they didn't win. The firm was Butler, Jefferson, and Frye. They felt I couldn't lose.

They decided I would be the key witness. I'd go up and tell my story. Even though Roxy and I were divorced, she agreed to come and testify about my rehabilitation and all that had occurred. We might also bring in a doctor or two, if we could get one to testify against another doctor—something that wasn't done, particularly in Orange County,

California, as conservative a place as has ever been. How were we going to successfully sue Dr. Ball, the doctor of the Angels, when the Angels' stadium was built on the corner of Katella and Ball Street?

I took the stand and told my story. Roxy, who was pregnant, got up and testified. When we brought in Al Campanis and Tommy Lasorda, the lawyers for the insurance company objected. Their lead defense lawyer was out of a Hollywood script, with snow-white, perfectly groomed hair and custom suits that flowed majestically as he walked around the courtroom.

"We don't want the jury to hear any testimony about how he was or how he wasn't. We don't know what happened there," said the lawyer.

The judge ruled that the jury should be out of the room when Al and Tommy testified. And when my lawyer asked me to pull up my pants and show my leg, the other side's lawyer objected and stopped me.

"They are just trying to play on the emotions of the jury," he said. "The jury doesn't know what they are looking at when they see his leg. Let the jury *just* look at the x-rays."

As though a juror can read an x-ray. But the judge concurred.

The ace up our sleeve was that we'd brought Dr. Paul Bauer, the orthopedic surgeon for the San Diego Padres, who testified that Dr. Ball's original procedure was up to standards but that he should have operated to straighten my leg when he saw how much the tibia had bent during the healing process.

"If in August or September something wasn't done to correct the angulation," he was asked, "was that acceptable practice within the community?"

"No," he said. "It was *not* acceptable."

Dr. Robert Kerlan also testified, and when he said that, after July, proper procedures were not followed, that the care was not up to the standard of medical practice in the community, it seemed like it was time to pop the champagne corks.

All that was left were the closing arguments. One of my lawyers called their lawyers to see if they wanted to settle. Not only did they not want to settle, they wanted to bring me back to the stand for a re-direct. To do so, they had to get my permission.

"I'm not sure I should go back," I said.

Over drinks, my lawyers decided that the jury really liked me, so for me to testify one more time seemed like a good idea.

"You really had a good story to tell," said my lawyer, "and they feel bad about you."

Reluctantly, I agreed. The next day I returned to the witness stand, and after a few questions asking how I was, and whether I thought everything was going well, the lead attorney for the insurance company pulled out a couple of pieces of paper and called my lawyers to the bench.

"Please allow these articles to be admitted into the trial as evidence," he said.

Holding up a piece of paper, he asked me, "Bobby, were you in Charleston, West Virginia, playing baseball last year?"

"Yes, sir. I was," I said.

"How did you do?"

"I did pretty well," I said. "I was really hot for a while, and then I cooled off. But it was a really good experience."

"Do you remember having an interview while you were in Charleston?" He showed me the article.

"I remember talking to the writer," I said.

"In this article, you said that your leg has never felt better, that you're running a hundred percent, and you couldn't wait to get back to the big leagues." I gulped. "Did you say that?" he asked.

"Yeah, I said that."

"Why did you say that?"

"Well, because I wanted to get back to the big leagues."

"So, your leg wasn't a hundred percent, and you weren't running as well as ever?"

"Of course not," I said. "You've seen my leg."

"Well, tell me again why you would say that."

"To get back to the big leagues."

With great deliberation he said, "Oh, so you were lying."

I paused and looked around. "I wasn't really telling the truth," I said.

He looked at the jury and said, "So if you weren't telling the truth then, why should we believe that you're telling the truth now?"

"It wasn't…Oh my. It was…" *Oh, shit.*

"One other question," he said. "When you were in the hospital, according to hospital records, you had a phone call from Dr. Robert Kerlan. Is that true?"

"Yes," I said. "That's true."

"Oh, and what did Dr. Kerlan have to say? Was he wishing you the best?"

"Yes, he was absolutely wishing me the best. He gave me encouragement that I could recover from this type of injury. And he wished me well."

"Did he also offer you his services?"

I thought for a second. This guy had just called me a liar. *I better not lie again.* Not understanding why this was such a big deal, I said, "Yeah. He said he would clear his calendar to get me in, if I needed him."

With that the lawyer for the insurance company approached the bench.

"Your honor," he said. "I would ask for Dr. Kerlan's testimony to be stricken from the record."

"Why?" the judge said.

In a loud voice that the jury could hear, he said, "Because it is an unethical practice of medicine within our community to solicit business, and Dr. Robert Kerlan solicited the business of this Robert John Valentine, and so his testimony should be thrown out on the grounds that this practice is malpractice." It was a jaw-dropping moment.

What? How? What is this? I was thinking. *What does one thing have to do with the other?*

The judge instructed the jury to disregard Dr. Kerlan's testimony.

I slinked off the stand. During the closing argument, their lawyer mentioned how unethical it was for Dr. Kerlan to call me while I was in the hospital. He said it four times. He also said that Dr. Bauer was not a member of the community that Dr. Ball practices in. Bauer was from San Diego, Ball from L.A.

"His testimony should not be used because he's not part of the community," the insurance company's lawyer argued.

We broke after his final testimony and went to lunch. When we came back, the other side asked to put on the stand a witness who was an intern for Dr. Ball. I had never seen him before, but he said who he was, and that he was in the room during the procedure. When he was asked about me, he said I was all in favor of what Dr. Ball wanted to do. Our lawyer didn't redirect, even though he had information that the intern had been on vacation in Hawaii, that he was lying through his teeth about his being in the room. My lawyer decided the best way to discredit the intern would be to do it in the summation.

During the summation, my lawyer took to the podium with a stack of his notes, multiple pages, and he was going through the notes, putting on a good show, but at the critical moment when he was to make the point about the intern, he dropped his pencil. He had been reading from a yellow legal pad. As he bent down, the pencil rolled across the floor. He moved to fetch it, almost lost his balance, then returned to the podium, and *turned the page*. In doing so, he never made the point about the intern lying about being a witness, present in Dr. Ball's office, when he actually had been in Hawaii. He finished his closing argument. I was sick to my stomach.

"How did you miss the point about the intern?"

"Don't worry about it. I think we're winning the case."

Pete Serino saw what had happened. "There are no grounds for a mistrial," he said, "but you should sue your lawyers for malpractice."

"No," I said, "I can't go through this again."

We got called back into court after a few hours, and the jury foreman announced that there was no malpractice. The case was final, closed, and I would have to take care of any and all medical expenses for the rest of my life.

I came out of the trial feeling guilty that I had lied to the reporter in Charleston, and that if I hadn't lied, perhaps I'd have won the case. I blamed everything on myself, and it took me years to come to the realization that either the whole thing was fixed, or it was just a bad job of lawyering.

The only footnote to the story came many years later. I was an analyst doing *Sunday Night Baseball* for ESPN in 2011. We were in Anaheim on a stage set up in the parking lot for a pregame show. During one of the commercial breaks, one of the producers came up on stage and said, "Bobby, this guy behind me says he has to talk to you."

"What guy?"

He pointed to a man in his sixties, who was there with a twenty-year-old boy. I waved to him. He motioned for me to come to the corner of the stage to talk to him, and so during the next commercial break I took off my headset and went over. I knelt on the stage, and the man introduced himself as a doctor.

"I was the intern testifying at your trial," he said. "And I'm going through the twelve-step program, and I need to make amends to those who I did wrong to. And my son is here as my witness. I'm sorry I lied at your trial."

I looked at him and said, "You've got to be shitting me."

I only had two minutes during the commercial break, and I said, "Thank you for doing that. Don't worry about it. I don't hold any grudges."

I went back up, put on my headset, and again said to myself, "You've got to be shitting me."

CHAPTER 12

Oh What a Year

Mary and I were engaged and ready for marriage. We found a house in San Diego and bought it, and then got back home for a January 1977 wedding. It was spectacular. We were married in the Chapel at Manhattanville College, and our reception was at the Westchester Country Club. We honeymooned in La Romana in the Dominican Republic, where we first met. The only thing more spectacular than the events of our wedding was my bride. Mary is one of the greatest people I have ever known, and she was on the top of her game for our wedding.

We were ready for spring training. I drove to San Diego one day during spring training and closed on our house. Mary went back early and got everything set up, and before we knew it a new season was underway.

I had no role with the Padres in 1977. I might have started five times. I didn't do very well, at that. I batted 67 times, had 12 hits, and batted .179. I was hanging around, trying to catch lightning in a bottle, but when you don't play, you have no rhythm, and without rhythm, you don't stand a chance. I knew it wasn't happening, anyway. Still, it was great to be in uniform with Dave Winfield and Rollie Fingers, Randy Jones, Gene Tenace, and to watch Billy Almon and Mike Champion play at the highest level of the game.

On May 28, John McNamara was fired, and Alvin Dark became the manager. I played for Alvin only a couple of days. We were playing Chicago at home in San Diego. Billy Buckner was over at my new house for lunch. The drapes for our new home had arrived that morning, and Mary and I were making plans to hang them. It was a happy day. We finished lunch and the phone rang.

The guy who had advised me to buy a home in San Diego the previous fall was asking me to come to the game early to see him. It was Buzzie Bavasi, the Padres' general manager.

"Sit down, son," Buzzie said. "You know, I know your heart is in New York, and so I made a trade for you to play in New York."

Holy shit, I thought, *I'm going to play for the Yankees!*

Buzzie then took a deep breath and said, "And the Mets want you to meet them in New York tomorrow."

I lived in that house in San Diego for three months. I was traded to the Mets during the "Midnight Massacre," one of the craziest days in New York Mets history. M. Donald Grant traded Tom Seaver—"the Franchise," the most beloved player ever to play for the Mets—to Cincinnati for Pat Zachry, Steve Henderson, Doug Flynn, and Dan Norman. He also traded slugger Dave Kingman to San Diego for pitcher Paul Siebert and myself, and he traded Mike Phillips to the St. Louis Cardinals for Joel Youngblood. When I and all the other traded players arrived at Shea Stadium, we were received with a cascade of boos. When I was asked, all I could say was, "I wasn't in the Seaver trade. I was only in the Kingman trade."

The fans didn't really miss Kingman because he was aloof and hard to understand. His baseball skill set wasn't appreciated, either. He walked and he hit home runs. He was a sabermetrician's dream, and he wasn't appreciated because he struck out too much. But I was damaged goods, and Paul Siebert wasn't going to win any awards. Not a good trade.

But losing Tom Seaver? That trade was a disaster. It broke the heart of every Mets fan. It was as bad as the day Walter O'Malley said the Dodgers were leaving Brooklyn. It was as bad as the day the Red Sox sold Babe Ruth. Seaver was beloved like no other Met before or since. It wouldn't have mattered who we got for him.

All the guys from Cincy who came over were nice players. Joel Youngblood was a nice player, but none of them had the personality for New York. When the fans faced the void of not seeing the face of the franchise, the greatest player who had ever worn a Mets uniform, the fans weren't just angry, they were spitting mad.

Steve Henderson was a .300 hitter. He hit the ball inside out. He played left field, didn't have much of an arm, but he was a really terrific guy. But he didn't have the personality of a .300 hitter. Dougie Flynn was a nice guy from Kentucky who had a good glove, but a really weak bat, and when you're losing 9–1, a good glove doesn't resonate much with the fandom. Joel Youngblood had a very good arm, could throw, had a little power, but he wasn't going to play every day and didn't give great interviews. Every time Pat Zachry opened his mouth, you knew he'd rather be in Texas than in New York. This is what the Mets fans had to be satisfied with. None of these were guys you wanted to boo. Dougie Flynn had a great smile, and Steve Henderson hustled all the time. Joel Youngblood always had a smile and worked hard, and Pat Zachry was a blue-collar, give-me-the-ball, I'll-do-everything-I-can-to-win-you-the-game kind of guy. The fans really didn't want to boo them. They also didn't want to root for them. They just wanted to boycott them. The attendance numbers went down and down and down.

We had some interesting players on the '77 Mets team. We had Lenny Randle, who stole thirty-three bases. I hung out with Lenny. I loved his smile, loved his enthusiasm. He always got dirty and played hard, though at the time, he had a little dark cloud over his head, because fans knew he had beat up his manager, Frank Luchessi, in Texas. The sportswriters, especially, never gave Lenny his due.

I was lucky enough to room with the best player and coolest guy on the team. Lee Mazzilli was a switch-hitting center fielder who could run, field, and hit with power, and had as good a look as any player in the game. Tommy Lasorda said to Maz the first time they met, "You probably get more ass than a toilet seat." Maz was incredible. He made basket catches in center field like Willie Mays. He was from Brooklyn, Italian, and, at twenty-one, he was the brightest star in the Mets organization.

Another Mets mainstay was Ed Kranepool, who was at the end of his career. He and Joe Torre, our manager, had been close. Eddie loved Joe. They were good friends. The two had roomed together before Joe got the manager's job, and Eddie felt Joe should have named him the hitting coach. They were tight, but seeing things from Eddie's perspective, he had been a Met since he was seventeen years old. He was a thinking guy's player, though he was a little outspoken. Eddie always felt there should have been a place for him in the Mets organization, and maybe there should have been. Did he have the skill set to be a general manager? I don't know. Could he have been a hitting coach? For sure. But it didn't work out that way. Eddie was the first one to criticize the Tom Seaver trade, and didn't ingratiate himself.

Eddie could hit. When it was cold, and a lot of our games in the spring and fall were played in the cold, Eddie would sit in Joe's office with his feet up on the desk, in full uniform, watching the game on TV. He'd come out to the dugout once in a while to say hello. When he saw a pinch-hitting situation might arise, he'd walk down the tunnel, grab his bat, and hit a line drive on the first pitch as often as not, and do it with grace.

My ankle was so damaged from the injury and the cortisone shots that I left the team early to get my ankle operated on. They tried to reconstruct my ankle so that it would adapt to my bent leg. It didn't work, but I had less pain playing the next season. The 1978 season was another bench-sitting year, but I had the great fortune to sit the bench with the finest human being I ever met, Tom Grieve. Tom was from Pittsfield, Massachusetts, and had been the number-one draft choice of the Washington Senators. We both had pretty lackluster ten-year careers in the majors. We also both knew it was the end of the line, and in spring training we struck up a friendship. He didn't know where he would live if he made the team, and I offered him a place to stay at my house until he found his own place. We sat the bench for about a hundred games together and talked about the other team, our team, the manager's moves, anything and everything you can imagine during the three hours of baseball. We had as much fun as any two bench-warmers could ever have.

Tom and I both loved the game. We had a true understanding of each other. We had a feeling that I was going to look out for him, and he was going to look out for me. Neither of us ever were thinking that one day he would be a general manager and I would get a call from him to offer me a manager's job. We couldn't even dream that something like that would happen.

CHAPTER 13

I Catch a Break

I didn't play very much for the Mets in 1978, and in '79 I was going to have to make the team again. I thought I played pretty well in the spring, even though I wasn't much of a player, but I had a few things going for me. One was that Joe Torre's Italian, Lee Mazzilli's Italian, and I'm Italian.

I was playing in an intrasquad game on the last day of spring training at Huggins-Stengel Field in St. Petersburg, and during the second inning, Charlie Samuels, the assistant clubhouse man, came over and told me that a guy named Bob Elmo, my stockbroker, was on the phone. I had given him $20,000, all our savings, to invest in a company called Ericsson International that was doing something with long-distance phone service.

"Tell him I'll call him after the game," I told Charlie.

In the sixth inning, Charlie came over to say that Elmo needed to talk with me.

"After the game," I said.

The game finally ended, and I called Bob. "What's going on?" I asked him.

"I've been trying to call you all day, Bobby," he said. "The stock went down to two pennies. We could have sold it at ten dollars when I first called you, and then we could have sold it at five dollars, but you didn't come to the phone."

"What the hell does that mean?" I asked.

"That means you've lost everything," he said.

That wasn't the worst of it. I walked into the clubhouse hoping to pack my bags and head north with the team. This time Herb Norman, the head clubhouse guy, was waiting for me.

"Joe wants to talk to you in his office," he said.

Oh shit, I thought. I went into Joe Torre's office, and he told me the Mets had decided to go in another direction, and he handed me my pink slip, my release. I had been traded three times and sent to the minors three times, but this was different. This was my release!

I was friends with many members of the press. Whenever they wanted an opinion or a scoop, they would come to me, and I would always try to give them something, usually on the record, but sometimes off. My scoop this time was that I was getting released, which wasn't the biggest deal in Mets history, but everyone gave me a cordial fifteen minutes in the training room while I tried to somehow say Joe was screwing me. I went to my rental condo to tell Mary that it was a good thing the bags were packed, but that I had no idea where we were going. I told her I was going to talk with my agent, Tony Attanasio, to see if there was a team that needed a player like me.

It was panic time. *What should I do? How should I do it?* I had no idea. After many teams said they had no interest, Tony called one of my old teammates, Jeff Torborg, who was managing the Cleveland Indians. Their spring training was in Tucson, Arizona. Tony talked me up, saying I was running great and la-di-da. I was about to call the phone company to disconnect the phone in my rental when Jeff Torborg called to say that if I could get to Tucson by 4:00 the next afternoon, he'd give me a tryout.

"I'll be there," I said.

I had no idea how I was going to get there. I had to book my own flight, which wasn't all that easy. I went to the airport and put Mary on a plane to New York, and I went around to the different airlines to see how I could fly to Tucson.

There were no flights that night. I had to wait for the morning, and that flight took me through Phoenix. There was a four-hour layover in Phoenix, which would get me to Tucson in time for the tryout. I thought I could make it. I bought the ticket and stayed in the airport overnight, sleeping an hour or two, and when I got to Phoenix, I took a cab to see my best friend, Tom Paciorek, who was playing for the Mariners in Tempe, fifteen minutes away. They were playing their last spring training game.

I walked into the clubhouse in Tempe to see Tom an hour before game time. He gave me a big hug, and then all of a sudden we heard someone screaming, as though he had just been shot. Everyone went running around the old lockers to the other side to see what had happened.

"This dude just closed his hand in the coffin," Tom said.

All the Cokes in the clubhouse were in coffin coolers, with the big latch that lifted up as you reached down into it to get a Coke. One of the Seattle players had closed the latch on his hand, and there was blood spilling all over the place.

"Who was that? Who caught his hand?" the other players wanted to know.

"That's Steinie," someone said. Bill Stein was the Mariners third baseman.

"Boy, who is going to play third today?" Paciorek asked. "We don't have anyone to play third. I tried to play third yesterday and almost killed myself." Tom said to me, "Why don't you go see Darrell [Johnson, the manager] and ask if you can play for us?"

Nothing ventured, nothing gained, I thought. I walked down the hallway and knocked on the manager's door. In his customary way, Darrell was smoking a cigarette at his desk. With his room filled with smoke and other odors, he said, "Yeah, what I can do for you?"

"Darrell," I said, "I'm Bobby Valentine. If you need a third baseman today, I can play."

"Why in the world would I need a third baseman?" he wanted to know.

With that, Lou Gorman, who was the GM, walked in to tell Darrell that Bill Stein had caught his hand in the cooler and couldn't play. As I stood there Lou said, "Bobby. Bobby. Bobby." Lou always repeated himself. "Bobby. Bobby. Bobby, what are you doing here?"

"I'm looking for a job."

"What do you mean?"

"The Mets released me. I told Darrell if you need someone to play third in the game today, I can play."

"Step outside for a minute," he said.

The game was starting in about a half hour. While I stood in the hallway, my world was spinning. My legs were shaking and I was saying a few prayers when Lou opened the door and said, "Hey, if you really want to play, we need a third baseman."

"I *really* want to play," I said.

"Go see the clubhouse guy and get a uniform."

I had my baseball bag and a little carry bag with me. I went over to Tom Paciorek's locker. They brought me a uniform, I put it on, and I went out and played catch. I started at third base wearing uniform number 40, with the name Housey on the back. (It had belonged to Joe Housey, who'd been released the day before.) When I came to bat, the stadium announcer said: "Now batting: Joe Housey."

This was a getaway game with about two hundred fans in the stands, but it was a very big game for me! I had a really good day, with three hits, including the game-winner in the ninth. After the game, radio announcer Dave Niehaus decided to interview me, to tell the listeners back in Seattle how it was that this new guy who played such a good game happened to be in a Mariners uniform. All the other players were rushing off to clean out their lockers.

The team had a dilemma. I was on fire that day, and my identity had been revealed to the Seattle fandom over the radio, and management didn't know what to do. I hung around, and finally someone in the front office came over and said, "Can you stick around? Darrell's going to have an intrasquad game tomorrow, and he'd like to see you play some more."

I had missed my tryout with Jeff Torborg and Cleveland. I was with Tom Paciorek, and he had a couch I could sleep on, so I said, "Sure. I will stay."

Darrell Johnson had an intrasquad game mainly to get his fourth starter, Paul Mitchell, a little more work. Mitchell was right-handed and had a really good curveball, a Burt Blyleven curveball, the real deal. The Mariners were trying to get me some at-bats, so I was the second hitter. I took a curve ball on the first pitch, and then on the next pitch I got a hit on a fastball.

Before the pitcher threw the first pitch, I heard the catcher say, "Hey, Bear."

I later found out that the coach, who was umping behind the catcher, was named Bear Bryant. The catcher would say "Hey, Bear" before a curve was thrown, so he would know what pitch was coming. I asked Wimpy why I heard "Hey, Bear," and we put one and one together and knew when the pitcher was throwing a curve. I got three more hits, all on curves, and impressed everyone.

The plane was leaving for Seattle that day, and I no idea whether I was going to be on it. After the game, Lou Gorman came over to me. "That was a pretty good showing," he said. "I have some good news, and I have some bad news."

"Lou," I said. "what's the bad news?"

"The bad news is we don't have a spot for you on the roster."

"What's the good news?"

"We have a spot for you on the plane. We need a little time to sort things out. Why don't you come with us to Seattle, and we'll see how things work out?"

I had no contract. I didn't even have a handshake. I was wearing a uniform with the name Housey on it, but it felt wonderful that when I went to the pay phone to call Mary, I could tell her, "I'm going to Seattle."

"Where are you?" she asked.

"Phoenix."

"I thought you were going to Tucson."

When the Mariners and I arrived in Seattle, they had to see whether Billy Stein's hand was healthy enough for him to play on opening day. The other third baseman was Juan Bernhardt, who was on the disabled list. If they could trade Bernhardt after he got off the disabled list, I was told, there would be room for me on the roster.

I spent five days sitting in the stands. They dumped a player, and I made the team. After I signed, I bought a house in Bellevue with my friend and teammate Bruce Bochte. Bruce, a smart Santa Clara guy, had a friend who was a local banker. Bruce and I put together some creative financial statements, and, with our major league contracts, bought the house for $65,000 in one of Bellevue's first developments.

Mary flew in, and we spent the summer in Seattle, which was spectacular. Not only did I get to play with Bruce, but I also got to play with Tom Paciorek. I was a real lucky guy.

I was sitting on the bench one day when catcher Bob Stinson caught a ball off his finger and had to come out of the game. Darrell Johnson sent in Larry Cox, the other catcher. Darrell was wondering who would catch if Larry got hurt, and as he walked down the bench, he said to me, "Bobby, you've caught before, haven't you?"

"Oh yeah, sure," I said.

The closest I'd come to catching was warming up the pitcher in between innings. Two innings later, when Larry Cox was bowled over at home plate and had to come out of the game because of a concussion, I went into my first major league game as a catcher. I had never even put on the equipment before, but I did well enough that Darrell put me in a second time, later in the season.

The hitting coach was Vada Pinson, my old left fielder when I broke my leg with the Angels. Willie Horton was Seattle's hitting star, and that year Willie hit his 300th home run. He also hit a ball that would have gone 500 feet if it hadn't hit one of the speakers hanging from the roof in the Kingdome and was caught for an out. It was also the year when a Tiger pitcher, Lerrin LaGrow, hit Willie with a pitch and Willie went out to the mound and tossed about eight opposing players into the air. They all landed. It was the most amazing fight. A whole bunch of people were trying to get to Willie, and one by one he tossed them around.

Seattle was a god-awful team. We finished the year at 67–95. We played in the Kingdome in front of about a hundred fans per night. My good friend from Spokane, Paul Pupo, and his family moved to Seattle to take Mrs. Pupo's recipes to the big city. Mrs. P was the best cook in the West, and Paul and his three brothers and one sister became family to me. Paul and his family opened a restaurant in Seattle, and I ate a thousand meals there. Three years later, he moved to Connecticut and became the COO of my restaurant business.

Other than reconnecting with Paul Pupo, I can't say much of interest occurred. When the season ended, so did my playing career. Once again I was waiting for the phone to ring.

In November of '79 I attended a charity dinner in Stamford, Connecticut, for multiple sclerosis, honoring Howard Cosell. Sitting next to me was a man who was Ricky Robustelli's neighbor. Ricky was an all-state quarterback in high school and a record-setting QB at UConn. He was also the oldest son of Andy. My seatmate at the dinner, Joe Romano, told me he had just moved his mainframe computer from his garage to a building in downtown Stamford.

Like so many others, he asked me what I was doing, and I said I was waiting for the phone to ring. He asked me what I was going to do if the phone never rang.

"I have no idea," I said.

"I just bought a building downtown," he said, "and next to my building is a derelict old bar called the Stagecoach Café." Joe said he had a computer company, and many of his female employees were afraid to work at night because of the bad crowd at the bar. He told me that the bar owner was in failing health, an old Italian guy, and then he proposed: "I think we can buy his liquor license, and if we buy the bar, I'd like you to be my partner. We'll put your name on the front of it, and we'll serve a bunch of lunches."

I had no idea at the time that this guy would play such an important role in my life. I made many friends, and I had a great many people help me on the field, but no one helped me as much in my life's work as Joe Romano. He taught me about life in the real world. His wife Rita and all the Romano clan are an integral part of my being.

"Let's go see the place tomorrow," I said.

We bought the place with a 2 percent loan from the feds, because we were in an urban renewal zone. It was the start of a forty-year venture. At one time, we had six Bobby Valentine's restaurants at locations across the country, and did about $200 million in business over the forty years.

By mid-1980, I was knee-deep in running this first restaurant. I cleaned bathrooms, poured beers, flipped hamburgers, and learned how to check out a waiter after a shift and how to balance the cash register. From the first day we opened, there was never an empty chair at lunch, and our nighttime business became a zoo.

One afternoon, the phone rang at the bar while I was bartending.

"Bobby, Bobby. How ya doin'? How ya doin'?"

It was Tommy Lasorda.

"You know, Tommy," I said, "the phone never rang, and I met this fabulous guy, and we opened a restaurant. I can't wait for you to be in New York so you can come and see it."

"Yeah, I know. I heard," he said. "But I need you to take a couple days off."

"I don't know if I can take a couple days off," I said.

"I want you to come to Youngstown, Ohio. We're going to be honoring Eddie DeBartolo Jr. at a dinner, and I want you to meet him and some of my friends."

I could never say no to Tommy, and so I covered for myself as much as I could, bought a ticket, and flew to Columbus, where someone picked me up and drove me to Youngstown.

Eddie DeBartolo Jr.'s family owned millions of square feet of mall space around the country. He and his sister were thinking of buying the San Francisco 49ers. When the Chicago White Sox were being sold by Bill Veeck, Eddie had wanted to buy them, but he was turned down by the other owners. Some thought it was because of his ethnicity.

There was no shortage of Italians at his dinner. I was at the head table. I was to introduce Tommy, and he was going to introduce Eddie. Tommy then gave one of his thousands of speeches that had everyone laughing and earned a standing ovation when he ended.

I sat next to Ballard Smith. He recently had been appointed president of the San Diego Padres. He was married to Ray Kroc's daughter. Ray was the founder of McDonald's and owner of the Padres. I didn't know who Ballard was, and he didn't know who I was, because he was new to baseball. By the end of the night, Tommy told Ballard that the first thing he should do when he took the reins of the Padres was to hire me as a coach. Before the night was over, Ballard said to me, "I'll have a job for you before the season starts."

I was honest about how much time I was spending on my restaurant. "It's going to be hard to get away," I said. "I'm going to need a flexible schedule."

"No problem," he said. "Be there when you can be there, and I'm sure we'll get our money's worth from you."

Jack McKeon was the farm director for the Padres. The Triple-A manager was Doug Rader. I worked with the younger kids in places like Reno and Walla Walla. I was given one special project: the Padres' first-round draft pick in the 1980 amateur drive, outfielder Jeff Pyburn from the University of Georgia, a blond kid who was very religious. He was playing in the Texas League for Amarillo. It was very hot, and those kids were taking twenty-hour bus trips. It was something out of *The Last Picture Show*. Everything seemed to be in black and white.

That was the job, but it was really a side job to my restaurant. It was my first adventure into the lower minor leagues, other than when I was a player in Rookie ball in Ogden. This was a different time and place. I was going to low-minor league cities, trying to provide a couple days of happiness for kids and coaches, and it was a rude awakening when I got to see what a hard life it was. Meal money might have been ten dollars a day more than it was in 1968, though the cost of living had increased three times. The bus rides were atrocious. There was never an off-day. In 1970, when I played Triple-A, we played 146 games in five months. Fast-forward ten years, and it was basically the same.

But I devoted my time more to the restaurant business than the business of baseball. My sign in every restaurant I owned was: *Remember the six P's: Proper Preparation Prevents Piss Poor Performance.* It wasn't original, but I loved it and used it, and everyone knew it.

I spent 1981 running my restaurant, and when Lou Gorman called and asked me if I would take on the same job with the Mets, I accepted. I split the summer working the restaurant and flying into the minor league towns of Mets affiliates. Darryl Strawberry, Dwight Gooden, Lenny Dykstra, Billy Beane, Steve Phillips, and others were in the minors, and I enjoyed my time with them.

In Connecticut, the restaurant was booming. We were selling more Budweiser than any bar in the state, and this was the year I "invented" the wrap. Yes, in 1981 I was in the kitchen working the grill for lunch. My banker ordered a club sandwich. We had no club on the menu, and our toaster was broken. We had just received a delivery of ten-inch tortilla shells. I took the ingredients of a club sandwich and rolled them up in a tortilla shell. I put American cheese over the top and melted the cheese in the salamander. I cut the roll in three parts and told the waitress to serve it as a "Club Mex." My manager Paul Pupo started calling it a "wrap," and years later went on the Food Channel and said that the Club Mex was the first wrap sandwich in America. The *Wall Street Journal* tried to prove him wrong, but could not. Ha!

Once again Tommy Lasorda stepped in to change the course of my life. He was the manager of the Dodgers, and he felt that Jim Lefebvre, his first-base coach and old Dodger second baseman, had betrayed him. Jimmy was undermining Tommy, thinking he could backstab him in the press and get his job. They went from kissing cousins to something very different. Tommy wanted me to replace Lefebvre, and he called Frank Cashen, the general manager of the Mets, because the protocol was that if you wanted to hire someone in a different organization, you had to offer him a better job than the one he had. That way no managers are stolen away to be managers, and no coaches are stolen away to be coaches.

When Tommy asked Frank if he could talk to me about being his first-base coach, Frank balked. "I can't grant you permission," he said, "because we already hired him to be the first-base coach of the Mets."

This was not the truth. I was not offered the major league coaching job until the day after Tommy asked permission to talk to me. Frank contacted me at the restaurant, and I bought a round of drinks for everyone at my bar, but it was a day *after* Tommy called.

That's how I got to be a coach on George Bamberger's 1982 New York Mets. I was thirty-two years old, coaching guys who were older than me. But working under George was a joy. He was fun to be around, and he never saw a cold one he didn't like.

George was just a placeholder. He was Earl Weaver's pitching coach in Baltimore when Frank was there as general manager. And he had done a couple of stints as manager of the Milwaukee Brewers. George literally came off a fishing boat and took the Mets managerial job. He was sociable and a really good person.

"We want you to work the way you work," George told me. "Bring some excitement to this group. You'll work with the infielders and the base runners, and we want you to be the first-base coach."

"I'm at your beck and call, George," I said. "Tell me when."

I was the first one to arrive at the ballpark and the last one to leave. We went through spring training and went to Philadelphia to open the season, and it was practice day just before the opener when George called me into his office.

"What's up, George?" I asked.

"You know, Bobby," he said, "I really like your energy. I like the way you're out there coaching first base, but you know what, I know something for sure."

"What's that, George?"

"I know that Frank Howard is the best first-base coach I've ever seen."

Frank was coaching at third.

"That's great, George," I said. "Do you want him to give me some tips? If there's anything you want me to do as a first-base coach, I'm ready to do it."

"No-no-no," he said. "I want Frank to be the first-base coach, and I want you to be the third-base coach!"

"Really?"

"Yes," he said, "but the only thing I want you to do is go out there and be yourself. I'm sure you can do a great job. And change the signs. Frank's signs are much too complicated."

This was the day before opening day, and I had never coached third. I couldn't use Frank Howard's signs for the bunt, hit-and-run, and take. It had taken me four or five days to digest and understand his signs. Most of the players didn't understand them. There were different signs for catchers, different signs for outfielders, different signs for infielders. And Frank was spectacular in the way he delivered them. At six foot nine and three hundred pounds, it was amazing how quickly he'd give those signs. He was totally animated, hands making all kinds of gyrations, very in-sync and practiced movements of touching a leg, touching an arm, and touching the top of his cap with both hands. Frank had it down. The only signs I felt comfortable with were the ones taught me by my Babe Ruth League All-Stars coach, Sharkey Laureno. If you touch your arm and use the same hand to touch your belt, and then if you go back and touch your arm, it's a bunt. Because belt begins with B, and so does bunt.

"When you first touch the arm," Sharkey would say, "that's the lock." After you give the sign and come back to the arm, that's like key that turns the lock. I changed the signs a couple of times, always making them easier. The truth was that none of George's players gave a shit about the signs.

It wasn't long before George Bamberger said to me, "Hey, Bobby, I really like your enthusiasm. I like the way you're sending these runners. You're making this team look really aggressive, but your signs are too tough. We need to change them."

I said to the players, "George says the signs are too tough, so I'm taking away the key. If I touch the belt, it's a bunt. If I touch my hat, it's a hit-and-run. If I touch skin, it's a steal. If I squeeze my hands together, it's a squeeze." These were my Little League signs, and now I was using them with the Mets.

I used these signs, and the players were still missing them. George told me to make them easier!

"How can I make them any simpler?" I asked.

Jimmy Frey, the bench coach, was sitting with us, and he said, "Why don't you use the claps?"

I looked at Jimmy.

"You know," Jimmy said with a grin, "the easiest thing for a player to get is the clap."

I figured it was a joke, but then Jimmy showed me the clap system.

"One clap is a bunt. Two claps is the hit-and-run. Three is a steal, and if you tighten your fist, that's the squeeze."

If I wanted a player to bunt down the third-base line, I'd clap once and point to the third-base side. If the first-base side, I'd point to the first-base side. I used those signs until I left the Mets three and a half years later.

In April 1983, my son Bobby Jr. was born. It is the greatest thing that ever happened to me, and I love him more than I can explain. I went into the 1983 season knowing the blessed event was going to happen sometime in April. I never wanted to disrupt my work with personal affairs. In 1983, one didn't get time off for personal days. If you were on the road, you sent flowers.

We had a game on April 23. Mary was nine months' pregnant and feeling great, and I asked my fellow coaches, Howard and Jim Frey, "Is there any way I can get home for the birth of my child?"

"Why don't you go and ask George?" they said.

I had been a coach for a short time, and I didn't want exceptions made for me, but I figured I'd give it a shot.

"When is it?" George asked.

"Any day now," I said.

"Just let me know," he said.

I was on the bus going from the hotel to the ballpark, and I said, "George, I think it's going to be any day now."

"For what?"

"Yesterday I was telling you about my wife giving birth."

"Oh yeah. Just remind me when it happens."

I had no idea. It was my first child, and I didn't know about child birthing. We played a doubleheader, and I'm running to the pay phone between games, and it was always, "Everything's fine. We'll be in touch. Everything will work out."

"Great," I said. "I believe so, too."

After a doubleheader in Atlanta, I called home before getting on our charter plane to Cincinnati. The plane gets to 30,000 feet, and the pilot comes walking back.

"Hey, are you Bobby Valentine, the coach?"

"I am."

"Well, congratulations. The tower just called, and they got the message that your wife had a baby."

This can't be, I thought. I went up to Arthur Richman, our traveling secretary, and we got the flight book, and we went page by page, airline by airline, trying to find a flight from Cincinnati to New York once we landed. The only way I could get to New York was to fly back to Atlanta and catch a flight to New York. I had fifteen minutes to make it. I talked to the pilot, who talked to the tower, so we could get off at a gate close enough for me to make the Atlanta flight. He landed two gates away, and I ran across the tarmac and went up the stairs of the plane without a ticket. They let me on the plane, and I flew to Atlanta and then to New York.

I landed at JFK very early in the morning. I got to a pay phone, called my house, and there was no answer. I called Ralph Branca, my father-in-law, and he answered.

"Ralph, what was it? Is it a boy or a girl?" I asked.

"What are you talking about?" he said.

"Didn't Mary have the baby?"

"No," he said. "We just drove her to the hospital two hours ago."

"The pilot told me—"

"Oh no," Ralph said, "we called the tower in Atlanta to tell you not to worry, that everything was fine."

I got to the hospital just in time to spend fourteen hours of labor with my wife. She had Bobby Jr. and it was glorious, the greatest day ever. I got a flight out to Cincinnati as soon as possible and arrived in the middle of the game.

The next month, we went to L.A. for a three-game series. We took batting practice on day one, and then we took infield practice—I hit infield practice—and everyone came into the clubhouse to drink Cokes, grab a cup of coffee, or have a quick rubdown. But on this day, George called a team meeting. Because I hit infield, I was responsible for bringing in the balls and throwing them into the ball bag to make sure we didn't lose any, so I was the last one in the clubhouse.

As I walked in, George was standing in the middle of the room. He started unbuttoning his uniform. When he finished taking off his uniform, we realized he had his slacks and t-shirt under his uniform. He then said, "Boys, I've decided to go fishing." He then left the clubhouse. We were stunned. *What do we do now?*

Frank Cashen was in George's office. He walked into the middle of the clubhouse and said, "Let's go, boys. We have a game to play." He then took the coaches down to the batting cage, which was outside the visitor's bullpen, down behind the left-field fence. It was a bit of a walk, and we walked rapidly. We arrived at the batting cage, and we all sat down. Frank Howard stood. "Boys, this is going to be fine," Cashen said. "Here's what we're going to do. We got a game to play. Frank, you are now the manager. Jim [Frey], you will be the assistant manager and continue as hitting coach. Monbo [Bill Monbouquette], you will be the pitching coach. Bill Robinson, you will share the hitting responsibility, and Bobby, you will do what you were doing."

We all walked from the bullpen. The team was already in the dugout. Frank Howard carried the lineup card in his rapid gait—which was amazing, in that Hondo walked with twelve-foot strides—not too late to hand the card to the umpires.

Frank Howard became the Mets' manager, much to the chagrin of Jimmy Frey, who was the brains of the team. Jim and Frank were an odd twosome, and a number of the players referred to Frank as "George"—as in the mentally challenged character from John Steinbeck's *Of Mice and Men*—and they called Jim Frey "Lenny." Neither of them ever knew. Dave Kingman, the resident intellect, was the one who said it first.

After Frank took over, we played better. Frank Howard was bigger than life, bigger than anything. He stood six foot seven and weighed about 300 pounds. He'd eat a couple of meals at a time. He could drink for five guys, and no one worked out harder than he did. Hondo would do his workouts in the sauna. He'd take dumbbells into the sauna, perspiring gallons of sweat, and he would do his entire dumbbell workout, often with a cigar in his mouth.

Frank's pitching coach was Bill Monbouquette, and he, too, was a piece of work. Monbo had great energy. He threw a lot of batting practice, would fight at the drop of a hat, and was really good to me, even though we were generations apart. Monbo and Frank spent a lot of time together.

One of the highlights of 1983 was the return of Tom Seaver, who was thirty-eight. Cashen realized that the fans were disguised as seats at Shea Stadium, and he had to do something to spark interest. In December 1982 he made a trade with Cincinnati to get Tom Seaver back in a Mets uniform.

For me it was great, because I lived in Westchester and Tom lived in Greenwich, and most days I got to pick up Tom and Skip Lockwood and drive them to the ballpark.

Tom started opening day 1983. He pitched six innings of shut-out ball and we won 2–0. Before the game, he received more than an ovation. The fans put on a display of honor and love. They stood and cheered, counting down the last pitches of his bullpen warmup, and as he left the bullpen they were standing and cheering. With each step he took, the cheers got louder. I have never seen such an outpouring of emotion and love aimed at one person. It was a *long* walk from the bullpen all the way to the dugout. I still get chills when I relive it. I had been a Met on the day after he left, and here I was a coach on the day he returned. It was an honor to play with Tom Seaver, and I never let him forget that the only time I was on *Kiner's Korner*, the Mets' postgame show, was the day I got the game-winning hit against him in 1971. Tom remembered it, too. Ha!

I was learning to be a coach, a father, and a restaurant owner. Joe Romano—my partner and one of the greatest men I ever met—and I took the profits from our first restaurant in Stamford and bought our second place in Milford, Connecticut. It was a one-story, 3,500-square-foot building across from the jai alai fronton. Mike Allegra, an all-state wrestler from Milford and the hardest worker I ever met, was the manager. Mike stayed on and made the Milford restaurant a twenty-five-year success! Milford was a thirty-minute drive from Stamford and an hour from Shea. I spent many a day and night with Mike and friends. The stories could fill an entire book.

One amazing story came in the winter of '83. At 3:30 a.m. I was closing the Stamford restaurant when the phone rang. An unfamiliar voice asked me to meet him outside the back door. He said it was very important. I opened the back door and saw a guy at the wheel of a late-model Cadillac. He rolled the window down and asked me to get in. He seemed to be a little younger than me, and rather nervous, as we drove around the block. He said in a very convincing manner that the baseball commissioner's office had a tape recording of me selling cocaine in New

York City. He said he could make the story go away for $25,000. That was a lot of money. This was Sunday night, and I had only until Tuesday afternoon to produce the money. I knew immediately there was no way I could come up with that kind of money, for anything, let alone a situation that I had nothing to do with. Extortion. Mob. 1983.

I tried to keep my wits together, as the sun was coming up, and called Joe Romano. We spent the next day finding out who my late-night visitor had been and who he was working for. Tony, as I found his name to be, was sitting at my bar at lunchtime on Tuesday. Even though the group that he was working for was formidable, I told him to go shit in his hat. Lunch ended, and I almost collapsed from the exhaustion and stress of the last two days. I had called his bluff.

I entered my basement office wanting a shoulder to cry on when the phone rang. I answered it. The voice on the other end introduced himself as a drug security investigator for Major League Baseball. He instructed me to come to his offices at MLB that afternoon.

I got in my car and drove as quickly as I could to the address I was given in New York City. I entered his office, and he began reading from a yellow legal pad notes that an undercover agent had given him with dates, places, and conversations. The written transcript stated that an undercover agent had asked me if I could procure an ounce of cocaine. Allegedly, I had said, "Of course, and more if you need it." After what seemed like an eternity of this line of accusation, I asked if I could listen to the tape that the transcript was based on. He said yes. He put a cassette into a cassette player, and together we listed to a voice that was not remotely close to my own. Immediately, he realized he had the wrong man and apologized for the inconvenience.

Driving back from New York, my head was spinning. I could never figure out how Tony "the Brains," who died in 2015 as an underboss of the Gambino crime family, knew of this MLB investigation.

We got through the '83 season with Frank Howard as manager, and during the winter Frank Cashen hired Davey Johnson to be the manager in '84. Davey had played for the Baltimore Orioles. He, too, was one of Frank Cashen's people.

Davey, who had been the Mets' Triple-A manager at Tidewater, Virginia, wasn't just a baseball player. He was a very intelligent guy who bought and sold real estate in Orlando. He was a wheeler-dealer, and when he was managing Tidewater, everyone knew he was going to be the next Mets manager.

When Davey took over, Frank Howard stayed as a coach. Mel Stottlemyre took over as pitching coach from Bill Monbouquette. Mel was the salt of the earth, one of the greatest people who ever lived, and a great pitching coach. Mel and I were Davey's conduits to the team.

Davey was on the cover of the Mets media guide with a computer in front of him in 1984! He was ahead of his time.

I can remember the year before, standing in line at the Tyrone Square Mall in St. Petersburg, waiting for the bookstore to open so I could get a copy of *The Bill James Baseball Abstract*. I would read James's book on the bus, and when I tried to talk to the other coaches about James's analytics, the coaching staff thought I was speaking Latin or Chinese.

When Davey got the manager's job, he knew what I was talking about. Davey played for Earl Weaver and believed in the three-run home run and didn't like to bunt. Davey let me handle the running game. When George Bamberger and Frank Howard were the managers, they always signaled me what to do. Davey trusted me enough that when I saw that the runner was timing the pitcher properly and could get a jump, I would give him the open hand. Davey put his trust in me, and I was loyal to him. We made a good combo. I continued to use Jim Frey's sign system of claps.

When Davey came up to manage the Mets, he brought with him a number of the players who had starred for him at Tidewater, such as fiery infielder Wally Backman. He was determined to bring up nineteen-year-old pitcher Dwight Gooden, among others.

One of the things that fueled Davey's fire was the way he liked to pit himself against Frank Cashen. Even though they had the usual manager-general manager relationship, Davey very often wanted to be the contrarian. Sometimes it was little things, and sometimes big things.

Davey won many arguments with his perseverance and his ability to use the "uniform card" on Frank. Eventually Davey would say, "We're in uniform, and we know what's going on." Frank often gave in.

Davey and Frank had a vision to build the team from within, using the Mets' minor league talent and adding a few from the outside to fill in the voids. Adding to the homegrown talent, the Mets acquired Howard Johnson. Howard was a switch-hitter, and Davey liked this flexibility in his lineup. Keith Hernandez added a Gold Glove and a middle of the order that was desperately needed. The final piece to Davey's puzzle came after the 1984 season when Cashen traded with the Montreal Expos for their All-Star catcher Gary Carter.

The standings were set going into the last game of the '84 season, and we improved but did not make the playoffs. We needed one more bat. Davey decided not to manage the last game and turned the lineup over to me. My first game as manager. It meant nothing in the standings, but it was important to me.

During that game, the Expos had runners on second and third, and Gary Carter was the batter. Gary was tied with Mike Schmidt for the league lead in RBIs. I walked him intentionally. I heard after the game that Gary was really upset, and then we traded for him. He finished the season tied for the lead. I anxiously awaited his arrival. When he arrived, I greeted him in the clubhouse by saying I was only trying to win the game, and it was nothing personal. He gave me his famous smile and a big bear hug. We became very good friends over the years.

During the off-season, we opened our third restaurant in Norwalk, Connecticut, halfway between Stamford and Milford. Frank Ramppen and Tom Kelly took on the managing chores in Norwalk. All three places were conveniently located near Interstate 95, and I was able to get to all three on the same day. During the winter I did this, and during the season I would work one for lunchtime business, and then another two after the game.

I was making $35,000 as a coach and hoping to make a lot more in my Connecticut restaurant business. Luckily, I convinced my friend Paul Pupo to move east from Seattle and help manage the three places. I was thirty-four years old and having a great time with great friends and lots of work.

On May 16, 1985, the Mets were playing in Houston. I was the Mets' third-base coach when Tom Grieve called me. Tom had been my roommate for a little while when I played and sat on the bench for the Mets, and after he retired, he became the general manager of the Texas Rangers. Tom had been a number-one draft choice of the Washington Senators, which then moved to Texas, and all during his career he lived in Arlington. So when he retired, he had a foot in the door, and the Rangers hired him as a ticket salesman.

"Everyone knows Tom Grieve," the Rangers brass figured. "He'll do great selling tickets."

Brad Corbett owned the team, and Brad got to know Tom and like him. Tom became a minor league coach, then the scouting director, and then the assistant general manager to Joe Klein. Eddie Chiles bought the team and brought over Mike Stone from his Western Company to run the Rangers organization, and they wanted to do it fresh. Mike Stone was from the University of Michigan, and so was Tom Grieve, whom he made the Rangers' general manager. Tom called me to say the Rangers were going to fire their manager, Doug Rader.

"Eddie Chiles and Mike Stone and I want to come see you and interview you to be the manager of the Rangers," Tom said.

"Yeah. Wow," I said.

"Don't tell anyone," he said.

I was in Houston, and the three flew from Dallas in Eddie Chiles's private plane to Houston's Hobby Airport. Eddie had more planes than most countries did. He had over twenty airplanes and more than three hundred eighteen-wheeler semi-tractor trailers for hauling the plastic pipe that he sold. Eddie was a self-made billionaire who worked his way through college ironing shirts for his fraternity brothers. He owned the

Western Company, which was an oil-rig servicing company. Though the price of oil was going down, he was still in high cotton, as he used to say.

The plane taxied into a hangar at Hobby Airport. The cab I took circled the airport for a while as I tried to figure out where I had to go to meet them. When we got to the right entrance, I got out and walked into a humongous building and found Tom, Eddie, and Mike. They brought me into the office for the interview.

I was so excited I don't remember much about it. I got back in the cab, rode to the hotel, and before I could get on the bus to go to the ballpark, Tom Grieve called my hotel room.

"There's going to be a ticket for you to fly to Chicago," he said.

CHAPTER 14

Texas

I was supposed to keep my hiring quiet, but I felt I owed Freddy Willis, the sports editor of *The Stamford Advocate*, a heads-up, and that really pissed off the New York reporters, including Murray Chass and Marty Noble. The Dallas writers weren't too happy about it, either. And this was even *before* I was the manager.

That night I coached third base for the Mets in the Astrodome, and I told Gary and Keith, as well as Mel Stottlemyre. After the game, I called Frank Cashen to thank him and tell him I was leaving. It all happened pretty quickly.

When I met the Rangers brass, I didn't know the first thing about them. I hadn't followed the American League at all since I'd played for Seattle in 1979. My memories of Arlington were how hot it was and that the usherettes wore little white cowgirl skirts. It was a Brave New World.

Before I took the job, I called Tommy Lasorda for advice.

"Ya gotta take it," he said. Tommy said he didn't think it would be the end-all job, but then he said, "If you have a chance to be a manager at age thirty-five, you have to take it."

I would have preferred managing the Dodgers or the Mets, but Tommy had become the Dodgers manager, and he wasn't going anywhere. Davey Johnson was the manager of the Mets, and he wasn't going anywhere. I didn't have many connections anywhere else. I took the Texas job and flew to Chicago to meet the team.

I had had an opportunity to manage once before, but the timing wasn't right, and I turned it down. Back in 1980, I was opening my restaurant in Stamford when Gabe Paul, the general manager of the Yankees, came to see me.

"George wants you to be his Rookie League manager," Gabe said.

I was knee-deep in the restaurant business, running around crazily, and I said, "Can I think about it for a day and call you in the morning?"

"Sure," Gabe said, "but you don't want to disappoint The Boss."

I just couldn't juggle the schedule. The Rookie League team played in upstate New York, and there was no way for me to leave my restaurant.

"I can't do it," I told Gabe. For years, whenever I saw George Steinbrenner, he would kid me about turning down that job.

Now I was the manager of my own team. The Rangers got off to a slow start, 9–23, and Tom Grieve had replaced Doug Rader with a thirty-five-year-old kid from Stamford.

I learned that Eddie Chiles had bought the Rangers from Brad Corbett during a poker game. Corbett had made a fortune in the oil business, producing and selling PVC piping. Brad was a transplanted Easterner who was gregarious and flamboyant, the opposite of Eddie.

"Eddie," Brad said, "you have all these planes, all those trucks, all that money. But I know something you don't have."

"What's that, boy?" said Eddie.

"You don't have a baseball team."

"By God, I don't," Eddie supposedly said. "How do I get one?"

"I'll sell one to you after the card game," Corbett said.

That was about as much as Eddie Chiles knew about baseball.

Everything was spinning so fast. I was trying to get to know the players while also navigating a management style that was changing. The traditional baseball management style was modeled after the armed forces, the greatest team in the world. Under that system, the manager was the boss, and it was either his way or the highway. The manager called his players "son." But things were changing. When Tommy Lasorda came in, Sparky Anderson—the old-school manager of Cincinnati's Big Red Machine—commented, "I've known Tommy a long time, and I see what he does, and I've heard what he does as manager; but I don't think he's going to be hugging his players in the big leagues."

Sparky was very wrong. Tommy not only hugged them, he learned the first names of their wives and kids, and he threw parties and had players over for dinner. He threw the book away, as far as what a major league manager was supposed to do and how he was supposed to act. By the time I was named the Rangers manager, I had played for four future Hall of Fame managers: Walter Alston, Dick Williams, Joe Torre, and Tommy Lasorda. The style I liked most was Tommy's.

I believed Tommy's style was the way to manage in 1985, and so I learned everyone's names, learned their wives' names, and spent a lot of time the rest of the season understanding my players and understanding myself. On off-days and during the All-Star break, I would drive to Oklahoma City to watch our Triple-A team play, and to Tulsa to watch our Double-A team play. I wanted to know as much about the organization as I could.

At the same time, Tom Grieve, the brand-new general manager, was trying to revamp the organization, and we were connected at the hip. The president of the Rangers was Mike Stone, a baseball outsider whom Eddie had brought in from his oil business. He was with us every step of the way. I could see that Tom and Mike were trying to do things outside of the box. They hired Craig Wright, a sabermetrician, to evaluate the team by the numbers, which is a standard today. Craig was not only evaluating players, he was evaluating games. He wrote spectacular essays on topics like stolen bases, lineups, pitcher usage, and bunting.

I, too, liked to think outside of the box. I was working for ESPN when I opened my first restaurant in 1979. I was the color man, doing the UConn versus Maine baseball game, when I found out about satellite dishes—that you could actually buy a fifteen-foot-round dish to capture news and stuff off a satellite in space. When I opened my first restaurant, I bought one of those satellite dishes so I could air sports events in the restaurant that were not broadcast on network TV. When I became the manager of the Rangers, the first thing I asked Eddie Chiles for was money to install a satellite dish, so I could record any and all American League games being aired.

At lunch, Eddie gave me a choice. "Son," he said, "you said you were going to scout teams with this satellite dish. We have paid a young man to scout teams for you. Are you telling me you'd rather scout the teams yourself than have him do it?" Eddie was looking at a ledger that indicated how his money was being spent.

"Between the advance scout or the satellite dish," I said, "I'd rather have the satellite dish."

"Okay," Chiles said. "You can have the dish, but you have to fire the scout."

The advance scout was a terrific guy, a lifer in baseball, but I fired him. Coincidentally, when I later got to manage the Mets, he was the advance scout for them, and when I arrived, he quit.

I put the satellite dish in and paid an hourly wage to a fellow by the name of Carl Hamilton, who had two VHS recorders. His job was to tape as many games as he could. I would take a VCR on the road and watch the games in my room. We were able to record games that no one else had.

༄

The first big issue I had to face as manager was whether I should keep Doug Rader's coaches. His coaches that year were Merv Rettenmund, Dick Such, Wayne Terwilliger, Rich Donnelly, and Glen Ezell.

In 1985, ESPN was becoming a household channel. We were watching TV at one in the morning to get the latest scores. The newspaper reporters were having a hard time accepting the fact that they no longer were the sole purveyors of sports in America.

The other change was the emergence of sports talk radio. Randy Galloway, the lead columnist for the *Dallas Morning News,* was becoming Randy Galloway, the fiery host of talk radio in Dallas. The talk radio station allowed Randy to put on his cowboy hat and enabled fans to call him so he could spew his venom and criticize the Dallas sports world. This was a time when Tom Landry was beginning to fade from his status as a sports icon. Randy was one of the reasons why. It was Randy who jumped on the concept that you could talk sports and create controversy even when the games weren't being played live.

I was an outsider and a young Yankee who spoke a foreign language. The foreign language was English. I hadn't yet learned how to speak Texan.

Doug Rader and Randy Galloway were drinking buddies. They were funny and smart, and loud. Well, Randy was loud. And now Doug was gone, and I came on the scene. It was the first time I ever experienced controversy with the media. In the past, all the media wanted to do was write nice stories about me. When I was a coach with the Mets, I was a fountain of information for them. They weren't going to get headlines from the third-base coach who was waving runners around, but if there was an opinion to give, I'd give it, and the one-liner either would be favorable or it wouldn't get printed.

In Texas, it was different. Arlington was smack dab in the middle between Dallas and Fort Worth, two towns that were diametrically opposite. There were three papers, the *Dallas Morning News,* where Randy Galloway worked; the *Fort Worth Star-Telegram,* where Jim Reeves wrote; and the *Dallas Times Herald,* where Skip Bayless worked. Early in my tenure, Bayless wrote an article that made it seem that we had grown up together. According to Skip, I changed my underwear three times a day, and I was going to totally destroy the Rangers organization and be run out of town within twenty-four hours, because I was Italian and a friend of Tommy Lasorda. Skip had an ax to grind, because he blamed Tommy for his departure from the L.A. sports media market. Bayless, along with a writer by the name of Gerry Fraley, were my true nemeses during my time in Texas. For about four years Fraley was a big supporter, and then one day he was talking to me before a game and said something about his mother wanting him to be more like me. On that day it seemed the page turned. After that, I couldn't do anything right. Gerry was going to rid me from his life and write anything he could to make sure I wasn't going to be successful. There were times when Randy Galloway loved me, and there were times when he hated me. He was either in favor of what I was doing, or he hated what I was doing. The sportswriters no longer could just write about the game, they needed to create controversy.

I had managed the team for a couple weeks, and the Dallas and Fort Worth sports reporters, Randy Galloway in particular, were writing articles on why I should keep the coaching staff. I was torn. Tom Landry came to visit me, because he and Andy Robustelli, my Stamford Godfather, had played together on the New York Giants football team in the 1950s and were good friends. I was a babe in the woods. Andy gave Coach Landry a call, asking him to stop in and make me feel at home.

I was in the Rangers clubhouse early when Joe Macko, the clubhouse guy, came in and said, "Hey, the Coach is here."

"Who?"

"Tom Landry is out there. He wants to come in and see ya."

I was flabbergasted. Coach Landry was a god. I stood up. He took off his hat when he came into the office and sat down. In his soft-spoken way, he talked about Dallas and Fort Worth and how they were closed communities, but that "they will open up their arms to you, if you show them that you care," he said. "Someone who gives a great effort is always welcome in the Dallas community."

"Thank you very much," I said.

We talked about other things, and as he was getting ready to leave, he put on his hat and said, "Do you mind if I give you a little advice?"

"Coach," I said, "I'd be honored if you'd give me some advice. Please."

"Make sure your coaches speak your language," he said.

I was sure he was telling me to get rid of Doug Rader's coaches and bring in my own. Soon afterward I changed the hitting and pitching coaches. I knew Merv Rettenmund, and liked him, but I disagreed with his hitting philosophy. As for the pitching coach, Dick Such, he was a great person. But as we stood side by side in a crucial situation in the eighth inning against the Tigers, Mike Mason, a left-handed pitcher was on the mound facing Alejandro Sánchez, a big right-handed hitter, and Dick let me down.

"Do you think Mike has had enough?" I asked Dick.

I didn't get a clear answer. I ran out to the mound to give Mike a pep talk, which seemed like the right thing to do. When I got back to the dugout, I had barely turned around when *bang*, Sánchez's bat hit the ball into the upper deck. We lost the game because of that home run, and during the press conference, one of the reporters said to me, "Didn't you know that in the last game, Sánchez hit two home runs off Mason?"

"No, I didn't know it," I said. "But I know it now!"

I was upset that I didn't get the information I needed, and at that moment knew changes had to be made. I told Tom Grieve I wanted a new pitching coach.

Tom House replaced Dick Such, and I had Art Howe replace Merv Rettenmund as batting coach. House, who had been working with Craig Wright, the sabermetrician, was Grieve's recommendation. Tom said his specialty was the mechanics of throwing. He was using high-speed video. He would put in a VCR tape and run it one click at a time to see a pitcher in slow motion. What House was seeing was different from what other people were seeing, and I loved it. He wasn't interested in what pitch to throw, a fastball or a curve. That was for me to decide. He dealt with the laws of physics and how they applied to pitching.

"There is only one correct way to throw a ball, and we just have to figure out what it is," House said.

I loved that. I had been going to college libraries in every town on the road trying to figure out the physics of the swing and the ball in flight. Tom had already done the research on the physics of the throw, so hiring him was a perfect match. He was also a USC graduate, and the guy who caught Hank Aaron's 715th home run in the Atlanta bullpen. I kept everyone else.

I enjoyed most of our players. We had Don Slaught, Pete O'Brien, Toby Harrah, Curt Wilkerson, Buddy Bell, Gary Ward, Oddibe McDowell, Larry Parrish, and Cliff Johnson.

But situations always arise, and the first was with Cliff Johnson, who was a really good hitter. He was thirty-seven, and he didn't need to learn anything new from a new manager, that's for sure. We were in Baltimore for a game, and if you're ever in Baltimore during the summer, you know it can feel like a thousand degrees with a thousand percent humidity. Cliff was my DH. In Baltimore there is no bathroom in the dugout. During the game, I had to pee, and I ran into the clubhouse, and Cliff was sitting in the air conditioning in a recliner chair, with a large tumbler half full of beer beside his seat.

"Cliff, you can't be that blatant about it," I said on my way out. I'm not naïve. A lot of guys shot a beer in the middle of the game, especially on a hot day. Some guys shook the can so there was an explosion going down your gullet. Guys thought it activated the key ingredient in the amphetamines they were taking. The alcohol and the amphetamines had a way of going together. Hell's bells, I did it. I knew it.

Cliff would take his at-bat and return to the clubhouse. I sent one of the coaches into the clubhouse, and Cliff was still sitting there with a beer in his hand, and I just felt someone had to get a grip on this. As a first-year manager, I had to show some authority, so I asked Tom Grieve to trade him. On August 28, we traded Cliff to the Blue Jays for three players.

Then there was the Buddy Bell situation. One of the best young players the Rangers had was Steve Buechele, who was John Elway's roommate at Stanford. Steve was a third baseman who was tearing it up in the minor leagues. Buddy was the elder statesman of the team. He held court every day after the game at his locker. Tom and I talked about Buddy's place on the team, whether or not to make him the captain and keep him around, or whether to make Buddy the DH, so we could bring Buechele up to play third base. This was before we traded Cliff Johnson, who was a DH, and we had Larry Parrish, who had his knee in a brace but who was a hell of a power hitter. We felt that Larry would be a really stable DH.

Tom called around and found that Cincinnati had an interest in Buddy Bell. Buddy's father, Gus Bell, had been a star in Cincinnati, and if there was a graceful way we could replace Buddy with Buechele, trading Buddy to Cincinnati seemed to be the answer. We had seen Jeff Russell pitching for Cincinnati during spring training. We liked what we saw, and Craig Wright was really high on Duane Walker, a left-hand-hitting minor league outfielder. The trade was made.

We still had a lot of work to do. At the end of the 1985 season, we finished 62–99. My record was 53–78. We needed to improve, and soon.

Tom Grieve and I had a plan to develop and play the young guys. The conventional wisdom at the time was that a player should play several years in the minors before being brought up. We disagreed. We thought: *Let's see how many of them we can get to the big leagues as quickly as possible.* I prided myself on my teaching, and Tom bought into it. Within the year, we turned over 50 percent of our roster. Of the core players, we kept Toby Harrah, Larry Parrish, Pete O'Brien, and Charlie Hough. They were going to be part of the future. Everyone else was a placeholder until we upgraded, through trades or from the minor leagues.

Toby and Tom Grieve were great friends and had played together. Toby may have been the most underrated player ever to play the game. He was a sabermetrician and Craig Wright's favorite player. He had total control of the strike zone, hit with power, played steady defense, and he walked more than he struck out. He also had a remarkably accurate arm and very good hands. Toby Harrah was the real deal, and he wasn't going anywhere. From day one Tom said to me, "You're going to love this guy," and I did. The only problem I had initially with Toby was that he and Buddy Bell were close, so when I traded Buddy, it wasn't Toby's best day. But Toby was a baseball player, and he got it, and, interestingly, it was Toby who replaced me when I got fired in Texas.

CHAPTER 15

Tom and I Have a Plan

1986 was my first full year as a manager. Spring training was in Pompano Beach, Florida, which had one redeeming quality—a dog track, where the gamblers, about 70 percent of the guys down there, would go to drink beer and bet on the dogs. The city field we played on was deplorable. We had announced to the town that we were not going to renew our lease, because the next year we were moving our spring training digs to Port Charlotte on the West Coast of Florida.

I was involved with the planning and building of the new facility with Tom Grieve, Mike Stone, and the architects. I was also kind of in charge of the groundskeeping in Pompano, because the city workers weren't doing much work on our field. I arrived before the players did and realized that there was no netting on our batting cage. I drove along the shore until I found a fishing village, and walked into a few warehouses to see if anyone would sell me some netting. Finally, I found an old guy who sold me as much netting as I could carry for fifty dollars. We put it up around the poles standing adjacent to the field. So the night before spring training began, I found myself on a ladder hanging netting.

It rained the day before opening day, and the field was a mess. We worked to get the puddles out, found extension cords and attached them to fans, and tried to blow the field dry. Just before game time it was almost presentable when the first-base umpire called time. "We can't play this game. When you take the lead off first base, it's too muddy," he said.

"Time out," I yelled. I ran over to a large pile of red clay, got on my knees, and with my arms and hands scooped up a huge amount and headed toward first base. The hundred people in the stands were watching. I was in full stride when I violently threw my hands up over my head, tossing all of it in the air while screaming bloody murder. It was a huge mound of fire ants.

Pete Incaviglia, the overall number-one draft choice out of Oklahoma State, came to camp. Pete set all kinds of records, and later, in 2000, he was voted the college Player of the Century. The Montreal Expos had selected him. As soon as the Expos announced their pick, Pete and his agent declared that he would not play in Canada and would not sign with the Expos. It had been ten years since the advent of free agency. Every player had an agent, and Incaviglia's was Bucky Woy, who lived in Dallas. Woy said the exchange rate and the lack of exposure were the main reasons he wasn't going to sign. His client, this good ol' boy from Oklahoma, wasn't going to be tucked away in a foreign country.

I had found a home in Arlington and moved my family. During the winter I drove to the ballpark every day, throwing batting practice to all the Ranger players who lived in the area. One day Tom Grieve called me and asked, "What would you think if we could bring Incaviglia to the team?" I didn't know the first thing about him, other than what I'd heard from the scouts who were videotaping players. Tom wanted to get the approval of Mike Stone and owner Eddie Chiles before doing something radical. Tom was a young general manager, who, like Tommy Lasorda, wanted to bring in young players, and he knew that Incaviglia was right up our alley.

I was an avid racquetball player, and some of the best courts were over by the airport in a development called Las Colinas. Racquetball was all the craze. I entered one of those cutthroat tournaments where if you won, you stayed. If you lost, you left and the winner played someone else. I ended up in the finals with a guy who gave me a hell of a match. Afterwards, we were totally exhausted, wiping off the sweat, and while we were sitting by each other, he reached over, put out his hand, and introduced himself as Bucky Woy. It meant nothing to me, absolutely nothing.

"I represent Pete Incaviglia, the number-one draft choice of the Montreal Expos," he said. "I also represent Bob Horner." Bob was also a number-one draft choice and a great hitter out of Arizona State. In a radical move later, during Bob Horner's prime, Bucky signed him to a lucrative multi-year contract in Japan.

"That's interesting," I said. "Is Pete going to sign or not?"

"Not only is he not going to sign with Montreal," Woy said, "but I'm going to do everything I can to see that he signs with the Rangers."

It seemed serendipitous, but I couldn't help but think it was planned, even though Woy had to win five games on the racquetball court to play me in the finals.

"If you're serious," I said, "I will deliver the message to Tom Grieve."

Within a week we had pulled off the trade, sending Bob Sebra, who had a really good curveball, and shortstop Jim Anderson to Montreal, then signing Inky to a nice contract. Pete was the only player in baseball history to be drafted number one and then traded by the team before he ever played an inning for that organization. When he arrived in Pompano Beach, it was quite a story for the Rangers and for baseball.

During batting practice at our decrepit field, with big sheets of rotting plywood making up the outfield fence, Pete came out to hit, and you should have seen the mob of reporters that came to see him. He put on an incredible display of power, hitting a ball *through* the fence in left-center. It became the lead for all the Dallas TV stations and a national story.

Pete was large, Harmon Killebrew large. He had big shoulders and a big back, with a lot of depth to his chest. He had hair coming out of his t-shirt and a beard that needed shaving a couple times a day. He was Paul Bunyan, exactly what the Rangers fans needed to start letting their imaginations run away with them on what might be.

The reason Bucky Woy wanted Pete to come with us was because the year before, we had brought up Oddibe McDowell, who had played a month in the minor leagues after being drafted out of Arizona State. Oddibe played a hundred games for the Rangers his first year, which was atypical. Bringing Pete to the majors was a big part of Bucky's dream playbook, and we played a part in it. We also brought up outfielder Ruben Sierra, who was twenty, and pitcher Edwin Correa, who was nineteen.

The model I was trying to build on was Davey Johnson's model. During the three years I was with him, Davey would say, "We're going to build from within. We're going to bring up the young guys because they're so talented. The fans are going to get excited."

What made managing the Texas Rangers really special for me was that I was managing Tommy Paciorek, who I was very close to, and also Charlie Hough. Not only did I have elder statesmen who were my disciples in the clubhouse, so necessary in every environment, but I had someone other than my coaches to socialize with.

I determined at the end of the 1985 season that I would clear the slate. I wouldn't bring back any of my coaches from the old regime. What I needed was someone to organize spring training. When I mentioned this to Tom Grieve, he said, "You know, Robbie [Tom Robson] is the greatest at organizing spring training and organizing anything you need organized." I badly needed someone to help me organize. I needed my players in spring training to be where they were supposed to be when they were supposed to be there. Tom Grieve said that Robson did that for the minor league program.

With Tom House as my pitching coach and Tom Robson my hitting coach, I embarked on my search for the Holy Grail: the perfect pitch and the perfect swing. Tom Robson jumped head-first into helping me analyze and collect videos so he could teach the new Ted Williams uppercut swing we were going to promote. Robson was the most unappreciated hitting coach in all of baseball. The naysayers who wanted to teach hitting the way we'd been taught, to swing down on the ball, were loud in their denunciation of me. Tom Robson was my saving grace.

In 1986, my Texas Rangers won 87 games, and I was the UPI Manager of the Year. *Voila!* But the improvement happened too quickly. We were changing a lot of stuff, and change is what most people dislike most in life.

The Rangers were actually getting some recognition. The Dallas Cowboys were on a downturn. We had brought in the young guys, and I was a young guy, and I went to every Kiwanis Club luncheon, every Rotary Club dinner, and every rodeo in town. I was out pounding the pavement, and my players were starting to stir the imagination in the fans' minds, something that had never happened before in Arlington, even though we were playing in a converted minor league stadium.

The community had never before given a damn about baseball. There were a couple months when the Cowboys weren't playing football, so sports-loving Texans went to baseball games. We were the absolute stepsister to the Cowboys, and then we began to gain some momentum. Reporters like Randy Galloway wrote about us and talked about us on the radio. Our problem was that Eddie Chiles was slipping financially. We went from an organization that was bought at a card game by this billionaire to being a team that was imposing austerity. We were going to build the bottom line, which I was fine with. I had no problem with marching to the organization's drum.

In 1986 we had sluggers Inky, Larry Parrish, Ruben Sierra, and Pete O'Brien, the heir apparent for the leadership role of the team. Pete O'Brien was a solid player who had come through our minor league system, and everybody appreciated him. He had the right *look,* a left-handed swing, and wasn't boisterous. He was just what the Texas fans were looking for in a cool, calm, and collected captain, even though he was never the captain. But that's how everyone viewed him.

We were supposed to take another step forward in 1987. Instead, we took a half a step back. The main reason—if you listened to Randy

Galloway, *the excuse*—was that good pitchers got hurt. In 1987, we finished with a 75–87 record. Edwin Correa and Jose Guzman, two Puerto Rican phenoms, got hurt. Correa threw a two-hitter against the Yankees his first time in Yankee Stadium. He threw a complete game, and soon thereafter in a bullpen session, his humerus—the bone that connects the elbow to the shoulder—snapped. He came back the next year but was never the same.

We were bitten by injuries, and Eddie Chiles was slowly going broke. The price of oil was dropping, his company was in decline, and his mental health was also in decline. He became very repetitive.

We often had lunch together, and at every meal during the second half of the season he'd say the same thing. Holding a pencil and turning over a napkin, he'd say, "Young men," looking at Mike Stone while talking to Tom Grieve and me, "I think you have a problem with your plan. When I was at university, I learned that success comes when a man knows where he is, knows where he wants to go, and then has a plan that takes him there. And I don't think we have a good plan." Eddie would draw on the napkin the cities of Chicago and Dallas, and he'd draw a line from one to the other, as though that was our plan. We were going to go from Dallas to Chicago in a straight line. Then he'd draw a cloud or two on the napkin and say, "Sometimes when you're going to Chicago, you can't stay on the same route. And if you have a good plan when you take off, you'll just go around that storm and get to Chicago on time."

Eddie—grandfatherly, professorial, and the old guy standing on the corner all rolled into one—was right. It was a great lesson. If you knew where you were and where you wanted to go, you've figured out the hard part. Now figure out *how* you're getting there, and be ready to take the fork in the road. You *must* change your plan on the way, otherwise you're just going to get bogged down in a thunderstorm and maybe get hit by lightning.

What should we do to get better? That's what Tom Grieve and I had to figure out. We were building our team with veteran hitting and young pitching, with Charlie Hough as the mainstay. After the first lunch with Eddie, Tom and I decided we had better be ready for the next luncheon.

Eddie said, "Well, boys, what are you going to do to keep the pitching healthy?"

In 1986, when I hired Tom House, we installed the first full-fledged weight room in Major League Baseball. I tossed out the ping-pong table, and a lot of players weren't happy about that. They used that ping-pong table regularly. By my second year we had the weight room, and there was a country-wide debate whether we were going to allow our players, especially our pitchers, to lift. Tom House implemented the program. We were going to do things *differently.*

House instituted pitchers playing catch in the outfield with a football. If you wanted to see disapproval from the old guard, it was having pitchers throw footballs. It was blasphemy. But we did it, and I take very little pleasure in noting that when Roger Clemens warmed up for the Yankees for his 2000 World Series start against my Mets, he was throwing a football. House showed us that when a pitcher releases the ball, the hand stops after it totally extends and pronates. A quarterback throwing a football does exactly the same thing. The laws of physics are the same, regardless of what you are propelling: a baseball, a football, or a javelin. All of our players bought into it.

I decided that the answer to Eddie's question, "What do we need to do to get better?" was simple: we needed to keep our players healthy.

We had a magnificent year from Ruben Sierra, who had 30 home runs and 109 RBIs. Larry Parrish had 32 home runs and 100 RBIs, and O'Brien and Inky also hit well. Our swing teaching was getting through, and we were transforming our roster in a rapid fashion. One of the decisions we had to make was whether to sign a talented relief pitcher named Steve Howe. Howe had been busted five times for cocaine use and suspended from baseball. He had pitched well as a Dodger, and Tommy loved him. Joe Ferguson, a coach on my staff as well as a former teammate of mine, had supervised Howe when they were with the Dodgers. Joe, whom I really liked and respected, thought we should sign him.

Howe had saved seventeen games during his Rookie of the Year season, a rookie record, and the next year helped the Dodgers beat the Yankees in the 1981 World Series. The downside was that if Howe got caught doing cocaine again, the baseball commissioner said he would fine the Rangers $250,000.

On the recommendations of Lasorda and Ferguson, and because it was a way to get an edge in talent, we signed him. All we had to do was keep him straight. I knew all about cocaine, Joe was here, and we had just hired Sam McDowell, a reformed alcoholic, to run our drug and alcohol program. We thought we had all the pieces in place. In 1987, Steve Howe was lights out. He was as good as any left-handed pitcher in the league. He would get to the park early, was being bed-checked and supervised, and everything was moving along,

Because we were bringing up so many young players, I had to release Tom Paciorek, who was like a brother to me. When Wimpy and I were in rookie ball together, Tommy gave one of his amazing clubhouse speeches, ranting and raving as he walked up and down, before ending his talk by saying, "When you guys go out on the field, and you cross the line and you're ready to play a baseball game, I want you to play the baseball game as though it's the last game you're ever going to play." From that day on, before a game, either Tom or I would say, "Hey, let's play like it's the last game we're ever going to play."

We were a month into the season, playing Seattle, and Tom was in the lineup against Mark Langston. Tom was shagging balls, and as I often did, I walked around the outfield to check everyone's pulse during the relaxed, pregame atmosphere. I stopped to see how Tommy was doing.

"Fine," he said. "How are you doing, Bobby?"

"I'm fine, Wimpy," I said, "But you have to do me a favor."

He was running, shagging balls and throwing them in, and he came over and said, "What do you need, Bobby?"

"Wimp," I said, "I need you to play this game like it's the last one you're ever going to play."

He ran after another ball, shagged it, and returned with an incredulous expression on his face. "Why?" he asked.

"Yeah," I said, "this *is* the last game you're ever going to play." Wimpy had had a twenty-year career. He knew he was at the end of the road.

"It is?"

"Yes," I said. "It is."

We both started tearing up, and as he walked toward the foul line, I walked toward center field. Tom hit a home run and a double against Langston, and we won the game. After the game, the Rangers released him.

Little did I know how different I was going to feel coming to the ballpark. There was a void. It was different, and weird. And lonely.

During the last couple of weeks of the season, I established the practice of conducting year-end interviews with my players. We would discuss their improvement during the year, and what I hoped and expected for their future. During one of these interviews, Pete O'Brien sat across my desk, and after we were done, he got up to leave, and said, "Skip, do you mind if I say something else? But I don't want you to be offended."

"Of course, Pete. Say anything you want." By this time, I knew everyone's wife's name. I was in the loop on when their kids were born, knew their kids' names. I was doing Lasorda 2.0, trying to be a different kind of manager.

Pete said, "Skip, I think you think about winning too much."

It felt as though a sharp object had poked me right in the middle of my eye. "Okay," I said. "Let me think about that for a while, Pete."

Initially, I was upset. *How the hell could a guy who I wanted to lead this team think that I was thinking about winning too much? What the hell else should I be thinking about?"* I was heartbroken and disappointed. I saw it as a personal affront.

During a lunch with Mike Stone and Tom Grieve, a light went on. I asked them, "Why didn't you tell me that I think about winning too much?" I realized that I wasn't working on the *little* things enough, the process. I was too concerned with the results, overemphasizing my thoughts and concentration on what happens *after* it's all done, and I shouldn't have been doing that. This was a significant awakening.

The plan for the future began the day the season ended. I continued to throw off-season batting practice as often as needed and met regularly with Tom and Mike to prepare for the MLB winter meetings.

In my spare time, I purchased a home that had plenty of land for a barn and riding arena for Mary, who was an accomplished equestrian. I also negotiated and purchased two new restaurant locations that would be converted into Bobby Valentine Sports Galleries. It was a great excuse to have my dad and mom visit, so my dad could convert the restaurants properly.

After the '87 season, Tom Grieve, Mike Stone, and a lot of scouts attended the winter meetings in December. I was having coffee one morning in our hotel and heard a distinctive voice in the booth next to mine. It was Jim Frey, who was now the general manager of the Chicago Cubs. Frey and his manager, Don Zimmer, were bitching and moaning about Rafael Palmeiro's style as a hitter. Zim was saying that during the last couple games, when the Cubs were battling for the pennant, there was a man on first, and instead of pulling the ball and hitting a home run to win the game, Rafael went for a base hit to left to win himself the batting title. After listening to this, I got up and walked over to them.

I said, "Hey, Jim, I'll take Palmeiro off your hands. If he's going to bug you that much, God bless. I don't want your blood pressure going up. Why don't we figure out something?"

"I'd take the wild-ass left-hander of yours that you have in the bullpen," Zimmer said. The wild-ass left-hander was Mitch Williams.

"Let me deliver the message," I said.

I went and found Tom Grieve. From my videotaping, I put together a collection of swings that I thought were teachable moments for others, because the batters did things so properly. Even though I didn't have much contact with him, Rafael Palmeiro was one of the models.

At the end of the season, I had moved Jeff Russell out of the starting rotation to the bullpen. Jeff was a tremendous athlete. He could punt a football sixty yards, throw a football eighty yards, play hoops, field his position, and was a good hitter. Jeff stood out in my mind as one of those pitchers who could close out a game, which made Mitch Williams expendable.

Mitch was the most amazing pitcher I had. He had spin rate before there was spin rate. He was able to propel the ball with the most abrupt and aggressive motion of any pitcher, and he was wild enough to be sure the hitter wasn't comfortable when he came to the plate. In fact, Earl Weaver, who was a chain-smoker, once told me, "Mitch Williams is more hazardous to a player's health than smoking." And Earl never put down a cigarette.

"You know they'd take Mitch for Raffy," I said to Tom. "We have to do that trade. We gotta do that trade."

At times I was wondering about the Pete O'Brien comment. By the time we got to the winter meetings, the light had gone on, and I got what he was talking about. But leading up to the winter meetings, I was thinking, *Maybe O'Brien is at the peak of his value. Maybe we can do something to get better at that position.* Trading for Palmeiro was getting better at that position. Tom Grieve met with Jim Frey, and they swapped Palmeiro for Williams.

Among my mentors with the Rangers was Bobby Bragan, who was in the front office, and Paul Richards, who was the senior baseball adviser. Bragan was a Branch Rickey disciple, the one Rickey handed the baton to. Richards was outside the family tree, but he was every bit the baseball lifer that Branch Rickey was. When Tom Grieve, Tom House, and I were trying to come up with protocols to keep our pitchers healthy, it was Richards who said to us, "Why don't you install a pitch count? I did it in the minor leagues with Baltimore for everyone under twenty-one years old, and they all got through their development stages."

The light went on. *Brilliant,* I thought. Dr. Jim Andrews and Tom House came back with an original plan of having a starter throw a maximum of 135 pitches, 15 per inning. If a relief pitcher threw fewer than 15 pitches, he could pitch the next day. If he threw more than 15 and fewer than 30, he needed one day off. More than 30, we'd give him two days off. The next spring training, and continuing through the season, we implemented the first pitch count in the major leagues.

We put in a wintertime workout program for pitchers in January 1988. We brought the pitchers in and tested them to make sure they were running properly, running two miles in the proper time, and doing sprints, so our trainers could check their recovery time. They were to throw in the bullpen to make sure they were developing a new pitch. All the wintertime homework in January was going to be checked before spring training. Among the pitchers in our program was Steve Howe, who was coming off a great half-season with our team. Steve had a great workout. He ran the two miles under the time prescribed, and passed the first day of tests with flying colors. But the next day he was missing.

We put out an all-points bulletin. We called all our friends on the police force, only to find out that he had left Lace, the notorious strip club in Arlington where Billy Martin famously got into a bar fight, and then showed up at the ballpark beaten and all bandaged up. Steve had left Lace with one of the girls who worked there. We found out the girl's name, and the next morning called her at her home in Waco. Steve was there. We asked him to meet us at the Marriott Hotel next to the stadium as soon as possible. After the phone call we were looking out our hotel window when, a couple hours later, we saw this girl drive up in a convertible. Steve was in the passenger seat with his shirt off, smoking dope.

Tom Grieve, Mike Stone, and I were fit to be tied. Not only was this going to be major egg on my face, but the Rangers were going to get hit with a $250,000 fine. Everything had been going so well. Pete Incaviglia hit 27 home runs his first year. Eddie Chiles was happy with our program for the pitchers and all the other little things that were going on, and now we had to deal with this disaster.

Mike Stone opened the door, and Howe walked in with a tattered t-shirt, glazed eyes, and a shit-eating grin on his face.

"Don't have me pee in that jar for a while," Steve said.

I might have mentioned I have a bit of a temper. I literally jumped over the couch in the hotel suite, ran at him, grabbed his t-shirt, and shoved him against the sliding glass door that went out to the balcony. We almost went through it. Then I left the room. I was just so pissed. I didn't want to hear any of his bullshit. I knew what had happened. I knew the look. And that was it.

It was the same look that my lifelong friend and Rippowan co-captain Darrell Atterberry had had when I found him on the floor of a drug den in the winter of 1971. Darrell had been on the road to recovery, living with Roxy and me during my rookie season with the Dodgers. He'd gotten a job at McDonald's, and for a year, things had gone great. He'd become the first black assistant general manager of McDonald's in Southern California. After returning from a road trip, I found everything was gone from our house. Because Darrell had needed to get back to La La Land, or wherever the hell he was, my TVs, my clothing, everything but one television and the drapes were gone. Only the keys to my car were left, so I knew how deep drugs could cut into a person's life. I should have learned from lessons past. As a major league manager, I'd made a costly mistake.

As for Steve Howe, I was mad at myself. I thought I knew better. I'd been around the culture forever. I had this big burn with Darrell, and thought I understood the culture, and here I was making the most stupid mistake anyone could make after everyone else had said, "Don't do it." I thought I could handle him. I felt that if anyone could handle him, I could.

Steve Howe was given one more chance, with George Steinbrenner and the Yankees, and he failed there, too. Early in the morning of April 28, 2006, a man driving through the California desert crashed his truck and was pronounced dead at the scene. Steve Howe was forty-eight years old.

In 1988, the Rangers' record was 70–91. What I remember most about that year was that Minnesota was getting better and Oakland was powerful Oakland. I had a strength and conditioning coach, because I wanted my players to be bigger and stronger, and yet every time we went to Oakland, their first-base coach, Dave McKay, looked better in his uniform than most of my players. I couldn't figure out why they were getting bigger and stronger and we weren't.

CHAPTER 16

George W. Bush

During the winter of 1988, Eddie Chiles gave Tom Grieve and me a call to action to get better. One of the best ways I knew to improve was to pick the right players available in the amateur draft, and we had the sixth pick in the June draft. Since we had such good luck with Oklahoma State slugger Pete Incaviglia, we concentrated on their team for our first pick, and selected the tall, right-handed-hitting shortstop Monty Fariss. Four picks later, the White Sox picked a third baseman from Monty's team, Robin Ventura. We'd also decided to become very active in the winter meetings. After first closing the deal for Palmeiro, we traded Pete O'Brien, Oddibe McDowell, and Jerry Browne to the Indians for Julio Franco.

Franco was a player who was able to hit the ball harder and more consistently than anybody I have ever seen. Julio walked with a pronounced duck-foot walk, with both feet pointing out. He was bigger than most in stature, with a small waist and a big chest, and was in the weight room all the time. There was a lot of suspicion about what kind of character he was.

One day at the end of the '88 season, Julio, who was with Cleveland, was in the Arlington clubhouse. Our weight room was right next to the exit of the parking lot. We had played a night game against the Indians, and the weather was lousy and hot, still close to one hundred degrees near midnight. As I was leaving, I heard a loud sound of weights hitting the floor. I went in, and there was Julio with more weight on the bar than I had ever seen, getting in his workout. The visiting clubhouse didn't have a weight room, but the visiting players could use our weights after the Rangers had left. I went in, surprised to see him, and sat down to watch. He was pumping iron and sweating. We began to talk, and I was amazed at the person I was talking to. He was telling me about his body, and how it was his temple, and how if he didn't get in his workout, he might be a step behind for the next game. His program was regimented, and he was hydrating. I was very impressed with him.

When we got to the winter meetings, we really weren't targeting Julio, but then his name started floating around. I told Tom Grieve about the meeting I had had with him.

"We need a veteran Latin player with a good head on his shoulders to mentor our young Latin players," I said. I thought Julio was a good fit, and Tom figured out how the whole thing worked, and since we had two left-hand-hitting first basemen, we made the trade of Pete O'Brien for Julio Franco move quickly.

The next day, we signed Nolan Ryan. The Ryan sweepstakes was being held that winter, and Tom and I determined we'd try to get him, even though we knew we couldn't be the highest bidder. Tom Grieve and Mike Stone had multiple plans of action, but you never knew what Nolan's side was doing. Dick Moss, the attorney for Marvin Miller, was Nolan's agent. Nolan had been injured a bit in '87, and at the end of the season he refused Tommy John surgery for a ligament tear and worked out especially hard. The pain went away. In '88 he had a 12–11 record with a 3.52 ERA for Houston. His health wasn't an issue.

Dick Moss set up a schedule for teams to come and talk to him, and we went to meet them in a hotel suite. The process was for each team to make its best pitch. There was to be no circling back, where you say, "I was kidding about my first offer." We were scheduled early in the process, but Mike Stone asked Dick whether we could be last, since we were the only Texas team bidding. Nolan was a Texas treasure, and we wanted the last shot at signing him. Dick granted us permission. We bided our time, and then we went up to the suite. Nolan and Dick and Tom Grieve and Mike Stone sat in one room, and I went into an adjacent room where Nolan's wife Ruth was sitting. I had known Ruth since 1973, when Nolan and I were teammates on the Angels, and I adored her. We were friends.

"Will you allow the kids in the clubhouse?" Ruth asked me.

At the time, Hal Lanier, the Astros manager, had a no-children policy. Nolan's kids were older than most players' kids, because at forty-two he was older than most players. I was thirty-eight.

As soon as Ruth asked that, I said, "Allow them? They can take batting practice if they want. They can be there every day. They can use my office if they want. I'll get another office." Her smile lit up the room, and at the press conference when he was asked why he'd signed with the Rangers, he mentioned my response. It also helped that we were making the last offer. The Chicago White Sox, we found out later, had offered more money.

I left the Ryan suite and walked down the hall to Mike Stone's room, and Mike told me that Nolan had accepted our offer. While we walked quickly down the hallway of the hotel, both of us jumped so high we almost hit the ceiling as we tried to click our heels.

In January 1989 we signed free-agent Rick Leach. Tom and Mike had gone to the University of Michigan, and so they invited Bo Schembechler, the famed Michigan football coach, to visit our new spring training facility in Port Charlotte. Bo invited us to Boca Grande, the island where he had his summer home. We had dinner and cocktails, and we were sitting on his deck discussing our team, when the subject of clubhouse leadership came up. Bo believed in it and said, "You know, I had a guy who didn't miss a snap in four years and went to a bowl game every year. He played quarterback, and there is no better leader in the world. And he's available.

His name is Rick Leach, and he's a left-handed hitter with the Detroit Tigers." Leach was thirty-one, but he totally fit the bill.

My Rangers were an interesting cast of characters. We had young kids like Juan González and Scott Coolbaugh coming up, and I couldn't help think that if we were in the Central Division, or somewhere other than the AL West, we'd be much more successful. In the West we were always up against that monster team in Oakland. They had bodybuilders like Mark McGwire and Jose Canseco, and even though we had Tom House, a master of strength and conditioning, and even though we had an actual strength and conditioning coach, a guy who did all his work in the weight room, we weren't getting anywhere as big as those Oakland players, or Minnesota Twins players Kent Hrbek and Kirby Puckett.

Early in 1989, during the lunches Tom Grieve and I had with Eddie Chiles, Eddie let us know that he was in serious financial difficulty. "Take my plan," he said at one of our meetings. "I always know where I am. I know where I want to go, and with the price of oil, I'm going to have to change directions." On April 21, 1989, Eddie Chiles sold the Rangers to a group of wealthy businessmen led by George W. Bush for $80 million.

Eddie was on the downturn, physically and financially. We loved him dearly, and we wanted everything to turn out right for him, and we thought the best thing was for him to sell the team. Eddie was a Republican donor. George H. W. Bush, who had been elected president in November 1988, was in the oil business, and his son George W. was, too. Billy DeWitt, whose family owned the Cincinnati Reds, was in business with George, and he bought George's oil business. Commissioner Peter Ueberroth was at the end of his term, and he didn't want to leave the Texas franchise without the proper ownership.

Tampa was a dummy franchise for teams that wanted to hold their city ransom. They had built a mausoleum there in St. Petersburg—the Suncoast Dome that became the ThunderDome that became Tropicana Field. The Chicago White Sox threatened to leave and move to Tampa Bay. So did the San Francisco Giants. Tom and I felt that maybe the Rangers could play the same cards in our attempt to get the City of Arlington to pony up some money for us to build a new, beautiful ballpark.

When George W. Bush's group came in, it was announced we were considering a move to Tampa if we didn't get the city funding we needed. Before the sale was approved, Commissioner Ueberroth declared that Bush would have to add more local ownership to keep the team in Arlington. Richard Greene, the mayor of Arlington, connected George with a local politician named Tom Schieffer, the brother of CBS journalist Bob Schieffer, and they hooked up with Fort Worth's Richard Rainwater, who, legend has it, was the ringleader of the Bass brothers' attempt to corner the world silver market. Bush got Rainwater involved, along with a Dallas takeover artist named Rusty Rose. George W. reached out and brought in his Yale roommate, Roland Betts, who was financing Disney movies at the time, and his partner Tom Bernstein, who now owns the Chelsea Piers in both Stamford and Manhattan. It was a group of wealthy people who invested millions to make millions.

We were really happy for Eddie. He turned his poker winnings into a jackpot. It was a great deal for George W., not because of the price, but because of his love of baseball. All George wanted was to be involved. I do believe he had aspirations to be the baseball commissioner. Just about every day, George would be in my office, because he was a jogger and his offices were up the street, and you don't run the streets of Arlington in the summer because the soles of your sneakers will melt. Instead, George ran the warning track inside Arlington Stadium. He'd get his five miles in and be finished by the time I got to the ballpark, around one-thirty or two, and usually when I came in, he'd be sitting at my desk in my office, because I had the best shower in the building. He was there to welcome me and talk baseball, trades, minor leagues, the previous night's game, or who we were playing that night. He loved baseball.

He never interfered with my work with the players but was always there if needed. Every game he sat in the front row right beside the dugout. He never once leaned over and questioned my decisions. He sat there as a fan with his wife Laura. We were lucky to have him as an owner.

You are always taking a risk when you make a trade. You can do your due diligence and have all your ducks in a row and still make a trade that disappoints. This was the case with Harold Baines. He had been the face of the Chicago White Sox and was elected to the Hall of Fame in 2019 as a White Sox. We traded for him in the middle of the season—on July 29, two days before the trade deadline—and he was disappointed to leave Chicago.

For Baines, the White Sox wanted either Sammy Sosa or Juan González. They weren't ready-made major-leaguers at the time, but they both had major league talent. I preferred trading Sosa for Baines, a proven left-handed RBI machine who we figured would complement Palmeiro and Ruben Sierra, a switch-hitter. From the right side we had Buechele, Julio, and Inky. We felt we needed one more left-handed RBI guy. We traded Sosa, shortstop Scott Fletcher, and pitcher Wilson Alvarez for Baines and Fred Manrique. I thought it was a great trade, one that was going to separate us from the pack. But when he played for us, Harold wasn't Harold. He was a real quiet guy, so quiet it was almost scary. We brought him to Texas to be an RBI machine, and he was anything but. I believe the trade broke his heart, so when he got to Texas, his heart just wasn't in it.

We had another situation involving drugs in September 1989, as we were wrapping a series against the Yankees in New York with a Sunday afternoon game. We stayed at the Grand Hyatt in Manhattan, near Grand Central Station. Most players just hopped onto the subway at Grand Central to Yankee Stadium, as the bus would often get caught in traffic in Harlem trying to get over the Macombs Dam Bridge. Rick Leach was one player who always took the subway. Sunday was getaway day, when everyone packed their bags and brought them down to the lobby before going to the ballpark to take batting practice. On Sunday, Rick wasn't there. We started asking if anyone had seen him that morning, but no one had.

An hour before the game he still hadn't shown, and we began to panic. Thinking he had overslept, we asked the hotel to check his room. He was not there but his belongings were, and a lot of anxiety set in. We alerted all the local authorities, who issued an all-points bulletin. We called the Port Authority and the New York Police Department and the commissioner's office, because we feared something bad had happened to him, that perhaps he had been kidnapped or murdered. We played the game, and Rick still hadn't shown up. It was time for the team to fly to Milwaukee. The next day was an off-day, so I stayed back to see if the authorities had learned anything about him. I wanted to be there for him, and I got a call in my hotel room at about four in the morning from the NYPD. Rick was found in one of the parks, on a bench, tattered, and more than hungover.

After what had happened with Steve Howe, the Rangers had a strict edict that nothing like that should ever happen again. This precipitated a clubhouse meeting in Milwaukee where I was upset, to say the least, and frustrated, not knowing what to do. I had visions of the owners coming in and purging me and the entire coaching staff.

"I have tried to get to know everyone personally," I said, "and I love you all like my own children, but when I'm betrayed, and you are betrayed by drugs, it really hurts. From now on"—I didn't use the zero-tolerance ploy, but it meant the same thing—"if I find out you have anything to do with drugs, it's going to be your ass."

Looking back, for me to say something like that was ridiculous, only because I had grown up in the drug culture. I had been around it and dealt with it, and it was part of my life, and a lot of players thought it was hypocritical, and others thought of it as "Let's spread the word that there's a new drug czar in town."

In 1989 and '90, players were getting involved with steroids. I became the bad cop, and it kind of stuck with me. I regret the situation because it wasn't really who I was, but it defined me at that time as a guy who was going to draw a line in the sand, so the Rangers wouldn't be known as this off-the-rail team whose players used drugs. Rick was remorseful and apologetic. It was a one-night binge that took him down the wrong road, but he remained in uniform. At the end of the year, we released him.

The Rangers finished the '89 season with an 83–79 record. Nolan Ryan and Tom House were a match made in heaven. Our pitch-count rules and Tom's strength and conditioning program, along with mechanical analysis, extended Nolan's illustrious career. He was remarkable, finishing 16–10 and leading the league in strikeouts with 301—at age forty-two! Ruben Sierra was also spectacular. He was a stallion, a switch-hitting Roberto Clemente who wore number 21. He was from Puerto Rico, played right field, had a great arm, hit for power, and had a great smile. Ruben was everything that anyone could want, and yet his play was always nitpicked and criticized by the Texas writers, who were especially tough on him and our Latin contingent.

I wish I could have done more to improve his relationship with the press. It might have made a difference in the MVP voting that year. The MVP race came down to the last day. Ruben hit .306 with 29 home runs and 119 RBIs. Robin Yount hit .318 with 21 home runs and 103 RBIs for Milwaukee.

We had Latin guys, and we were playing in Texas, which is not the most multicultural-friendly environment in the world. The *major leagues* weren't the most multicultural-friendly environment in the world. I don't think there was a single Latin sportswriter. So it all came to a head when Robin Yount, the white guy from Milwaukee, beat out our Latin star from Texas as the American League MVP. Even so, as the year ended, I was really happy with the improvement of the team and the additions we had made to the roster.

Fifth grade at Ryle Elementary School.

1964 Stamford American Babe Ruth World Series team.

Dad with his parents, immigrants from Italy.

Pam Dempsey and me at the 1964 Dance Championship in Florida.

Sport Magazine *Athlete of the Month with Mom and Dad (far left).*

1970 - SPOKANE INDIANS - 1970
Pacific Coast League – Northern Division Champions

Best Minor League team ever? 1970 Spokane Indians were a team for the ages.

1968 Ogden Dodgers. Buckner, Lasorda, Garvey, and me.

1970 Spokane with Tommy, Eddie Minasian, and Steve Garvey.

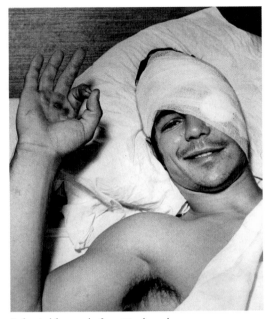

In hospital for a week after getting beaned.

Leading the Angels in hitting before my leg injury, 1973.

The Bridgeport Post *coverage of my injury, May 18, 1973.*

With Tommy at my first restaurant in Stamford, 1980.

Working for NBC with Bob Costas on his first broadcast, 1980.

1983 Mug Shot

In 1989, the Texas Rangers were purchased by George W. Bush. Sitting on floor left to right are Team President Mike Stone, me and GM Tom Grieve.

At Ground Zero two days after 9/11.

Me and Joe Torre at Ground Zero twenty years later.

TOP: Soon to be $5,000 poorer.

LEFT: At Shea with Mary and Bobby Jr.

Victory Parade in Chiba on Valentine's Way after Japan and Asia Championships.

Tommy and I with Ronald Reagan in the Oval Office.

With George W. Bush in the Oval Office.

Tommy, my attorney Phil Hersh (far left), and me with Governor Pataki.

Stamford native and Hall of Famer Andy Robustelli.

CHAPTER 17

Why This Job Is So Hard

S teroid use was booming through the '80s and into the '90s. Ignorant as I was, I had fired my strength and conditioning coach because the Oakland A's had much bigger and bulkier players, and I thought it was his fault we weren't looking like them.

George Mitchell, a United States senator from Maine, conducted a bogus investigation while he was getting ready to become a director of the Boston Red Sox. He promised that any information brought to him would remain confidential, but his report named ninety players. The MLB Players Association had agreed to anonymous testing, only to find out the list of positive results had been turned over to Mitchell and publicized.

One of the biggest scams of the investigation was the testimony of Sandy Alderson, who was general manager of the San Diego Padres. Sandy testified that the baseball owners had *no idea* what was going on at the time. When Sandy was the general manager of Oakland, he drove past the BALCO offices every day on his way to work. This was a guy who knew how many baseballs were used in batting practice in Double-A, yet he didn't realize that Jose Canseco had come back thirty pounds heavier and stronger and faster, and that the goons hanging around with Canseco and McGwire in the batting cage every day were so steroided-up that they looked like Bluto and Popeye? Alderson was a Dartmouth man and a military man to boot. He crossed every "t" and dotted every "i." Sandy had *no idea*?

There was no leadership from the commissioner or from ownership. Not once did I get a memo or take a class on what to look for if someone was doing steroids. You never heard a peep from the Giants' owner or general manager when Barry Bonds bulked up and hit 73 home runs in one season. You didn't hear from Tony La Russa or the Cubs' general manager when McGwire and Sammy Sosa were battling to see how many home runs they could hit in 1998. La Russa and Alderson both have law degrees.

When the steroids craze started, I didn't know what it was. I knew that my players were making concoctions in blenders, but I never knew what was in them. But there was stuff going in those blenders with the bananas and the grapefruits that made them bigger and stronger and helped them recover faster. For a long time it wasn't illegal. It was so out in the open that McGwire had his stuff in his locker in full view. That's when the line got blurry. McGwire thought it was okay. But it wasn't okay.

I blame no one except everyone. If steroids were a problem, then I blame myself. I blame my organization, my trainers, the general managers, the owners, and the commissioner's office. If we were supposed to know, and we didn't, it's our fault. If we knew and pretended we didn't know, it was our fault.

We can't put Barry Bonds in the Hall of Fame because he took steroids? Really? He is the best hitter I've ever seen.

In the 1970s, many players were taking amphetamines. I remember one Hall of Famer on the other team as he walked past our dugout. He stuck out his tongue, and on it were six or seven little green hearts. Each was five milligrams. Most of us took two. His tongue was covered with them. I used to take amphetamines to watch the game when I sat on the bench, so I wouldn't be bored. Conversations were always more exciting when you had a little extra fuel in your tank. It's all hypocritical and convoluted.

We thought all those steroid users would be dropping dead by now. I didn't think the players who were older than me would live to seventy. The word was that those who took steroids would die at fifty. They did not. Football players took ten times what the baseball players took, stacked them, and they never got busted. Only baseball players. "I get it," I used to say. "We're the bad guys. But that football player who's three hundred twenty pounds and does the forty in four-point-four and bench-presses six hundred pounds is *not* doing steroids?" We were led to believe that football players and basketball players were all natural. Give me a break. It was terrible the way baseball handled it. Baseball drew the black eye on itself. I never could understand that.

All I know is I watched the Mitchell hearing, and I thought it was bogus. I was managing in Japan then. The day I was introduced as Red Sox manager in 2012 up in the club box, I was introduced to George Mitchell as a director of the team. Oh, of course, Mr. Mitchell. I felt bad for some of the accused players, and none more so than Rafael Palmeiro, who was one of the great hitters of our time. Palmeiro had come to us and fit in like a charm. He was all in on our desire to use the biomechanical studies that we were knee-deep into, as we were figuring out how to launch the ball rather than just trying for a hit. Raffy had incredible eye-bat skills and hand-barrel skills. He was able to center the ball with the good part of the bat at a very high level. This man was a hitter. And now they're saying his hits were illegitimate because of something he said at those stupid hearings? Are you kidding me? Meanwhile, Bob Dole was doing Viagra commercials. Now there's a performance-enhancing drug. I'll bet every male in Congress was trying to improve his performance.

In 1990, Ruben Sierra came late to spring training. He was a holdout. I was sitting in my office early in the morning on spring training day three or four when I looked out the window. Walking down the sidewalk was a player I almost recognized. I had to go outside to make sure I knew who I was looking at. It was Ruben. Over the winter he had gained twenty-five pounds, all muscle. He was wearing this dago t-shirt, as we used to call them, and his gold chains were dangling down. This once sleek thoroughbred of an athlete—he of the most graceful running motion, the Roberto Clemente of his generation—looked like a bodybuilder. He had transformed himself in four months into someone I hardly recognized. I should have known why. People were talking, but I wasn't listening. I just didn't get the message that this was the result of steroids. I thought it was the result of Ruben having a really proficient weight trainer.

At batting practice, he now had a slow, cumbersome swing. We had just put in our winter protocol for our pitchers after the Steve Howe screw-up. I was upset we didn't put in the protocol for our hitters. This was really disturbing, but the thing that was most disturbing was that I didn't understand what was going on. And the main reason I didn't understand it was Steve Howe and other drug incidents of recent years. I'd gone out on a limb for Steve and cost our owner $250,000. And I had egg on my face with Rick Leach; he was the guy I'd brought onto our team to be the stabilizer. I was going to stay away from anything drug-related. Everyone thought I had turned into this drug czar, the guy who was going to turn anyone in if he found out about the drugs they were using. And I wasn't getting as close to the players as I once did, because I didn't want to know what was going on. *I didn't want to know!*

I remember the day when I should have connected the dots. Julio Franco and Ruben Sierra were playing dominoes with two other Latin players. They were slapping down their tiles, and Julio won.

Ruben said, "Ah, you don't know shit about dominoes."

Julio said, "I might not know shit about dominoes, but I know something in my heart for sure, and that is, when you get old, you are going to be bald and you're going to be fat."

It was a *Huh?* moment. Julio understood that to be the legacy of the players who took steroids. They often lost their hair, à la Barry Bonds, and their muscles turned to flab. But at the time, it didn't resonate with me. It was an inside joke that I was not in on.

1991 was an improvement, albeit a small one, over 1990. We won 85 games and lost 77, despite player moves that were unpopular with some players and especially with the press. In March we released Pete Incaviglia, who in 1990 had hit 24 home runs and drove in 85 runs. He had also hit .233 and struck out 146 times. Part of our decision to let him go had to do with money, and part of it had to do with the quality of his replacement, twenty-year-old Juan González.

Pete had taken the Rangers to arbitration that winter and won. He was paid $800,000 in 1990 and wanted more. Pete was my guy. We were together from the start, and I threw more batting practice and had more lunches and dinners with him than any other player. I was never godfather to his kids, but we were close. About his fourth year in the big leagues, he plateaued. The league now understood Pete Incaviglia, and I didn't see him making the adjustments he should have been making, even in batting practice. Ownership and I had a meeting. Inky wanted a three-year deal. We wanted a six-month deal at our price. Evaluation on the Rangers was constant. Tom Grieve and I always talked about players' progress and their level of ability and where they would top out. It was a guessing game.

Player evaluation was fun and exciting, and in 1991 the worst evaluation of a player I ever made was of our pitcher Jamie Moyer. He wanted to be a starter, and one year I started him seventeen times, but he didn't throw hard, and because of that I wanted to move him, trade him, or release him.

"Do you think he can be a number-three starter in the major leagues?" Tom asked me.

"I don't think a pitcher whose best pitch is his changeup can be a number-three starter," I said. "The only pitcher I knew who could do that was Al Downing." But Downing also had a 90-mile-an-hour fastball and a pretty good curveball. Jamie didn't have any of that in his arsenal. He just had that changeup. And then he had the changeup of his changeup.

It was a mistake that I didn't put Jamie Moyer on my pitching staff. His father-in-law was Notre Dame basketball coach Digger Phelps, and as soon as March Madness was over, Digger would pop in. I really liked Digger, and Digger liked Jamie, but I just couldn't envision having Charlie Hough, a knuckleballer, and Jamie Moyer, a changeup pitcher, in the same rotation and win a championship. It was a blunder. A really *big* one. Jamie pitched another twenty-five years and finished with 269 wins.

We tried to sign Inky to a one-year, team-friendly contract, but Pete's agent, Tony Attanasio, played hardball and went to arbitration. It took big balls to go to arbitration in the early '90s. Players and agents were fearful of arbitration, because a lot of negative, hurtful things were said during the hearings. Ownership would bring out negative charges from the closet that hurt the player personally, and a lot of those wounds never healed. We went to arbitration during spring training, and Pete won $1,675,000, a little less than what Nolan Ryan was making. Before the case, we tested the market to see if we could trade him, and there were no takers. The other GMs were seeing what I was seeing. Pete had been the number-one draft choice, had never played a game in the minor leagues, and had hit thirty home runs in his first year. Six years later, he hit twenty-four home runs. His output wasn't worth the money he was asking.

We had three choices once he won arbitration: keep him and pay him, trade him, or release him. The rules stated that if you released a player before the end of spring training, you only had to pay part of the salary. We released him before spring training. We thought we were on the hook for only $415,000. Inky's agent tested our decision, and we realized a little late that the rule did not apply to a player that had won in arbitration, and we had to pay him the entire $1,675,000.

I was still licking my wounds from some of my decisions that had cost the Rangers money, like my signing of Steve Howe. Releasing Pete seemed like a way to save the organization some money. I also felt I could platoon Jack Daugherty and Kevin Reimer to fill the void until Juan González was ready to join our team. Daugherty had had a good year the previous season and Reimer had good power. We had Gary Pettis to play center field, to make up for any deficiencies Juan might have in left, and we had Ruben Sierra in right. Releasing Pete wasn't the worst move I ever made, but it wasn't popular, especially with Randy Galloway, who had the loudest media voice.

Randy was pro-Southwest. He was pro-Cowboy. Inky was the kind of Southwest Texas cowboy persona. Inky had established himself as a bigger-than-life Texas Ranger hero. His release was a surprise to Randy and all the baseball writers, which meant his sources weren't good enough, his intuition wasn't good enough, and when a writer is surprised, he gets angry. Randy was beside himself. He was in my office screaming and yelling and questioning my knowledge and wisdom.

"I can't believe you made a decision like that in isolation," he said. "How can you not go to the senior members of your team? How could you not reach out to see if anyone agrees with you?"

Of course I had talked to the other team officials. I had even gone to a couple of veteran players to talk to them about it, and I told Galloway that, though I refused to tell him which players. I had spoken with Nolan Ryan, and he agreed that Inky had seen better days, but he wasn't in favor of releasing him just to save money.

After Randy's second or third article, it became an integrity question. I had talked to other players, but I wasn't about to throw anyone under the bus. I knew Galloway would go to the players, so I said to them, "You do what you think is right. You don't make the decisions, I do, and whether I went to you or not doesn't matter. I was going to make my decision anyway, so if the press comes to you, answer the question any way you wish."

Randy went to the veteran players, and they said, "No, Bobby didn't come talk to me." I said I had talked to them. They said I didn't. It was a real mess, and it was stressful, to say the least. The easiest thing in the world for me would have been to say, "Let's keep him and let's live with him," because Pete was the one person other than Tom Paciorek who I had become closest to, and it seemed as though I had totally be-trayed him. For what it was worth, having a young, suave Latin player who didn't speak that much English take his place—regardless of Juan González 's 27 home runs and 102 RBIs—wasn't met with approval in the clubhouse or in the community. I'm not saying anything bad about either the clubhouse or the community. It was just the state of affairs in Texas in the '90s, and around the league and the country, for that matter. In that I seemed to favor the underdog, or even the non-English-speaking players, that I didn't hunt and fish, and that I was Italian, in some circles made me a bit of an outlier.

1991 was an incredible year for forty-four-year-old Nolan Ryan. On May 1 he threw his seventh no-hitter. Nolan, as with most players, had a ritual every time he pitched. He would always warm up and then come into the dugout, take off his hat and dry his hair, and then he'd put on his hat with his back to the field, and once he put his hat on properly, he would turn and go up the stairs of the dugout and enter the field to a standing ovation. Nolan would get his private ovation right after the team entered the field, and it was always a standing ovation because he was like no other player of his time.

On this day, he was drying off his hair, ready to put his hat back on, and he looked down to me at the other end of the dugout and said, "You better get somebody ready. This might be the end." He then turned and jogged out toward the mound. With that, I turned to find Tom House, our pitching coach, who had watched him in the bullpen. Tom looked like he had just seen a ghost.

"What's going on?" I asked.

"He can't reach home plate," Tom said.

I watched Nolan warming up, and, sure enough, he was bouncing the ball in front of the plate. I got on the phone to get Dale Mohorcic ready in the pen. "Get the Horse ready," I said.

Nolan reached the plate with his last warmup pitch, and the catcher threw down to second. Nolan performed his customary ritual of getting the ball, walking toward the hitter, picking up a pebble or sunflower seed between the mound and home plate and throwing it away, then turning to head back to the mound.

On his first pitch he threw the ball 96 miles an hour for a strike, and the next thing I knew, he had struck out Roberto Alomar of the Blue Jays for his sixteenth strikeout and seventh no-hitter. Nolan was the oldest player ever to throw a no-hitter. My horrifying feeling had turned into elation.

Nolan and I were very close. I had played with him in '73, and then I managed him. I had separate rules for Nolan, and I thought he deserved them. Guys complained, and I took the heat. Later, Cal Ripken stayed at a different hotel than the other Orioles, because he didn't want to be besieged with autograph hunters. His manager was criticized for that, because there is this mythical idea of team unity. But I didn't think giving Nolan special treatment was going to affect us that much, except that Goose Gossage made a stink about it. I was allowing Nolan to have his own travel and workout program, and Goose didn't think it was right. I believed that the most unfair thing you could do was to treat players who are totally different exactly the same. Everyone would have a common code of conduct, but a twenty-year veteran was treated differently than a twenty-year-old rookie.

It wasn't the first time Goose disagreed with me. Mid-season, we were playing the White Sox at Comiskey Park, and I got wind that the Sox were stealing our catcher's signs and relaying them to the hitter by flicking on a certain light on the scoreboard. I had a team meeting and said, "Listen, we have to change the signs. Let's make it real simple. If the hitter's uniform number is even, we'll go with the first sign. If his uniform number is odd, we'll go with the second sign." Goose, a future Hall of Famer, thought it was ridiculous. He wasn't going to have anything to do with it, because he had used the same signs all his career. And he pitched that day, and Robin Ventura hit a grand slam off of him. Goose was all upset, mumbling and grumbling about the signs being changed and how stupid it was. We went from Chicago to Oakland, and he was at the bar with other players, holding court while I was walking through the bar. He saw me and made a comment that the other players could hear.

"I played for Billy Martin," he said to me. "And you're no Billy Martin."

It wasn't the place for me to react, so I walked to where the players were and quietly said to Gossage, "Why don't you come and see me in my office tomorrow when you're sober?"

Goose came the next day. I closed the door and yelled at him real loud, for all the other players to hear.

"You've got a big mouth when you have a beer in front of you," I said. "I'm giving you a chance to say something to me."

He didn't say anything. He walked out of the office. That was that.

In the spring of 1991, George W. Bush and I discussed the situation with the scouts. I told him, "I'm not sure that Sandy Johnson and these scouts are what the organization needs as evaluators." George was interested in making the entire organization as good as it could be. Uniformed personnel, the scouts, and some front office staff were not always on the same page. There were draft picks that came into question. I wanted the Rangers to be one of the top-tiered scouting teams, but I didn't have a say. All I had was input.

Before the 1989 draft, a scout brought me into his office to watch a video of a big kid from Auburn named Frank Thomas. He was a pro-quality defensive end as well as a home-run-hitting baseball player. The scouting bureau tape showed him hitting home runs to right and then to left but not much else. The tapes weren't great, but you could see the balls going over the fence. I favored Thomas for our number-one draft choice, and so did Tom Robson, my batting coach, who himself was a 6-foot-$4^1/_2$-inch behemoth weighing 250 pounds.

"What are we doing with that big guy who hits the ball over the fence?" Robson asked Sandy Johnson. Johnson responded that Thomas didn't have a position. When I said we had the DH, he and everyone else said that Pete Incaviglia should be the DH. Thomas wasn't on our list.

Instead, the scouts favored a Texas Tech outfielder by the name of Donald Harris. He came to the ballpark and took some batting practice, and the scouts seemed really excited when he hit the ball hard. I was lukewarm. He was a good-looking athlete. He had been a defensive back at Texas Tech, but he hadn't played college baseball. No one else had him on their radar, and so our plan was to swoop in and draft and sign him. I got myself in a little hot water when I said something negative about him, but I didn't care, and what I said didn't matter. We drafted Harris number one, and the White Sox took Thomas. Harris played for three years and disappeared, and Frank Thomas went on to a nineteen-year Hall of Fame career, hitting 521 home runs.

I was kind of on the outs with the scouts, but I was an optimist. I loved Tom Grieve so much. I believed in myself so much, but I didn't think it was my job to expose the organizational problems. My mistake was keeping my big mouth shut.

We were doing a great job in Latin America. We'd signed Ruben Sierra, Juan González, Pudge Rodriguez, and Sammy Sosa. George saw the disconnect, and he decided we should have a think tank, a collective meeting of all departments.

"Let's all get together and go to this island off Mexico," he said, "and we'll be secluded, and the ownership group and the scouting group and the minor league directing group and the major league group will all be together, and we'll figure things out."

We got on a private plane and flew to Mexico. The Ayatollah Khomeini had put a fatwa on the Bush family, so we had six Secret Service agents hanging out with George W. all the time. This little island had wonderful cabanas and tennis courts. We were in hammocks, playing cards, and every three hours we held group sessions and came away a better group. It was an amazing three days of fun in the sun. I came back with a real appreciation of George W. I thought he stood out as a leader. Still, I didn't think I needed the help of George W. or anyone else. But I did.

The next issue I had with one of my players came in August 1991, before the trade deadline. Steve Buechele was another of my favorites. We had traded Buddy Bell so Boo could play third base. He came up and did well, and he became one of my go-to guys. Boo was one of my younger-generation disciples, and I loved him, as I did Incaviglia and Geno Petralli—guys who lived in Arlington who were going to spread my gospel. I knew what it was like to play for someone who cared, and

I wanted my players to thrive because of me. My wife Mary and Steve's wife Nancy were close. Steve was a baby machine. He and Nancy had five in about seven years. During the winters, I'd throw batting practice to him, and we'd do things socially.

Boo had been with the Rangers for five years and was approaching free agency. Tom talked about trading him. For weeks Boo would ask me whether he was going to be traded, but I stiff-armed him, because I didn't know. I knew his name was out there. There was talk we wanted to make a trade with Pittsburgh, because they had two pitchers we coveted and pitching was what we needed. We had traded Wilson Álvarez for Baines, and we wanted to replenish our supply. The deadline was August 31 to trade for any player that you wanted on your playoff roster. The clock was ticking, the rumors were mounting.

On August 30, Steve called and said, "Let's have lunch before the game." He and his wife came to my restaurant across the street from Arlington Stadium. Pete Moore, my manager there, who always did a great job, was sitting with us when the bar phone rang. It was Tom Grieve.

"Tag," I said, "This is the day of reckoning. Steve and Nancy are here. What can I tell them? He means too much to me not to give him an answer. If we're going to trade him, please let me know. I can tell him and his wife face to face, and live in the future knowing I've done the right thing."

"Pittsburgh rejected trading us the two players we need to get for Boo," he said. "We're not trading him. Don't worry about a thing."

We had lunch in a round booth outside the bar, and I told him, "Boo, there are a couple of pitchers we have designated as premier talent, and if we can get them for you, we're going to make the deal. But Tag just told me you're not going to get traded. You're going to stay with us, and you're going to be our guy."

We finished lunch and hugged, and Nancy was crying because she was so happy, and then we went to batting practice. Boo was in the starting lineup. We started the game.

In the fourth inning, Tom Grieve called. "Take Boo out of the lineup. We just traded him to Pittsburgh."

When he came off the field, I told him, "Boo, you just got traded to Pittsburgh." I was all in if we could get the two pitchers we wanted. Pittsburgh traded us Kurt Miller, and a week later Héctor Fajardo.

Before the game, Steve had told a few of his teammates, "Bobby told me I'm not getting traded. I'm with you guys."

Not only did that break my heart, but it destroyed my credibility. Inky was the first nick in my armor cred, and then Boo. It was a bad day. There's no doubt about it.

By 1991, I had been ejected from games nineteen times and was causing some headaches, arguing with umpires and getting thrown out of games. Bobby Brown, president of the American League, heard about it and called Tom Grieve. Then he met with me about my temper flare-ups. As 1991 came to a close, I was learning many things, but maybe not quick enough.

CHAPTER 18

Fired

When I began the 1992 season with the Rangers, I really believed I was going to be the manager there forever. I really thought things were going to fall into place that year. At the halfway mark we were over .500. At one point we were six over. Twenty-year-old Pudge Rodriguez was the starting catcher. Rafael Palmeiro, Juan González, and Ruben Sierra were all ready to take off, and Kevin Brown, Charlie Hough, and Nolan Ryan were all pitching well. But it was being held together by a wing and a prayer.

In 1991 we finished 85–77, ten games behind the Minnesota Twins in the American League Central Division. Obviously, I was disappointed we hadn't advanced further, and things were starting to get stressful. I never wanted to be the cause of the stress. I always wanted to be the one to relieve the stress of others, but over the years in Texas it wasn't working out that way.

In the Dallas-Fort Worth universe, the writers were either for me or they were against me. Media coverage was expanding, and everyone was looking for an angle. ESPN was on the map. Sports radio was growing. All these outlets needed material, and all things Bobby V became a topic of conversation and often controversy.

It continued to really bother me that our scouting staff was trying to justify their picks by moving them up the ladder. I wasn't always in agreement with their picks, and I really didn't like the idea of not being part of the selection committee. In 1990 I was sitting in my office on the day of the draft, and T. R. Sullivan, a reporter for the *Fort Worth Star-Telegram*, said, "What do you think of your number-one draft choice?"

"Well," I said, "he looked pretty good to me."

"When did you see him?" T. R. asked me.

"I saw him on television last night pitching for Stanford."

"Oh really," he said with a chuckle. "That's not who you drafted."

"You've got to be kidding me," I said.

"He didn't pitch on television," T. R. said.

"Who was I watching?" I asked.

"You were probably watching Mike Mussina, the guy you wanted to take, but the Rangers took Dan Smith instead."

Stanford and Creighton had played in the same College World Series. Mussina starred for Stanford, and Creighton had Daniel Smith, a left-handed pitcher who played baseball and hockey and who showed some real grit on the mound.

Our scouts—Doug Gastoway and Brian Lamb—decided that Mussina didn't have the heart he needed, because he gave up four runs in the fifth inning of a series game. So instead of taking Mussina, the guy I was told we were going to take, we took Dan Smith.

That grated me, and I was embarrassed.

It didn't take a private detective for them to learn I wasn't a fan of our choice. A couple of times I said something to the wrong people in our organization. A couple of times I might have said something on the radio or to the newspapers.

I voiced my opinion. I alienated the scouts. I didn't care. They should have been fired.

On July 8, 1992, the day before I was fired, I was in the dugout before the game. I could see Gerry Fraley, who wrote for the *Dallas Morning News*, talking with Rangers president Tom Schieffer at the other end of the dugout. I was never sure whether Tom was on board with me.

The Rangers, with my help, had gotten the new stadium bill passed. The half-percent tax increase was in the bag. We had been six games over .500, but we lost two games to the Cleveland Indians, and I was playing a player by the name of John Cangelosi in center field. He was a hard-nosed switch-hitter who dove and stole bases. Our top draft choice, Donald Harris, was at Oklahoma City. I was still angry we hadn't signed Frank Thomas, and I didn't think Harris was much of a player.

When Fraley left Tom Schieffer, he came over to me and questioned what I was doing in center field. Juan González was playing there. John Cangelosi was playing there as well. Fraley had a way of rubbing me, and when he asked me about who was playing in center field, I said, "I think we can make some matches and get by. We'll get offense from other players. Cangelosi will play defense."

"Why don't you call up Donald Harris?" he asked.

I was abrupt. "We already wasted a draft on him. I'm not going to waste my time playing him."

Fraley then walked over to talk with Tom Schieffer, wrote all of this in an article, and the next morning I received a call.

Our record was 45–41, and we were sure to get better. When I saw Tom Grieve, who was the most wonderful person who ever lived, I knew it wasn't his decision, knew he would quit if I wanted him to, but I stopped that in its tracks.

"Don't even think about it," I said. "You're going to stay here and finish what we started.

I needed to clear my head, so I turned off my phone and for several weeks performed manual labor at my ranch outside Arlington. I built retaining walls. I bought railroad ties eight feet long and six inches square and nailed them together with spikes and a sledge hammer. When I wasn't doing that, I visited my two restaurants during lunch and dinner.

I listened to the Rangers games on radio and watched them on TV, and I rooted for Toby Harrah, who took over as manager, and all my guys.

Tom Grieve and the Rangers organization gave me a great opportunity. I worked 24/7 and gave them everything I had. I did everything humanly possible to help get the stadium bill passed so there would be a new place for the Rangers to play. The people of the Metroplex treated me like one of their own. Pete and Jeffrey, Paul, and others kept the restaurant alive and well for thirty years, and Mary and Bobby Jr. and I made friends for a lifetime.

I wasn't bitter. It was time.

CHAPTER 19

A Year in Japan

With two weeks to go in spring training of 1993, Jim Bowden, the general manager of the Cincinnati Reds, called me. I had opened a total of six restaurants, including ones in Stamford, Norwalk, and Milford, Connecticut; Middletown, Rhode Island; and two in Arlington. He asked if I wanted to be the advance scout for the Reds.

"It's nothing I've ever done before," I told him.

"Come on down for a couple weeks of spring training," he said, "and I'll show you all the reports. It'll be easy. I'd really like to have you in the organization."

I told him I'd give it a try and went to Plant City, Florida, where the Reds trained. Bowden showed me what he was looking for, and I went on the road and started scouting the teams the Reds were going to play. The advance guy travels ahead of the team and sends back reports on who is hot, who is not, who is injured, and what pitchers our team are likely to face in the next series. In those days, information was hard to come by.

The irony was that as manager with Texas, I'd chosen to do away with the advance scout so I could get my satellite dish!

The job was pretty easy. Once the season began, I would watch the next opponent for a series. If our team was coming to that town, I would leave my reports at the desk of the hotel. I never had face-to-face contact. I would then go to the next city where the Reds were playing and scout that team. Jim Bowden was the first person I knew who was collecting information. He had friends send him articles from local newspapers around the country. He had a staffer collect every mention of injuries in those newspapers. He would collect this information and track it, and it became part of his evaluation system when he made trades. You didn't get medical records in those days. It was buyer beware.

I was scouting the Colorado Rockies, and that team was going to Cincinnati. The protocol was that I would scout the team, write my notes, and then go to Kinko's and fax the reports to the Reds. There was a Sunday doubleheader, and the games ran late, and when I arrived at Kinko's, it had closed. I didn't get my reports faxed until the next morning. This wasn't a major problem, except it happened on the day Cincinnati manager Tony Pérez was fired. I heard that my reports, arriving late, were part of the reason he was fired. Bowden hired Davey Johnson to replace Pérez, and Davey called me.

"Why don't you get off the road and become my third-base coach again?" he said.

When I arrived, it was uncomfortable. Tony Pérez was *beloved* in Cincinnati. He was a main cog in the Big Red Machine, and he'd only been allowed to manage for about six weeks. The fans were in an uproar. I didn't like being part of this situation.

There was a lot of craziness. The Reds players were a fun-loving group. When we got to Chicago's Wrigley Field, in the middle of the game pitcher Tom Browning said to me, "Make sure you look around when you get out to third base." I looked over the right-field fence, and on top of the one the buildings outside Wrigley, Tom Browning was doing jumping jacks in his Cincinnati uniform with a bunch of Cubs fans. I didn't tell Davey, and Davey didn't see him. This was a crazy group.

Rob Dibble, another pitcher, threw one hundred miles an hour, and he was different. Chris Sabo was a real interesting character. I don't think he said ten words to anyone on the coaching staff the entire year. Ray Knight was on the coaching staff, and he wanted to manage. Ray liked to second-guess, and Davey knew it. Davey was committed to jumping in with both feet and doing everything he did in New York. The Reds had finished 66–48 in 1994, and in '95 Davey led the Reds to an 85–59 record. Davey always liked to say, "The only way to have a good team is to have good players, and the way to have good players is to let them play."

That was his skill. He didn't mess with the players. He would mess with the front office instead. Davey liked to be confrontational with the decisions that were being made, and he insisted on having the last word, which he often did—until he'd get fired. The last word to Davey was always, "Goodbye."

It was a helter-skelter season. Marge Schott was the Reds owner. She was different from any other owner in baseball, being the only female. She never left home without her 200-pound Saint Bernard, Schottzie, by her side.

The one consistent benefit of the season was watching and enjoying the play of Barry Larkin. Davey was not a Red. He was not part of the Reds tradition. Sparky Anderson, the longtime manager, was beloved; and Tony Pérez, the Reds first baseman who replaced him, was loved; and from out of nowhere the Reds had hired this stranger. Don Gullett, a Red through and through, was the pitching coach. Dave Miley, the bench coach, was a Reds minor league lifer, and they were really stuck on tradition. Davey was up against it. It was tough for him.

I tried my darndest to bridge the gap, but I was in a tough spot. I had managed for eight years, and I was looking for another manager's job. Moreover, I had left my restaurant businesses behind, and I was in Cincinnati, Ohio. It was hard for me to be fully committed. Davey was bucking the system, and by the end of the year, I decided I wanted nothing to do with returning to Cincinnati. I finished out the season and thanked Davey and Jim Bowden for the opportunity.

That winter of 1993 I was having dinner at the home of Phil Hersh, my attorney, and sitting at the dining room table was Joe McIlvaine, the general manager of the New York Mets. The Mets had fired Clint Hurdle as manager of the Norfolk Tides, and Joe asked if I had any interest in the Triple-A job. I interviewed with Jack Zduriencik, the Mets' minor league director, and he offered me the job. I went to Norfolk to manage the Tides. We had a very engaging owner named Ken Young, and a lifer general manager/part-owner named Dave Rosenfield. Rosie had been in baseball forever, and he was bigger than life. He carried every bit of three hundred pounds, was jovial and smart, and cared for me and the players. There weren't a lot of minor league lifers. Everyone seemed to either be on the way up or on the way down.

It was back to managing 24/7 with young guys who were working hard to get better. They looked forward to my batting practice. We'd fool around in the outfield kicking a soccer ball. The World Cup was going on, and I'd play goalie, and during batting practice they'd try to kick the ball by me, and we would laugh and have a great time. We had players such as Butch Huskey, Aaron Ledesma, Jeromy Burnitz, and Quilvio Veras. We finished the 1994 season 67–75.

I didn't know it at the time, but the general manager of the Chiba Lotte Marines baseball team of Japan's Pacific League had come to the United States for the express purpose of hiring a manager who wasn't a Japanese national. His name was Tatsuro Hirooka, and he had been the star shortstop for the legendary Tokyo Giants and a championship manager and general manager in the Pacific League. He played alongside Sadaharu Oh and third baseman Shigeo Nagashima.

Lotte is a $50 billion family-owned business that sold chocolate, candy, and gum in Asia. One of the sons, Akio Shigemitsu, was in charge of the baseball team, and he had been educated in the United States. His team moved from Kawasaki, Japan, in 1992 to its current location in the prefecture of Chiba, which is forty-five minutes outside of Tokyo. Chiba is a new city, halfway between the international airport and Tokyo. It is also two minutes from Tokyo Disneyland. The town of Kaihin Makuhari was built on reclaimed land—Tokyo Bay was filled in with all the rubble of destroyed buildings from World War II. Twenty years later the land was stable enough to build on. They built a new city, and it was beautiful. It had twenty-story office buildings, wide streets, and beautifully lit billboards. It's on Tokyo Bay, so it has an amazing view of Mount Fuji and the Tokyo skyline.

But the Chiba Lotte team was going nowhere. After moving from Kawasaki, the team had never finished higher than fifth. Hirooka-san was ordered to come to the States and find the guy who would be the first non-Japanese manager in league history.

I first met Hirooka-san in 1986, because he had heard what I was doing with pitch counts, and wanted to know more about it. I was invited to speak to all the Japanese pro and amateur coaches at the time about things we were doing with the Rangers. In 1986 I went to Japan to coach with Davey Johnson, who was managing the U.S. All-Star team against a team of Japanese All-Stars. On our team we had Tony Gwynn, Dale Murphy, Jose Canseco, Ozzie Smith, and other MLB stars. I did clinics for kids. Some Japanese baseball people knew me because in 1977 I had been the first American player in Major League Baseball to use a Mizuno glove.

I was on his radar. Hirooka-san scrutinized me, coming to about fifteen games in different cities where I was managing for Tidewater. He took amazing notes, and then we'd have dinner and he'd ask me a series of questions about why I made the moves I'd made during the games. Other than Tommy Lasorda, Hirooka-san was the most well-rounded baseball person I was ever around. He had a body like Joe DiMaggio and dressed as impeccably as Joe did. He looked like he had just come off a fashion runway. Hirooka-san was a class act.

At dinner with Hirooka-san, right before the end of the Tidewater season, he said, "I've seen one hundred sixty games this summer. I've interviewed a lot of people. It's my conviction that you are the person most suited to be the first non-Japanese to manage in Japan. Will you accept the job?"

Without any salary mentioned and without any terms, I said yes. What I didn't know when we shook hands was that I wouldn't be home very long, because the Japanese run what they call Fall Camp. After resting at home in October, I would have to fly to Japan for five or six weeks, working in a little ballpark in Urawa, adjacent to a Lotte factory. It was hard on Mary, because we had a young Bobby Jr. I was off on my own. Mary came to visit for a week, did some shopping, and went home.

I loved every aspect of being in Japan, other than the fact that I was thousands of miles from home. I was learning to slurp my noodles, which went against everything my Aunt Doris believed. She hated when you made noise chewing gum, and always admonished me to eat quietly.

During Fall Camp, perhaps one hundred people, eighty players, went into this heated assembly hall that had picnic benches inside. They had their soup and ramen in front of them. No one was talking, and everyone was slurping. I was horrified. Then I adapted. I learned to slurp my noodles and join them.

After Fall Camp, Hirooka-san suggested to our owner that we spend three weeks of spring training in the United States so I would feel at home managing. He had worked out a deal with the San Diego Padres, who had built a new facility in Peoria, Arizona. It was no small feat to fly a hundred people from Tokyo to Arizona, along with all our equipment and tons of rice, which I found crazy until I learned how food-centric the Japanese are. We rented an entire motel in the middle of Nowhere, Arizona. It was hardly developed, and we set up camp. We played on the fields during the day and used the hotel pool area and parking lot for night practice. We spent three weeks getting fit.

I had seen a pitcher in our Fall Camp by the name of Hideki Irabu, and I invited Nolan Ryan and Tom House to come to Arizona to watch him pitch. With the Japanese press standing by, Nolan said, "He has one of the best arms in the world."

Irabu was one of the few pitchers in the world who could throw one hundred miles an hour. There were always oohs and aahs when he pitched, but he was always met with a frown from our general manager Hirooka-san, who was all things Japanese. Irabu was anything but disciplined and straight-shooting. He was bigger than most, and his dad wasn't Japanese; he had been a U.S. serviceman. Irabu was also overweight and didn't run hard in the sprints, and he loved to drink beer.

Tom House and my hitting coach Tom Robson were with me in Peoria. Between the morning practice and the night practice, we had dinner, and then we had meetings of all the coaches and the general manager, and everyone evaluated what they had seen that day. We also began to discuss the first team we were to play when the season started, the Orix BlueWave. For an hour and a half, we went through all their pitchers and hitters, took a five-minute tea break, and for the next hour we went over one player, Ichiro Suzuki. At the time, the name on the back of his uniform was Suzuki. Then Orix hired a new manager, Akira Ogi. Ogi-san was revolutionary and a little radical, especially for the Japanese, and the name on the back of Suzuki's uniform was switched to Ichiro. It was perfect timing. I hadn't heard all that much about Ichiro or Suzuki.

"Wait till you see Suzuki." It was Suzuki this, Suzuki that, and then I watched the films of what he'd done the year before. He hit .385 that year. He was twenty years old. His numbers jumped off the board at me. One of those numbers was that he had 210 hits. When I was twenty, I had 211 hits. He had 29 stolen bases. When I was twenty, I had 29 stolen bases. He had 80 RBIs, and when I was twenty, I had 80 RBIs. He was doing it in the Pacific League of Nippon Professional Baseball. I was doing it in the Pacific Coast League in the States.

It was really weird sitting there for days going over Suzuki's performance with a translator as one of our coaches stood in front of a large white board and a little TV monitor, speaking Japanese. They put up all these charts of where he hit the ball and which pitches he hit. Everyone had an immediate fascination with him, and with good reason. Ichiro played one year in the minors and the next year led the Japanese major leagues in hitting. He was a phenom before phenoms were phenoms, because in Japan you weren't allowed to play in the major leagues until you paid your dues. Ichiro was different. *Very different!*

When we faced Orix and Ichiro, we tried everything to stop him. I pitched Irabu. He threw one hundred miles an hour. Ichiro should have been in the big leagues earlier, but his former manager thought his hitting style too unorthodox; but when I watched him live, I was infatuated. In one game, Ichiro hit a ground ball to Julio Franco at second, a regular ground ball, and he beat it out. When I looked at my stopwatch, which I carried with me in the dugout to time runners, he got down to first base in 3.4 seconds. It's what I always heard that Mickey Mantle could do when he first came up to the Yankees.

There was no stopping Ichiro. I had a 6-foot-11-inch-tall left-hander by the name of Eric Hillman who I brought over from the States. He had pitched in Norfolk for me the year before. At six-eleven, I figured at least things were going to be different. Ichiro hit him, too. I marveled. He hit everyone.

Orix went on to win the championship. We finished second. There were no playoffs that year.

While in fall camp in Urawa, I told Hirooka-san I wanted Hillman to pitch and Julio Franco to DH and play second. He agreed. Julio finished second to Ichiro for the batting title. Hirooka-san also wanted a right-handed-hitting power hitter.

"You had one in Texas," he said. "He hit thirty home runs, and he's available."

He was talking about Pete Incaviglia. Hirooka-san was infatuated with American right-handed hitters who could hit the ball over the center-field and right-center-field fences, because Japanese hitters, for the most part, pulled everything.

"I don't think it's going to work," I said. "Inky and I didn't part best of friends."

But Hirooka-san insisted that Pete come over for a tryout. Pete was represented by my agent, Tony Attanasio, so it was real easy to get ahold of him. Inky came to try out. They put their best former pitcher on the mound to throw batting practice, and on the first pitch he threw, Inky hit the ball over the center-field fence. Hirooka-san's eyes opened up. He began smiling. He was sure Inky was the right guy for the times. The deal was sealed. I returned home for the Christmas holidays.

On January 17, 1995, I landed at Narita Airport to give a press conference about being the new manager of Chiba Lotte. My press conference was held at the airport before I went through customs. Forty members of the press attended. I was escorted off the plane right to this area with my good friend and lawyer Phil Hersh. It was televised throughout Japan.

During the press conference, the media members heard that there had just been a 7.2 earthquake in Kobe. Freeways collapsed, whole towns collapsed. It was devastating. Coincidentally, our very first game was against Ichiro's team in Kobe, the site of the earthquake. I took a ride to view the devastation. We went to the top of a mountain and looked down upon the valley, and there was destruction as far as I could see. Trees had collapsed on cars, roads were made impassable, and trucks were overturned off the side of the highway. The ballpark was tucked up in a little hillside and had minimal damage, but all the infrastructure leading up to it was destroyed. I couldn't imagine that in three months, when the season began, I'd be able to walk to the stadium, never mind drive to it.

Miraculously, this little country worked to get the infrastructure rebuilt so we could have a ball game. They fixed the roads and made repairs to the ballpark, and how they did it so quickly, I will never know. We drove to the stadium for our first game, and not everything had been rebuilt, but the highways were passable, the sidewalks were rebuilt, and we had opening day in Kobe.

After a month in Arizona, we completed spring training in Kagoshima, in southern Japan. Our ballpark was within sight of an active volcano that simmered more days than not. The Sakurajima volcano was so close that an Inky home run could land in its crater.

Our season went pretty smoothly. There were six teams in our division, the NPB Pacific League. In it there were two classes of major league teams. After the season ended, three teams were designated Class A. The last three teams were Class B—fourth, fifth, and sixth. Chiba had been Class B for thirty of its thirty-one years.

In 1995 we returned to the Class A division. We came in second to the Orix BlueWave led by Ichiro. Our hitting stars were Kiyoshi Hatsushiba, a third baseman who hit 25 home runs and drove in 80 runs; Koichi Hori, our second baseman, who hit .301 with 11 homers and 67 RBIs; and Julio Franco, who hit .306 with 10 homers, 58 RBIs, and 11 stolen bases. On the mound, our best three starters were Eric Hillman, who had pitched for me in Norfolk, and who finished 12–9 with a 2.87 ERA; Hideki Irabu, who was 11–11 with a 2.53 ERA; and Satori Komiyama, a twenty-nine-year-old vet who finished 11–4 with a 2.60 ERA. In the bullpen we had veteran pitcher Toshihide Narimoto, who finished 9–3 with a 2.00 ERA and 21 saves.

In 1995, I brought my AOL disk to Japan thinking I would have the internet at my disposal. How could I not? One of my buddies connected me with the Compaq computer company. I did TV and magazine commercials for them. The theme was, "We're going to change the world." The double meaning was that the Compaq computers would change the world and I was going to change the world of baseball in Japan. They gave me a big desktop computer with a dial-up mechanism for my AOL disk, and for the entire year experts from Japan and America tried to get me connected to the internet. These were high-tech people. Computers weren't in vogue in Japan, because no keyboard could deal with the thousands of kanji and katakana and hiragana that comprise the Japanese written language. Three sets of different characters! We have twenty-six. They have thousands. They were just making computers. And they couldn't get mine to work.

Trying to meld two societies into the Chiba Lotte baseball team also resulted in a disconnect. I was American, and despite our success, it wasn't easy for my Japanese general manager to understand some of my methods. Hirooka-san signed Pete Incaviglia because he saw his power in batting practice. But Pete personified the ugly American. He wanted the entire country to conform to him, and that wasn't going to happen. He struck out 74 times in 71 games and only walked 23 times. He had weaknesses in his swing that the opposing pitchers exploited. They put him in the rocking chair—hard in and soft away. He hit about .180, with 10 home runs and 31 RBIs. Pete didn't play much in the second half, and Hirooka-san was upset with me because the club was paying him $2.5 million.

Hirooka-san was a remarkable person, but he stood for all things Japanese and all things Japanese baseball. He wasn't totally invested in having an American as the manager. He didn't mind if I succeeded, but it had to be on his terms. He was part of the old guard. I had a two-year contract, and toward the end of the first season, Hirooka-san and I were having disagreements about my resting of players. We had this long stretch during the hot summer without many off-days. The weather was ridiculously hot, and when we finally got an off-day, I told the team, "There will be no practice tomorrow on the off-day."

The elder statesmen on the team whom I spoke to about it said he thought it would be okay. Some were thankful. The next day, the "off" day, I walked out to the stadium to get my bicycle. I was taken aback when I saw the team was on the field with Hirooka-san leading the practice. I spent the next two hours of practice riding around the inside warning track of the stadium without saying a word. My choosing to give the players an afternoon off became a media circus. I was challenging the samurai mentality of the Japanese culture. Many saw this as opening a wedge between the East and the West. They opined that this sad experiment of my giving my players the afternoon off should never happen again.

Despite the criticism and distractions, the Chiba Lotte Marines finished strong. We were second in the league with a 69–58 record—an A-class season and one to build on. The controversy of my American methods led to many discussions on philosophy, which were becoming quite stressful. At the same time, I got a phone call from Carmen Fusco, the assistant to Joe McIlvaine, the general manager of the New York Mets.

"Can you get out of your contract?" he wanted to know.

"It's a two-year contract," I said. "I have another year."

"Yeah," said Carm, "but Joe wants to know if you can get out of it, because he's going to fire Dallas Green. And he wants you to manage the Mets."

I could not believe this was happening.

Maybe this experiment in Japan should come to an end, I thought. *Maybe I should be home managing the Mets.*

"Let me think about it," I said.

CHAPTER 20

You Want Me to Manage Where?

E thically, the Mets should never have contacted me. Our correspondence never should have happened. This is considered tampering both in Japan and the US, as teams are not supposed to steal another team's manager. They had a manager in place, and I was under contract.

I talked myself into deciding that this American manager experiment in Japan wasn't going to work, and I communicated that to Hirooka-san. He agreed, and there was an announcement in the press that I would not be coming back to Japan for a second year—not that I had quit or that I had been fired, only that I wasn't coming back.

In the next three weeks, the Marines' fans collected 20,000 signatures in support of my staying. In one year, the fans and I had really connected. I had a fan-friendly policy for my players, and it really resonated. This was a difficult decision. I felt like I was leaving something behind, as I had wanted to fulfill the two years of my contract, but I was going home to manage the New York Mets.

When I landed at JFK, I promptly called Carmen for instructions. I got no answer and left a message. I went home to sleep, something I really needed. The next morning, I got a call that the Mets wanted me to come to Shea Stadium. I got there and Joe McIlvaine was not in. I was told to talk to Steve Phillips, the minor league director. Steve offered me the job managing the Triple-A Norfolk Tides. I was flabbergasted—more than flabbergasted. I was left holding the bag.

I couldn't say, "What the eff are you doing?" because if I did that, I would never get the Mets job. When I interviewed for the Triple-A job, I thought to myself, *I'll be the Mets' manager-in-waiting. Really? For $60,000 I left a job paying $600,000. Boy, was I duped!*

I was not a happy camper when I got to spring training, even though I was with the major league club during spring training, which is standard practice for all Triple-A managers. I could not let on to anyone what had happened, because I would look like a fool and probably never get a job in either place in the future. I bit my tongue and went to Norfolk.

The Mets threw me a bone when they traveled to Arlington, Texas, to play the first exhibition game in the brand-new Arlington Stadium. I flew with the team and coached first base. I had helped design the stadium and helped convince the people of Arlington to vote for a tax increase to fund it, and I wanted to be there for the opening ceremony. I also wanted to go back to Texas to see my restaurants and friends.

Returning to Florida, I assumed my role as Triple-A manager. We had a really nice team led by Matt Franco, who hit .323 with 81 RBIs, and Roberto Petagine, who hit .318 with 12 home runs and 65 RBIs. But I'm proud to say the players whose careers I most affected were Benny Agbayani and Rick Reed.

We played games every day during spring training. One day, as our game was to start at our minor league complex, I saw Benny leaving the clubhouse. I was intrigued by him because he had skills, even though he looked different from most players in uniform. He looked fat and moved slowly. Benny was on the Binghamton Double-A team. I had injuries on my team and had sent a couple guys to the Mets for their spring training game. I yelled over and asked Benny what he was doing.

"I've been released," he said.

I needed an extra outfielder, so I told him to get back in uniform and play in my game. Benny played and did fine. That night I went to the minor league meetings and asked to keep Benny until the end of spring training. I wanted to see if he could make my team. The brass was skeptical, but I got my way and Benny made my team. I'm happy he did. One reason Benny might have been released was the player strike in 1994. Some minor league players had crossed the picket line when the teams were trying to build a player pool, so they could play the season without major-leaguers. The picket line crossers were called scabs, strike-breakers, and Benny had been one of them. That didn't matter to me.

This was also the situation with pitcher Rick Reed, who I thought was a really good pitcher. Rick lived in Huntington, West Virginia. His family was in need, and he saw a way to help by crossing the line. I remember hearing something about Rick going to the major leagues for a week and having to dress in the New York Jets locker room, because after the strike ended, the other players wouldn't let him dress with them.

I was promoted to manager of the New York Mets on August 26, 1996. We had just finished playing a game in Scranton/Wilkes-Barre in Pennsylvania, when I got a call from Joe McIlvain.

"Bobby," he said. "We want you to be the big-league manager."

"That's great news, Joe."

"But we don't want you to come in tonight, because the press is hot on the story. We want you to come in tomorrow."

"What should I do?" I said. "The Tides are leaving Scranton/Wilkes-Barre tonight. We're going to Pawtucket."

"Take the bus to Pawtucket," he said. "Rent a car and drive down to Shea Stadium tomorrow morning, and at noon we'll have a press conference."

As awkward as it was, I couldn't say anything to my players. I was allowed to take Bob Apodaca, my pitching coach, with me. That night, when we got to Pawtucket, I was able to tell Bob that we were going to get up the next morning and drive to New York to take over the Mets.

As we were getting close to New York, I said, "Let's hear what they're saying on the radio." Talk radio was alive and well in New York. Mike Francesa and Christopher Russo's *Mike and the Mad Dog* was the most listened-to sports talk show in the country, and I was trying to get their show on the radio. As we approached the city, we could hear the speculation as to who was going to be the next manager, because Dallas Green had been fired and no replacement had been named. Some callers speculated it might be me. Some wanted someone with more experience. I turned off the radio. I couldn't listen to it anymore.

We pulled into Shea Stadium and had the press conference. Bruce Benedict took over for me at Norfolk and took the Tides to the playoffs against the Columbus Clippers, the Yankees' Triple-A farm team.

Bruce was my coach in Norfolk. He had an eleven-year career as a catcher with the Atlanta Braves and one of the greatest senses of humor. When I became the Mets manager, Bruce called in the Tides' game report to me every night. We won our division and had a three-game series for the league championship against the Clippers. We had split the first two games against them, and I was looking forward to Bruce's call about the final game. Kevin Flora, an outfielder and one of the fastest players in the Mets organization, broke his wrist the last week of the season. We decided to keep him on the playoff roster in case we needed a pinch-runner.

When the final game of the series finished, Bruce called and left the game report, offering a play-by-play account of how the last inning went down. His message said, "With the score tied, Shawn Gilbert is at the plate, and the count is two and two, and he hits the ball into right-center field, and the Columbus outfielders are converging on it, and Kevin Flora, my pinch-runner from first base, is racing around second, and here comes the relay, and Flora's racing around third, and there's not going to be a play at the plate, and we're about to win the championship. But wait! Flora falls down. He's on his knees. He gets up, he falls again, and here comes the relay, and the relay man throws home, and Kevin is crawling to the plate. *And he's out.* First-pitch home run for the bad guys in the next inning. We lose!!!"

The guys were running out of the dugout to congratulate Kevin at the plate. Everyone was jumping up and down. And then he fell, and he started crawling. He would have been on all fours, but he had a cast, so he was on all threes. It was heartbreaking. These players were really good guys. A lot of them came up to the Mets in September and played the next year in the big leagues.

When I replaced Dallas Green, his record was 59–72. Dallas was old school, my-way-or-the-highway kind of guy. I was nothing like Dallas Green, who looked really good when he was dressed up, with that silver hair. He had a real deep voice, but I thought Dallas was full of it. When I was with him during spring training and watched what he did with the players on the field, I wasn't the least impressed. So I wasn't worried about having to take over for him, though I knew he had loyal coaches and others in the organization who were loyal to him, and I knew I would have to deal with that.

My first day on the job, I met with each coach individually for a briefing on their department. Tom McCraw was the hitting coach. I had played with Tom in California, and he was a little standoffish, but he was okay. Frank Howard was the first-base coach, and Chuck Cottier the third-base coach. Bobby Wine, who was very nice, was Dallas's guy. They had traveled together, and he was the bench/infield coach and gave good evaluations. Mike Cubbage wasn't going to be an ally. Mike felt he should be the manager, because he had been the Triple-A manager when Davey Johnson was manager. He felt he had put in his time.

Frank Howard and I had coached together in the '80s, and I loved Frank's enthusiasm, style, and baseball acumen, but there was no chance Frank was going to be a coach of mine. Sure enough, Frank gave his evaluation the first day, and two days later he quit, out of loyalty to Dallas.

I kept everyone else on, and we worked together. I didn't play many cards at all. I decided I would take the rest of August and all of September to spend time with the team and just evaluate them. Three weeks into my tenure, in mid-September, Joel Sherman—a young, aspiring, go-getter, street-fighter of a newspaper reporter—came into my office during one of my private times.

"I've been watching you since you took over," he said, "and you have done nothing. Whatever it is you're supposed to do, I haven't seen any action at all."

"Is this for an article or just for my tombstone?" I asked him.

"No, I'm writing an article."

"Make sure you write in your article that you have no idea what you're talking about, because I've done a lot since I've been here," I said. "I've collected information. I've evaluated, and I'm going to put a plan in motion how to make this team, and this organization, one that all Mets fans will be proud of." It was all I could do to bite my tongue. To this day, Joel and I are friends, and he recalls this little meeting.

I met with every player, three players a day. Sometimes I'd skip batting practice so I could hold these meetings. I just wanted to hear what everyone had to say. I was surprised that there was a small group of players who were up in arms about the amount of smoking in the clubhouse. Jerry Dipoto, one of our relief pitchers and a cancer survivor, expressed his displeasure that every day in the clubhouse, someone to his left or his right was chain-smoking.

"If you can't separate the smokers from the nonsmokers," Jerry said, "I want to go and dress somewhere else. I don't even want to be in the clubhouse."

Other players expressed displeasure that some teammates weren't taking as good care of themselves as they should, mainly because we provided beer and liquor in the clubhouse after the games, and at midnight the clubhouse became a fraternity house. I had a beer with the guys, but I wasn't going to hang around the clubhouse. I was never there at midnight because I would drive to Stamford to oversee the closing hour of my restaurant. I hated the smoke as much as anyone, and it prompted me to have discussions with the front office during the winter. Some of the executives worried about their liability if a player was drinking, went out into the parking lot where the autograph-seekers were standing, and something bad happened.

"I think we should do something about the drinking," said someone in the front office.

"Hey, listen," I said. "That's not my territory. I'm not going to tell guys they can't smoke or can't drink. That got me in trouble in my last job. I don't want to be part of that."

I had a partner who was in the sign-making business. He had a lathe that made cool signs out of plastic. He made one that said, "By ordinance of the City of New York, smoking in a public building isn't allowed." I brought it into Joe McIlvain's office, and when the team came back to Shea after spring training, these signs were posted in the clubhouse. If a player bitched, I'd tell him, "If you don't like it, go to town hall and complain."

Adjoining the clubhouse was the laundry area. There were washing machines and dryers for the uniforms and towels. We let the smokers and drinkers go in there, a small closet tucked away from the main clubhouse. It was not a cure for the problem, but it created a little safer clubhouse environment. Putting that sign up was a big deal. I did take the heat for it. Once again I was accused of playing the morality cop, but it was worth it.

The 1996 Mets team had a lot of offense from three guys. Catcher Todd Hundley had 41 home runs and 112 RBIs. Bernard Gilkey had 30 home runs and 117 RBIs. Lance Johnson had 69 RBIs. That's a lot of hitting. I brought in Tom Robson to be our hitting coach, and he came in with a new hitting style. The guys were receptive. They could hit, but it wasn't the kind of team I thought could make a dent in the National League. We were competing with the Atlanta Braves, who led with NL East with a 96–66 record. Montreal was 88–74, and even the Florida Marlins, at 80–82, were ahead of us. We finished 1996 at 71–91.

We needed to change things, especially in the bullpen, which was atrocious. We did have some offense, but it was a mature offense a little long in the tooth, while the pitching was young, promising, and highly touted. We had three young pitchers who we were supposed to ride to the promised land: Bill Pulsipher, Paul Wilson, and Jason Isringhausen. They were said to be the three starters we could build a franchise around. The last thing I wanted to do was count on them to bring us to the promised land, because from the reports I read and everything I heard about them, they were not of the quality we needed to build around. This was a *major, major problem*, because there were people in the organization who had invested in them and a lot of reporters had written glowingly about them, comparing them to Seaver, Koosman, and Gary Gentry. Or they were supposed to be Gooden, Ron Darling, and Sid Fernandez all over again.

I had played against the '69 Mets pitchers and coached the '85 Mets pitchers, and I just didn't see it, though it was hard to figure out how not to give them the ball every fifth day. It took a while, but eventually I was able to convince the front office I was right. Wilson got hurt, and Pulsipher was a left-hander who floundered a little, and Izzy was a late bloomer, an immature kid with a really good arm. None of them started the next year.

The Mets made a significant leap forward in 1997, and we finished with 88 wins and 74 losses. Joe McIlvaine was rather aloof. In Texas, Tom Grieve and I had been in contact all the time. We'd have lunch, he'd come into my office after the game, and if there was a tough loss, he'd be there to say, "Hang in there." Joe was a good guy, but he was never around. He pretty much let me do what I wanted to do, and in the off-season after 1997 he asked me, "What do you think we ought to do?"

"We need a whole bunch of different looks in the bullpen," I said. "We need to have pitchers who don't throw the same, guys who throw different pitches, so we can mix and match." And so we changed the entire bullpen.

Joe Crawford had pitched for me at Norfolk. I loved his changeup, and my intent was to use him as a Jamie Moyer type. I brought up Ricky Trlicek, who had a slider I could utilize, and we brought Turk Wendell over in a trade.

I had to make peace with John Franco. Johnny was Dallas's boy initially, and why not? Tough as nails, he took the ball whenever asked and saved games. I loved giving him the ball, and he went from being Dallas's guy to becoming my guy without missing a beat. No one else pitched in the ninth. Every day I checked with him to make sure he was okay to pitch. He always said YES!

On offense, one of my favorite players was Carl Everett. To this day, I think that Carl had as much talent as anybody who ever wore a uniform. He was a switch-hitter, had power from both sides, and had an incredible arm. He played a shallow center field, like Gary Maddox, and nothing got over his head. He could bunt and he could steal. There was hardly anything in his repertoire that he wasn't better than average at. But Carl was a little different. He was a loner who didn't drink or smoke. His family was key to his existence. I went all in on Carl, and that bugged some of the players. Lance Johnson had a nice résumé, but we traded him because I favored Carl in center field.

Our biggest star was Todd Hundley. I was good friends with his dad, Randy. In 1997 Todd hit 30 home runs and had 86 RBIs, but Todd had a serious problem with alcohol. He had already been to rehab once, and he wasn't supposed to be smoking or drinking. There were days, usually day games after night games, when I wouldn't play Todd because he didn't get enough sleep the night before. Todd was a really good guy, but he had a problem. I went to the New York Sportswriters dinner in 1997. The sportswriters were presenting Randy and Todd Hundley with the father-and-son award. Randy and I were in a back room, ready to go on stage and sit at the head table. It was a black-tie affair, and Todd came in and he was feeling really good.

His father came over and said to me, "There are some things that fathers just can't handle with their sons. Todd is having a lot of trouble sleeping at night. Do you think you can get my son some help?"

"Sure," I said. "I'll do what I can." This, I knew, was going to be one of those lose-lose situations for me.

After a day game when I didn't play Todd, the press came to me and asked, "Why isn't Todd in the lineup?"

"He has a little trouble sleeping at night," I said. "Day games are a problem."

There were headlines, and when they went to Todd and asked him about it, he said, "Hell no, I don't have a problem sleeping. I'm ready to play every day." The next day the headline in *The New York Post* read: "I'm not Sleepy, Dopey."

Speaking of the back page of *The Post,* when I was first hired, I had a meeting with Mets owner Fred Wilpon.

"One of the things we need you to do is work all year round," he said.

"I do that, Fred," I said. "Don't worry. I'm not taking the winters off." Many of the other managers couldn't be found during the wintertime. They were fishing or playing golf, and if the club needed them to visit a hospital or speak at a Kiwanis luncheon, they weren't around. Fred thought that if the manager was going to make a big salary, he should work twelve months a year. I was all for that.

Fred also said, "We have to capture the back pages more, because the Yankees own the back pages."

Our team was led by Todd Hundley. He had a fan club, a great smile, and a great bat. He had it all going for him. He was what the team needed, except that he hurt his elbow and needed surgery at the end of '97.

We were also led by John Olerud, our solid first baseman, who hit 22 home runs and had 102 RBIs. He was one of the greatest people I've ever been around, a model player who I tried to build the lineup and the team around. He was tall and an extremely athletic first baseman, with range at the bag.

This was a specular group of infielders, and there might have been a bad infield throw or two, but it was always saved by John at first. We had different defensive looks, what today are called shifts. The infield would shift as the ball was being pitched. John had adopted the philosophy that I thought would work to keep runners from stealing bases against our left-handed pitchers. The years John was our first baseman, our left-handed pitchers, except for Kenny Rogers, had poor moves to first base.

They were easy to steal on. Al Leiter hardly had any move at all. John Franco was quick to home, but he didn't have a good move to first. Mike Hampton had a decent move, but Glendon Rusch did not. Dennis Cook did not. And so I tried to neutralize it by employing Olerud off the base. Instead of holding the runner on, he would stand parallel with the base runner and just a bit in front of him. John had impeccable timing. As the pitcher would lift his right leg to deliver the ball John would make a little move toward first as though he was going to the bag, and that would freeze the runner, thinking the pitcher was going to throw to first. It negated a lot of stolen-base attempts, and it was also controversial. Some umpires declared it illegal. Managers wanted to protest the move, but it was perfectly legal, and it worked really well.

Olerud's offensive style was also exactly what I was preaching at the time. I wanted hitters in my lineup who walked as much as struck out. At the time, there was hardly any appreciation for the walk, but I favored it, from my days with Craig Wright, the sabermetrician who taught me to appreciate it. Olerud walked eighty-five times in '97. He was the model hitter. I had known him from the American League, and now I had him, and I *never* wanted him to leave. When John did leave, against my advice, it was gut-wrenching.

We had Rey Ordonez at shortstop. The first Cuban fence-jumper in major league baseball, he was another piece of the puzzle. He literally jumped a fence while playing in a tournament in the U.S. and defected from Cuba to come to America to play in the major leagues. Rey was an interesting person in that he could make a regular play look difficult and make a difficult play look spectacular. He had the uncanny ability of catching pop-ups with his back to the infield, as good as anyone this side of Derek Jeter. But Rey was a challenge offensively. He swung at everything. He didn't believe in the walk. He didn't think the signs applied to him. He was different, but I didn't mind the difference, though I never did appreciate that he didn't buy into the team concept. I would think about where Rey had come from and give him a pass. He'd left his entire family behind in Cuba and hadn't seen them since. He was learning a new language.

We also had another Cuban, Alex Ochoa, who was the number-one citizen on earth. Alex was a mentor to Rey. Alex was also Joe McIlvaine's favorite player. When Joe traded for him from Baltimore, he touted Alex as the Second Coming, the next five-tool player. Alex was a late bloomer who finally hit his stride in Japan. He was getting close to being that guy in the major leagues playing for the Mets.

A lot of crazy stuff happened in 1997. On July 16, Joe McIlvaine left as the Mets general manager and was replaced by Steve Phillips. All I knew about McIlvaine leaving was that one day Fred Wilpon had come into my office and said, "Joe is no longer the general manager. Steve Phillips is going to take over." It was that abrupt. There were rumors in the media that I had pushed Joe out, but nothing could have been further from the truth. I always wanted to get the story from Joe about why—when I was in Japan—Carmen Fusco had asked if I wanted to manage the Mets, and after I quit Japan, I ended up managing Norfolk instead. Then Joe got fired. To this day I don't know the answer.

Two months later, in August, when Carl Everett was really coming into his own, I faced another "situation." Carl was batting third or fifth in my lineup. During one game, we were getting ready to bat in the bottom of the ninth, and Carl was getting ready to hit. Charlie Samuels, the clubhouse guy, who was in on everything and knew everything that there ever was to know, came over to me, pulled on my shirt, and said, "Bobby, we have a problem." I thought he was talking about the relief pitcher the other team had just brought into the game.

"No," I said, "I think we can hit this guy."

"We have a problem, Bobby," Charlie said. "You gotta bring Carl up to the Jets' locker room. The police just took his children away from his wife."

"What?"

"Yeah."

Carl was walking over to the bat rack. It had taken me a lot of work to get close to Carl, but I had done it. I grabbed him and said, "Hey, Carl, you're not hitting this inning." He thought I was pinch-hitting for him, and he looked at me with disbelief. "No, Carl," I said, "we have a personal situation we have to take care of."

I had no idea what Charlie was saying to me. All I saw was the troubled expression on his face. I knew how close Carl was to his wife and children, and so I turned the lineup card over to Tom Robson, and Carl and I went up the runway, crossed the concrete tunnel, and went into the Jets' locker room. I opened the door, and Carl and I walked in together, and standing on the back side of the clubhouse was a uniformed NYPD officer who had mirrored sunglasses on, with two policemen on either side of him. He was holding both of Carl's crying children in his arms. His wife was being held back by a female Human Services officer as she was crying and yelling. We walked into this horrific scene, and Carl sprinted across the clubhouse. Carl could have been an NFL running back. He had thighs the size of Earl Campbell's. He was 215 pounds of muscle, and he took off across that clubhouse, and the only reason he didn't get to the policeman holding the children was that four other NYPD officers tackled him and wrestled him to the ground.

Outside on the field, it was the bottom of the ninth, and I could hear the yelling and screaming, and in the room there was screaming and crying, and my head was totally spinning. I calmed Carl down. I got two inches from his face. I was hugging him, holding him.

"Carl, this is me. It's okay. Carl, relax. We will take care of this. Carl, it's okay. Carl, it's okay."

After seconds, minutes, seemingly hours, Carl calmed down enough that only two policemen were holding him as one of the other policemen explained to me what was going on.

"What do we do?" I asked. "Where do we go from here?"

"We have to take the children to the hospital to be examined," he said. "They will not be in Carl's custody until they are cleared by Human Services."

It wasn't easy to digest. Carl's wife came over to us.

"Carl," she said, "they saw bruises on the children's arms."

Bernard Gilkey's wife, it was said, had turned them in to Human Services. The police told us what hospital they were taking the children to, and Carl and I went back to the locker room, changed our clothes, got in my car, and drove there. We went to the waiting room, and we wound up sleeping on the marble floor of the adjacent room, where we had to wait for the doctors to be called in to examine the children. During that time, I got to talk to Carl.

"Do you hit the kids?" I asked him in a fatherly, brotherly way. "What's going on? Is your daughter safe?"

Carl wasn't very talkative. The only thing he would say was how much he loved his kids. His young son had come with the team on a couple of flights, and the entire flight he ran up and down the aisles. The boy was active, and Carl's way of disciplining his children was to shake them like his daddy had shaken him. He'd grab them by the arms and shake them to get their attention. On their arms you could see bruising. Carl had to go on family leave, and in December we traded him to the Astros. All I know is that it made me ill, and the next time I saw Carl, he was in a Red Sox uniform. I got to see him in the players' parking lot, and I gave him a big hug. I asked him if he was all right, and he said he was. He was back to being a good player.

There were situations like the one with Carl that maybe I became more involved in than I should have, and I would end up with more yolk on my face or blood on my hands, however you want to describe it. Maybe I was too involved, but I was only doing what I felt I ought to be doing. In the case of Todd Hundley, when I swore I wasn't going to get involved, I knew a crisis was brewing. He was burning the candle at both ends and ready to crash and burn, and I went to Mets co-owner Fred Wilpon to tell him what I was seeing, and Fred determined that he was going to be the peacemaker. He loved Todd, he told me, and he was going to figure out how to take care of him.

A few days later, Fred told me he had "taken care of the situation." I asked him how. Fred said he had invited Todd and his wife over to his house. He said he told Todd that as a show of his love, he was going to let Todd wear his 1986 World Series ring, if he would promise to modify his lifestyle and be a good citizen. Todd agreed, and I was told they celebrated by drinking two expensive bottles of Fred's wine. I wanted to wash my hands of the situation, and I said "Okay," knowing that it could have been handled better. It wasn't about Fred's words. Todd was an addict. "He promised me," Fred said.

It wasn't Fred's fault. The Mets had hired Dr. Allan Lans, a psychiatrist specializing in addiction, who was supposed to take care of these situations. I shouldn't have been involved at all. I'm not a choirboy, and certainly not the smartest guy in the room, but I was always caring. I always tried to do the right thing. I never did anything for the wrong reason. I was just flipping the coin. But it was heads I lose, tails I lose.

CHAPTER 21

We Trade for Mike Piazza

I n 1998 we started to get some pitchers with genuine name recognition. The Florida Marlins were dumping, getting rid of their good players and trying to sign young players. On February 6, Steve Phillips seized the opportunity to get Al Leiter. Al had already earned some stripes, and he stepped right into our rotation along with Rick Reed, Bobby Jones, and Masato Yoshii. Leiter was a godsend for me. He looked the part. Always emotionally connected to the game, he was intelligent, and he had that cutter, a pitch that was new on the scene and hard to hit. Al became one of the best pitchers in the league.

We also had Masato Yoshii, who we signed on a flyer. I didn't know Yoshii from Japan. He pitched in the other league, but I had good reports. Sad to say, one pitcher we didn't sign was Kogi Uehara. I wanted to leverage my year in Japan by signing some jewels. Jae Weong Seo, who was Korean, was a stud. He was a hard thrower, with a slider that was lights out, and a good split-finger. We were going to sign him. The other pitcher we were going to sign was Uehara, who I wanted to sign right out of college.

We thought Seo was good enough to offer him half a million bucks. I flew over to Korea to help with the courting of the coach and the father and the brother and everyone else. We struck a deal verbally, and I agreed we'd also sign his brother, a non-prospect, which would give Jae another Korean-speaking player while he played in the minor leagues, someone who could eat with him and keep him company. At the time, Chan Ho Park was lighting it up with the Dodgers. Seo and Park played on the same Korean national team that finished second in the World Games. We brought him to New York to have a signing and press conference over the Christmas holidays. He brought an entourage of twelve: his family, his high school coach, his college coach, his interpreter, and members of the Korean press.

There was a Christmas party at Shea Stadium, so we put off the signing for a day, and unbeknownst to me, Steve Phillips told Seo he had to have his arm examined before the press conference. The conference was going to be held at 4:00 p.m., and I waited for everyone to get there. I greeted them, and then we went in to have a private meeting before the press conference. During the meeting, Steve said, "By the way, we can't give you what we said we were going to give you because the MRI came out bad. We're afraid you're going to have arm problems."

This couldn't be real. Steve removed a zero from our offer. There was one member of Seo's party who spoke English, his agent, who was also the trainer on his national team. Seo had brought all these people over, and there was no way he was going to walk out of the room without signing that contract.

"Steve, I can't believe we're pulling this shit," I said before walking out of the room.

Seo signed the contract. He played that year at St. Lucie, and in a playoff game against the Yankees farm club, he came close to throwing a no-hitter. We agreed he could pitch in the winter National Tournament in Korea. A gold medal would have exempted him and his teammates from military service. He wound up getting hurt, and even though it wasn't the injury predicted by the MRI, he became less of a pitcher.

The next year, our scout, Isao O'Jimi, convinced us to sign Koji Uehara out of college. O'Jimi was going to make the pitch to his family with our contract, and right before he went into the parents' home, Steve again took a zero off our offer. O'Jimi refused to go in, and Uehara signed with the Tokyo Giants for $5 million as their number-one pick. As a rookie he went 20–4 for them.

I was furious that we didn't sign Uehara, but on May 22, 1998, Steve made up for it when he performed a miracle, acquiring catcher Mike Piazza from the Florida Marlins for Geoff Goetz, Preston Wilson, and Ed Yarnall. The Marlins had owned Piazza for a week. They had traded Bobby Bonilla, Jim Eisenreich, and Manuel Barrios to the Dodgers for Piazza and Todd Zeile. The reason the Dodgers let Mike go was that Tommy Lasorda, who was like a father to Mike, had had a heart attack, and he wasn't managing in '98.

Lasorda was close friends with Vince Piazza, Mike's father. I can remember my first year with the Rangers, Tommy had called me and said, "I have a buddy who has a kid playing at Miami Dade Junior College. Get your scouts to look at him. Try him out." When Tommy said to do something, I did it. Mike and his dad came to my spring training site in Pompano. I got all our scouts to watch the kid take ground balls and hit. He was a switch-hitter, but he looked terrible. He broke bats in batting practice and couldn't catch a ground ball. Mike went back to school for another year, and Tommy begged the Dodgers to sign him, and they did after drafting him in the sixty-second round. The rest is history. Piazza played sixteen years, had a lifetime batting average of .308, and hit 427 home runs.

In 1998, Bill Russell, the same Bill Russell who took the shortstop position from me on the Dodgers, took over the team for Tommy, and somehow Mike was traded. Mike told the Marlins, "I don't want to play for you." We had considered trading with the Dodgers, when Steve Phillips asked me what I thought of Piazza. I considered that we had

Todd Hundley, an All-Star catcher, but he was rehabbing from an arm operation. Even though Todd was projected to come back strong, I said, "Piazza? Are you kidding? I love Piazza. How could you not love Piazza?"

"I think we have a shot at him," Steve said.

"Good luck."

I then heard the Dodger trade for Piazza was off the table, and I was surprised when he got traded to the Marlins. I was sitting on the pot in my office at Shea when Steve came into my office.

"You better hurry up and flush," he said, "because we just got Piazza."

The Marlins liked the players we offered, but it looked like the deal wasn't going to get done because of Piazza's salary. Then co-owner Nelson Doubleday said, "We're not going to let money stop us from getting this guy." Earlier, Nelson had been standing with me around the batting cage when he asked, "Can Piazza really help us?" It was the only time Nelson Doubleday talked to me about baseball.

"Yes," I said confidently, even though I knew this was going to cause one hell of a shit show with Todd Hundley.

The first thing I said to Steve when I got out of the bathroom was, "What are we going to do with Todd?"

"Let's make him the left fielder," he said.

Todd had a lot of strengths. Catching a pop-up wasn't one of them, even as a catcher. I didn't think that was going to fly, and it didn't. Todd was embarrassed and upset. He was recovering from his arm injury, and he came in to see me. He hated the idea of playing left field.

"When I come back and my elbow's better," Todd said, "give him one day and give me one day, and I'll win the job after a month."

I went to see Steve, and I said, "Mike Piazza didn't come here to play every other day. If he's going to play every other day because Todd is here, we're going to have a major problem."

Todd was traded in December, and I took the brunt of that. I was afraid his fan club was going to slit my tires, or worse. They were really upset with me, carrying signs, saying this was all my idea. I'd love to take credit for it, but I had absolutely nothing to do with it. I wish I had, because Mike Piazza turned the entire franchise around.

Recall that I had taken Randy Hundley's concern about Todd to Fred Wilpon and Dr. Allan Lans, and Wilpon's answer was to let Todd wear his World Series ring if he curtailed his extracurricular activities. I was hoping Wilpon would get Todd real help, but instead, Todd and his agents took great exception to what I did. I had turned him in, if you will, exposed his problem to ownership and the organization. His agents, Sam and Seth Levinson, were lawyers from Long Island. The two brothers founded ACES, an agency that represents many top athletes. The Levinsons thought what I had done was bogus, that it was their job to handle Todd.

Steve Phillips traded Todd to the Dodgers, along with Arnold Gooch, on December 1, 1998, in exchange for Roger Cedeno and Charles Johnson, who was immediately sent to the Orioles for Armando Benitez. The Levinsons hated me, and they did everything they could to try to ruin my career. This story may sound a little complicated, so bear with me.

When I took over as manager of the Mets, they had an archaic video system with one video recorder in a little closet recording Mets games. Once in a while, a player would go into the closet and look at the game from the night before. When I saw this, I said, "This is ridiculous." During the off-season, I designed a plan to incorporate a video system much like I had at my restaurants. I wanted to put multiple televisions in the clubhouse and designed it for six, three facing the pitchers and three facing the hitters. I had the hitters sit on one side of the clubhouse and the pitchers on the other. I wanted the pitchers to watch the opposing hitters and my hitters to watch opposing pitchers, all orchestrated through one control room.

Steve told me there was no budget for it. "We can't spend any money. The union contractor was too expensive because the union electricians are so expensive, and the budget cannot handle it."

"What if I have it done after hours?" I asked.

"If I don't know about it," Steve said, "I won't worry about it."

I hired a guy named Larry Slote, who was a customer at my Norwalk restaurant, to be the electrician. Larry had been Mr. Fixit whenever something went wrong with my satellite dish or TVs. He came into the Mets clubhouse at nine at night during the winter to install the six TVs, the satellite dish, recording system, and a couple of cameras. The cameras were next to the dugouts on each side of the field, so the players could see themselves from a good perspective, not just from a TV perspective. If I wanted to see what the third-base coach was doing, I could move the cameras to watch him. I could even look at the manager in the other dugout to see what signs he was giving. I also bought, out of my own pocket, a big Sony printer that could print sixteen frames of sixteen seconds of movement on one sheet of paper. It was very helpful to the hitters and pitchers, who could look at themselves in stop action.

Larry often came in to fine-tune the cameras or fix the TV setup, because he was the only one who knew how the whole thing was wired. During the season, every once in a while, Larry came in while players were still in the clubhouse because the beer wasn't gone yet. Larry ended up becoming friends with Todd Hundley. Cut to the winter after Todd was traded, and Larry was house-sitting Todd's Long Island home while Todd was in Florida. While he was there, Larry teamed up with the brother of Kirk Radomski to run a business selling satellite dishes. Kirk Radomski was working in the Mets clubhouse when I took over as manager. When I asked Charlie Samuels, our clubhouse attendant, what he did, he said, "He gets the guys anything they need when they need it." In 2007, Radomski pleaded guilty in district court to money laundering and illegal distribution of anabolic steroids, human growth hormones, and amphetamines. *Oh good*, I thought.

"Fire him," I said. "I don't want him in the clubhouse."

It doesn't take much imagination to figure out how my man Larry and Kirk's brother hooked up. The business the two had started revolved around selling small network satellite dishes. These dishes were new at the time and not easy to get, especially in Canada. Larry worked a deal with a guy in Canada to sell him a hundred. The buyer sent the money, but Larry never delivered the dishes. At the same time, Larry was installing an elaborate speaker system in the home of one of the Levinson brothers. He was asked to put stereo speakers in every room. Instead of putting in the speakers, Larry just cut holes in the ceilings and put up little caps that looked like speakers. He scammed the Levinsons as well. Why did he do this? Because he was a scam artist, and scam artists are stupid and crooked. The Canadian buyer hired a private investigator to track down Larry and Radomski in an attempt to get his money back. The investigator found them, turned them in to the police, and the police arrested them. The private eye is a guy I went to high school with in Stamford.

At Larry's arraignment in Stamford federal court, he got bailed out by a guy who was a regular at my bar, and he hired Mickey Sherman, a Stamford lawyer, as his counsel. Mickey had represented Michael Skakel in a highly publicized trial in Connecticut in the '80s. This tangled web was being woven unbeknownst to me. The Levinsons called Marty Noble, a beat reporter from *Newsday*. By this time, Marty had turned anti-Valentine. The *Stamford Advocate* was owned by the same company that owned *Newsday,* and Marty wrote an article from information supplied by the Levinsons that said that *I* was the one who had funded Larry for the scam on the Canadian buyer and supplied the $10,000 that bailed him out.

I'm going to lose my job, I thought. *I'm losing face in my hometown, and the worst thing is my dad and mom are embarrassed!*

It was worse than terrible. And this happened during the 1998 season. The article came out in the Stamford paper and was read by my dad. My dad opened my restaurant in the morning and made sure the cleaning people cleaned properly. He knew Larry because Larry was often there in the morning fixing the electrical systems. My dad hated Larry. He knew to his bones that Larry should not have had anything to do with my restaurant, but Larry had the keys to the kingdom because he knew where the wires were.

When this hit job came out in the papers, I was told by friends in the media that it was the Levinsons' doing. After one of our games, I heard that one of the Levinson brothers was waiting in the lobby outside our clubhouse. I went out, grabbed him, and put him up against the wall. He wasn't a very big guy. I lifted him off the ground and said some unpleasantries. I didn't punch him. I'm sorry I didn't. I should have. From then on, I never wanted to see that guy again. It was more than distaste. I wanted him out of my life *forever*. The problem was that he represented ballplayers, some of whom played for me. I intended to get a list of all the players he represented so I would better be able to watch my back. Finally, I thought, *I'm too big for this kind of thing. It's not about the agents and me. It's about me and the players, so I will just have to make it right with the players*. But talk about a distraction!

Larry and Radomski's brother went to jail. They were put on trial, and there was a guilty plea. I had nothing to do with the thing. I did know the guy. The guy worked for me. He installed everything. I admitted that to the press, and I was never investigated by the police. It was a made-up story, and if you connect the dots, it came from my association with Todd Hundley and the Levinsons.

CHAPTER 22

Steve Is Suspended

n 1998 we finished 88–74, which was still not good enough for me to have job security. What occurred in the winter of that year made my job even more precarious.

It started when Steve Phillips had to take a leave of absence in November. The papers weren't clear about what exactly happened, except that he was married and a woman had accused him of sexual harassment. This was right before the general managers meetings in Naples, Florida, the place where many trades were made and teams were rebuilt. Steve could not attend the meetings. Not a good sign.

Bobby Jr. was ready to make a decision on college, and we were going to visit some universities. We were in Chapel Hill, North Carolina, where my wife had gone to school, when I got a call from Fred Wilpon. He wanted to pick me up that evening to go to the meetings.

"Jeez, I have only casual dress," I said.

"Pick up a sport coat," he said. "We'll pick you up in Winston-Salem."

I bought a sport coat and went to the airport. I got picked up by their private plane. When I got on the plane, I was told that Steve had a personal problem and that everyone on the plane was going to pull together to get all the work done. It seemed the entire organization was on that plane—Dave Howard, the vice president; Jim Duquette, an assistant general manager; Omar Minaya, an assistant general manager; Carmen Fusco, another assistant; Gary LaRocque, the scouting director; Jay Horwitz, the outstanding PR director and the greatest person I met during that stretch with the Mets; and Dr. Allan Lans, the psychiatrist for the team.

Fred Wilpon said we were to meet with Frank Cashen, our special senior adviser, when we got to the hotel. For the two and a half years I managed the Mets, I had only seen Frank a couple times in spring training. He had not been heavily involved with the team. We had Steve's files and notes, along with some leads he'd developed, and we were to conduct business as normal, even though this wasn't normal. When Frank came in, Fred introduced him to everyone.

"Frank is going to run the meetings," Fred said. Then he left and went back to New York.

"Let's get one thing straight," Frank said. "Cocktail hour starts at five o'clock."

The idea was for each of us to set up meetings with other teams in order to get information on what the other teams needed, who they wanted to trade, and who they might be interested in. We decided to meet every morning and give Frank our information. Among the things we had to do was sign Masato Yoshii. We did, but for two years, when he would have signed for one. But first we needed to talk to the Dodgers about a Mel Rojas for Bobby Bonilla trade.

When the '98 season ended, Tommy Lasorda, who was then the Dodger GM, came with the team to New York for a series. He asked me after a game, "Why are the fans so unhappy with Mel Rojas?"

"He gave up a big hit to Paul O'Neill in the Subway Series in '97," I said. "They don't forget that."

Tommy said, "Every time Bonilla comes up to the plate, they boo him."

"Maybe we should think about making a swap," I said. "How much is he making?"

"He makes five million."

"Rojas makes about five million, too," I said.

I went to the ballpark, mentioned this to Steve, and Steve and Tommy agreed to talk about it at the winter meetings. It was one of the notes that Frank received, and he was excited. When he was the Mets GM in 1992, he had given Bonilla a $29 million contract. Bonilla had been traded a couple times since and was older, but Frank thought it would be a good idea to get him back. We went to a meeting with the Dodgers. Tommy was no longer the GM, and Kevin Malone was negotiating for the Dodgers. Frank, Carm Fusco, and I sat down with Malone and did the mating dance.

"How was your winter?"

"How is your team?"

"How is your health?"

"How is your owner?"

"By the way, do we match up with anything?"

"What's the possibility of exchanging Bonilla for Rojas?" Frank asked.

"There's a lot of possibilities," said Malone.

"Do we have a clarification on the contract?" I asked.

"Yeah," said Malone. "Bonilla makes five million dollars a year."

"That's for two years, right?" I asked.

"Yeah," he said.

During my conversations with Tommy, I had said to him, "Rojas only has a one-year contract."

"Listen, if we make this trade and you don't like him," Tommy said, "I'll convince the Dodgers to take him back or pay the money."

"Great," I said.

Steve understood this, but this time Frank Cashen was in charge, and when I brought it up to him, he said, "That doesn't matter."

"Frank, oh no," I said, "that really does matter." I was getting emotional. "Ask Tommy. Tommy agreed it's one year, and if we don't like him, the Dodgers will eat the second year."

Kevin was now in charge, and it didn't matter what Tommy had said. The meeting got a little heated. There was a pause, and everyone agreed to revisit the deal the next day. We went out and walked down the hall to get a cup of coffee. I again explained the whole thing to Frank, and again Frank made it clear he didn't think it mattered.

The next morning Frank went to the meeting without me and made the trade. We got Bonilla for two years for one year of Mel Rojas. After the 1999 season, Bonilla was released. Jeff Wilpon, who was a friend of Bobby Bo, worked out the deal for the second year that paid him for the next twenty years. He's still getting paid today.

Bonilla hit .160 with 4 home runs and 18 RBIs. Like many players, Bobby was the last to know that his career was over. And like many players, he became a real pain in the ass. Bobby was bigger than most, and his problems were bigger than most.

We moved Edgardo "Fonzie" Alfonzo to second base, because we'd signed Robin Ventura as a free agent. Robin's agent, John Boggs, had been close to Lasorda, Tommy Paciorek, and me, and he got the idea that Robin playing for the Mets would be a good fit. It was. Robin was another left-handed batter and, together with John Olerud, gave our lineup balance. Robin had been one of the great college players of all time. He set the all-time consecutive hit record at Oklahoma State and finished number two to Pete Incaviglia as the best college player of the century. Robin was the real deal, and we felt we would be making a run at the pennant in 1999.

We weren't finished. We signed Rickey Henderson as a free agent. Rickey was the best all-around player I ever managed, but he was also at the end of his career. When I managed against him in his heyday in the American League, he was the most dominating player I ever saw on the field. He still showed glimpses of that.

We had Roger Cedeno, a leadoff switch-hitter. Roger could run and steal a base. He and Rickey combined for over fifty stolen bases. Even though he wasn't an everyday starter, Rickey was a very good piece on the '99 team, though there were times when he was less than the player we'd hoped for.

We got Orel Hershiser that winter, too. We were building a team, trying to do it from within, but we decided that if we could fill some of the pieces with veterans, we just might have a chance. It was going to be impossible to go up against the Braves with just a young team. The veterans would play a big part.

Orel loved the game of baseball, and he became another coach. He loved to talk baseball when he wasn't pitching. He was a thinking man's player, always contributing to what the hitters should be thinking and what the pitchers should be thinking.

Melvin Mora came into his own as a hitter that year. I used him as a utility player, who played more and more as the season went on, as did Benny Agbayani, who became a regular toward the end of the season. Benny hit .286 with 14 home runs and 42 RBIs in a part-time role. Jay Payton was a big contributor, too. Things really seemed to be coming together.

The questions of the day, and every day of the meetings: "What is going to happen with Steve?" "Is he going to be replaced?" "How are we going to get through the season?" "Is Frank going to be our general manager?"

I was told explicitly that Frank was only going to be in charge for the meetings. I had no other information, and neither did anyone else. It was in Fred Wilpon's hands. After one meeting, when everyone was talking about who was going to be the general manager, I went around the table asking everyone there if they felt they were qualified for the job. Only one exec, Gary LaRocque—the minor league director and a young guy, a terrific guy who went on to have years of success with the St. Louis Cardinals—said, "No, I still have a lot of learn." Everyone else said, "Yeah, I could step in. I can be the general manager." I saw that as a problem.

"Well, guys," I said, "what we need to do is get through these meetings. We can't be concerned about anything except getting the work done, otherwise the moment is going to pass."

Everyone except me, it seemed, wanted to be the general manager. I had execs in the organization come to me and say, "Will you back me if I go to Nelson and Fred and ask for the job?"

"Let's see what happens," I would answer.

Later that night, I was with Carm Fusco and Omar Minaya. We were walking by the hotel pool, and I was asking why certain information wasn't getting to Frank. One of those two was charged with talking to the Indians, but we did not have the Cleveland intel. The only topic they wished to talk about was Steve, and whether he was coming back.

"Listen," I said. "Fuck Steve. If we don't get this done, it isn't going to matter."

I knew if the Mets weren't successful in 1999, I wasn't going to be there, and a lot of them weren't going to be there, either. I also was wondering about the GM status, and at midnight one night I knocked on Brian Cashman's door. The Yankees GM was fighting with owner George Steinbrenner over his contract, and I asked him, "If this thing doesn't work out with Steve, is there any chance I can bring your name to the ownership?"

"Let me wait until breakfast to answer you," he said. "I'll meet you at breakfast."

When we met, Brian said he was flattered but that he was going to stay with the Yankees. I ran into a couple of the other general managers, Oakland's Billy Beane and Ed Lynch, who was with the Chicago Cubs. I was a coach with the Mets when Billy was a minor league player, and Ed and I had played together on the Mets. I knew them well. I tried to set up meetings with Oakland and the Cubs, and when they asked about Steve, I told them, "I don't know the situation."

After the winter meetings Steve was reinstated, and I was really happy for him.

Fred Wilpon called me to say, "Steve is being reinstated, I want you to know. I want you two guys to work together."

"Great," I said.

I thought it miraculous that we had gotten through the meetings in pretty good shape. We made a couple trades and signed some significant free agents. I went to Shea and met with Fred, and then I went to see Steve. I walked in feeling good, welcoming him back. He was seated at his desk, and I could see he wasn't real happy to see me. I sat down and asked him if he was okay and if I could do anything, and he said to me, "I hear you were trying to be the general manager and take my job at the meetings."

I was hurt and insulted. When I had that meeting with Gary LaRocque, after Gary said he didn't want to be the GM, I said to all the guys, "Just for the record, I don't want to be the general manager, either." Never, not on one day of my life, did I aspire to be or think of myself as the general manager. So where did that come from? It had to be either Fusco or Minaya, because someone told Steve that I had said, "Fuck Steve."

From that day on, our relationship went south. I mentioned there was a division in the press, the writers who liked me and the ones who didn't, and now they could either be for Steve or they could be for me. It became stressful, and some of the writers lived for it. They enjoyed throwing kerosene on the fire. The season had more drama as it played out.

CHAPTER 23

My Coaches Are Fired

Any season has its ups and downs, but the one for me in 1999 was more like a Busch Gardens suicidal roller coaster. It was early June, and we were playing the Yankees in an interleague three-game set. We were six games over .500, but a seven-game losing streak after Game 2 of the Yankee series put us one game under .500. After the postgame press conference, we took the bus from Yankee Stadium as the police stopped traffic for us to make the trip unimpeded.

Arriving at Shea Stadium, I jumped in the shower, and three of my coaches, Tom Robson, Bob Apodaca, and Randy Niemann, were sitting in my office waiting for me, still in uniform.

"We'll get them tomorrow," I said.

"*You'll* have to get them tomorrow," Tom said.

"What's that supposed to mean?"

"We just got fired," Randy said.

"Who said?" I asked.

"Steve."

I called Steve in his office. He wasn't in. These were my guys, and we sat in my office for hours.

"If you want, I will quit with you," I said.

"No," said Robson, "you should stay on and get us a bonus check at the end of the year."

Tom had been with me for most of my managerial career. He was the guy who filled out my lineup card, the organizer of my baseball life. He was just a terrific human being who preached what I thought was just the right hitting philosophy. And Bob Apodaca was my minor league pitching coach in Norfolk.

The next day, a Sunday, I had a meeting scheduled in the morning at the Westchester Country Club with my good friend Bobby Castrignano to discuss my idea of starting an internet business. Without any sleep, and feeling pretty miserable, I met with Bobby and other potential investors. Before the others arrived, Bobby emphatically talked me out of whatever thoughts I had about quitting the team. I pitched the business to Anthony Scaramucci, Glen Fuhrman, and Doug Romano, and raised $250,000. After lunch I went to Yankee Stadium for our Sunday night game.

I met Steve as we were walking to the pregame press conference. I asked, "What's this all about? I don't agree with what you're doing." Together we met the entire New York press corps, and Steve explained the firing of my coaches. I sat quietly and said nothing.

As the press conference ended and I was walking off the stage, Murray Chass of the *New York Times,* who by this time had become my personal nemesis, said, "Why didn't you show some loyalty to your coaches, if they were such good guys, and quit?"

"I thought about that," I said, "but they wanted me to stay and turn the thing around."

"Yeah," Chass said. "You've played fifty-five games and have fifty-five more before September first. Can you turn it around by then?"

As I was walking off the podium, talking over my shoulder, I said, "Yeah, we'll go forty and fifteen."

"And what if you don't?" asked Chass.

229

"I'll quit," I said. What a blackhearted fuck he was.

We went out and won the game against the Yankees. A few days later, I had new coaches: Dave Wallace, who had been the Dodgers pitching coach; Mickey Brantley, the Mets minor league hitting coordinator; and Al Jackson. Dave was a Connecticut guy and one of Tommy Lasorda's favorite people. Sandy Koufax, Fred Wilpon's friend from high school, was a great supporter of Dave. Fred and Sandy were teammates on the Lafayette High School baseball team, and Fred always claimed he, not Sandy, was the number-one starter. I knew Mickey from spring training, and Tom Robson had shared our hitting philosophy with him. Al, a lifelong Met and one of the nicest guys in baseball, replaced Randy Niemann in the bullpen.

I didn't know what the story was with these coaches. Were they there to give Steve information? Were they there to get me fired? Or were they just coaches? A lot was going through my mind. I was trying to be polite, but I wasn't happy with the situation.

After the firing, we got off to a good start, winning that Sunday night game against the Yankees with the help of a Mike Piazza home run off Roger Clemens. We won the next two games against Toronto, and I was hoping we were on our way to 40 wins in the next 55 games.

In the fourth game, on June 9, David Wells, pitching for the Blue Jays, started the ninth inning with a three-run lead. Robin Ventura got a big hit in the bottom half of the ninth to tie the game. In the twelfth inning, with a runner on base, I called a pitchout. Piazza went to catch it, and Randy Marsh, the umpire behind the plate, started waving his arms as Mike threw to second. I thought someone had called time-out. Mike started arguing with him, and I ran out of the dugout to keep Mike from being thrown out, not yet understanding the call. I asked the umpire what was going on.

"I called a catcher's balk," he said.

On the advice of Sharkey Laureno, from the time I was fifteen, I read the rulebook twice a year. I had read about the catcher's balk but had never seen it called. It was an obscure call which had never been called in my major league career. I couldn't believe what was happening. The runner was awarded second base, and the batter was awarded first. I was beside myself. Even though I hadn't slept much the last few days, I was trying to be on my best behavior, because the spotlight was on me. I knew if I did anything radical, like punch the umpire on the chin, I'd give the Mets a reason to fire me. So after calming down Piazza, I asked Randy if I could get thrown out for what I was thinking.

"No," he said.

I then told him what I was thinking. I said it was a horseshit call, and he was fucking horseshit for making the call. Nothing more needed to be said. I was ejected.

Now I had the dilemma of who to turn the game over to. I needed someone to manage in my place. My trust and knowledge of my three new coaches was limited. I gave the lineup card to Dave Wallace. I stormed into the clubhouse, and when I got there, I threw a chair across the room and yelled something in frustration. Robin Ventura happened to be there. I had pinch-run for him, because while Robin had a lot of skills, putting his left foot in front of his right foot in rapid fashion wasn't one of them.

"What the hell are you doing here?" Robin wanted to know.

"I just got thrown out of the game," I said.

Orel Hershiser then came running into the clubhouse.

"I'll be your runner," he said.

That meant he would run down the runway to the dugout to take my game instructions to Wallace.

"Nah, the hell with it," I said. "Let them do whatever they're going to do."

"No," Orel said, "they don't even know who's in our bullpen."

It was true they weren't as versed in the makeup of the bullpen as Orel was.

"Why don't you go down to the dugout?" Robin asked me.

"Because they'll throw me out of the league if I go down there."

"Yeah," he said, "but take off your uniform and put on these sunglasses."

He threw me a pair of dark sunglasses.

"Yeah," said Orel. "And put on this hat."

He threw me a hat that wasn't a Mets hat.

"Pull down the hat, put the glasses on, and go on down there," Orel said. "You won't be in uniform."

I walked into the trainer's room to look in the mirror to see what I looked like. On the table below the mirror were little black adhesive strips used to reduce the sun's glare during day games. I took a couple of them and put one on the right side and one on the left side under my nose, where a mustache would grow. I looked in the mirror. I looked over at Orel and Robin, and they said in unison, "They'll never know."

The plan was for Orel to stand on the stairs of the dugout in front of me to block the view of the umpires. It was a good plan, except I was in full view of a TV camera that filmed from the third-base side of the infield. In the thirteenth inning I was recognized on television. The announcer, Fran Healy, an ex-player, had a good sense of humor and was amused by my disguise.

"Oh," he said, "it looks like Bobby Valentine has returned."

When I got to the dugout, I knew I had done the right thing, because when most of the guys looked over and saw me, they were laughing. Even the stoic John Olerud cracked a smile. It was rare for John to show that much emotion.

Ah, I'm doing the right thing, I thought. *Maybe everyone's going to loosen up.*

In the bottom of the fourteenth inning, Rey Ordonez got the game-winning hit. Everyone ran out on the field, and I went out on the field in my disguise. As the umpires walked off, two of them saw me. They smiled and gave me a thumbs up. However, the one and only Murray Chass wasn't going to stand for it. He decided that this was the most despicable, disrespectful thing that anyone had ever done on a baseball diamond, and he let his voice be known in his column the next day. The league office had to respond.

I was summoned to the principal's office. Leonard Coleman was the president of the National League, and he sent me a fax that said I was going to be fined $10,000 and suspended three days. Along with my father-in-law, Ralph Branca, I went to see Leonard. Ralph knew Leonard better than I did, from their association with the Jackie Robinson Foundation. After a thirty-minute conversation, Leonard said, "I will reduce it, but I can't cancel it." He reduced the fine to $5,000 and the suspension to two games.

"Do me a favor," I said. "Allow me not to serve the suspension on the road, because the pressures of the other guys managing might just crack the whole team. Could I split my suspension between two cities?" He agreed.

My disguise became a focal point of some writers, who continuously asked me for the rest of the season, "How could you disrespect the game?" My answer was that I was trying to bring levity to a tense situation.

I served my suspension, one game in Cincinnati and one game in St. Louis. I was allowed to be with the team during batting practice, but as soon as batting practice was over, I had to put on my civilian clothes and stay out of sight. I went up to a suite to watch the game. I completed my suspension and returned home on June 20 with our record at 39–31. We had gone 12–3 toward my objective of 40–15.

During the next home stand, Robin Ventura needed a day off, and the only other third baseman on the roster was Bobby Bonilla. After batting practice, I was walking to the dugout with Bobby Bo, who said he didn't want to play. I told him he was the only healthy guy we had to play third. It was minutes before the national anthem. I said the team needed him and that if he wasn't going to play, he should tell the starting pitcher himself.

"No," Bobby said. "I'm not going to play."

We stood on the top step of the dugout for the national anthem, and I sent someone to get a new lineup card. I was standing next to John

Stearns, my coach, a tough guy. Bonilla was standing a couple of players away. I was hot, and I knew Bonilla was hot, and I said to Stearns under my breath, "Dude, tell me something. If I hit him with the first punch, is he going to go down?"

There was a long pause. John looked at me and said, "I don't think so, Bobby." Then he said, "Don't worry, I'm here for you."

I was sure Bonilla and I would come to blows as soon as the national anthem was over, but it was Korea Day at Shea, and we first had to stand for the Korean national anthem. After that, Bonilla jumped down into the dugout and hightailed it to the clubhouse. According to Charley Samuels, our clubhouse guy, Bonilla took a chair and threw it in anger at the door of my office. From that day until the day they knocked Shea Stadium down, that office door had a big dent in it. Right above the dent, it read Manager's Office.

I had never seen Melvin Mora play third, but I put him in and tried to cool my heels. I realized I had a situation. I complained about it to Steve Phillips, but he said he wouldn't release Bonilla until after the season.

"You won't have to worry about it next year," he said.

That got me to thinking. *Is that because they're going to get rid of Bonilla, or is it because they're going to get rid of me?*

CHAPTER 24

We Come So Close

A t the All-Star break in 1999, our record was 50–39. Just before the break we had another three-game set against the Yankees. If we were to have a chance to play them again in 1999, it could only be in the World Series. To do this, we had to get through the Atlanta Braves.

The Braves were an incredible team. They had three Hall of Fame starting pitchers: Tom Glavine, Greg Maddux, and John Smoltz. They had a relief pitcher having a Hall of Fame season in John Rocker. They had a well-rounded offense that was led by all-time Mets killer Larry "Chipper" Jones. This team had won the National League East four consecutive years, and would go on to win it eleven years in a row.

We had a heated rivalry, and one bone of contention was what the Braves did with the batter's box. As soon as the Braves catcher came out to start the game, he would erase the lines of the batter's box. He did it every game. My players would come back to the dugout complaining that the balls that were called on them were not strikes. They were outside pitches.

Mike Piazza went as far as saying he couldn't reach a couple pitches that Tom Glavine threw him. You could see it on the videotape.

We weren't the only team that complained. It was a running complaint. Maybe I complained louder than others. Maybe I yelled from the dugout to get the attention of the umpires, but the fact was, when we played the Braves in Atlanta, we couldn't win. It was very frustrating, and there was no love lost.

Bobby Cox, the Braves manager, had a way of creating an environment that intimidated the umpires. Rarely was I thrown out of a game complaining about balls and strikes. Early in my career when I was a coach, it seemed that when I complained about balls and strikes, it only made things worse. I had a loud voice, and if I complained about a pitch being low, the next pitch would be lower, and the umpire would call it a strike. I felt the umpires were human, that they made mistakes. I would argue about plays I thought I could get changed, or I'd make a point to get the next one called in our favor.

Bobby Cox, on the other hand, from the first pitch of the game was all over the umpires arguing balls and strikes. He dictated what the strike zone was going to be, and he got thrown out four or five times more than anybody else, mainly for arguing balls and strikes. I actually marveled at that, and I was jealous that he could get away with it, that he could control the strike zone and that his pitchers benefited from it.

John Smoltz didn't do that as much because he had stuff. He came into the game and tried to dominate, but Maddux, Glavine, Denny Neagle, and Mike Remlinger were really good pitchers who figured out how to game the system. Sabermetrics will tell you that the pitch on the 1-and-1 count is the most important of the at bat. Whenever it was 1 and 1, the Braves catcher would crouch off the plate a few inches, and Maddux and Glavine and a couple others had an incredible ability of hitting the catcher's glove perfectly. With Bobby all over the umpire on that call, the Braves would get that call. The count would go to 1 and 2, instead of 2 balls and 1 strike. The advantage went to Atlanta. It was a game within a game, and the Braves won that game, and I regret I wasn't able to combat that.

Returning to the critical 55 games that were to determine my future, after a win against the Brewers on August 4, our record was 66–43; 39–15 over our last 54 games. I came to Shea Stadium for the next game, ironically against the Dodgers, committed that I would resign if we lost. I would keep my word in the Murray Chass challenge, even though our record was 23 games above .500. With Piazza and Olerud hitting back-to-back home runs, rookie Octavio Dotel starting, and Armando Benítez closing, we won one of the most personally gratifying games of my career, 2–1, and had achieved my 40–15 prediction.

We had our sights on the division championship with twelve games to play in September—six against Atlanta, three against Philadelphia, and three against Pittsburgh. Atlanta had two more wins than us, at 92. Cincinnati, our competition for the wild-card playoff spot, had two less wins. We proceeded to lose seven straight games, three to Atlanta. This left us holding on to a wild-card chance. On September 29, we were described as a "sinking ship." After taking two of three games from Atlanta, with three games of the season remaining, we were out of the division race and two games behind Cincinnati for the wild-card spot. The last games were at home against Pittsburgh. Cincinnati was playing St. Louis. We needed to win three and they needed to lose at least two for us to have a chance at the playoffs. We went 2–0 and they went 1–1 in our respective series, going into the last day of the season. A win for us and a loss for them would tie us for the wild-card spot.

Orel Hershiser started the last game. We had great relief work from Dennis Cook and Pat Mahomes (the father of All-Pro, Super Bowl-winning quarterback Patrick).

The Pirates' Kris Benson was spectacular, allowing one hit and one run in seven and a third innings. The score was tied in the bottom of the ninth. We had 50,000 screaming fans at Shea Stadium, and we loaded the bases on a single by Melvin Mora, a single by Fonzie, and an intentional walk to John Olerud. Mike Piazza came to the plate. Pirates pitcher Brad

Clontz came into the game, and his first pitch was wide of the catcher and rolled to the screen. Melvin came in to score the winner. It was reported in the papers as Mike's "most important at-bat of the year." Mike finished the regular season with 40 home runs and 124 RBIs.

Our victory came on October 3, which was the same day that my father-in-law Ralph Branca threw that home-run pitch to Bobby Thomson to lose the '51 pennant. His was in a must-win situation. We were in a must-win situation. It was not a good day in Branca family history. But here I had my first chance to get into the playoffs, and I got the win. We finished the season 96–66, the same as the Cincinnati Reds, prompting a playoff game to determine who would win the wild-card berth. We had survived to play a one-game playoff against those talented Reds, led by Barry Larkin, Sean Casey, and Greg Vaughn. We lost the coin flip and had to play the game in Cincinnati. This was the biggest game of my managerial career and my first postseason appearance.

We scored two runs in the first inning on a hit by Rickey and a home run by Fonzie. In the third, Fonzie walked and John Olerud doubled him home. We scored two more runs on bases-loaded walks to Mike Piazza and Robin. Al Leiter pitched one of the iconic games of his career, shutting out the Reds on two hits in a 5–0 victory. The Mets were in the playoffs for the first time in eleven years.

We had our work cut out for us against the Arizona Diamondbacks, a team of talented left-handed pitchers. We were only four games above .500 against left-handers. We were thirty games over .500 against right-handers. The odds were against us. We were playing in our third different city in three days. We went from New York to Cincinnati and then to Phoenix to face Randy Johnson.

When we got to the playoffs, Joel Sherman from the *New York Post* thought that Arizona manager Buck Showalter was the greatest thing since sliced bread. He got to know Buck when he was the Yankees manager, and he felt that Buck should have been the Yankees manager for eternity.

Our starter was Masato Yoshii. We were playing a best-of-five series. The score was tied in the ninth inning, when Buck decided to leave Johnson in to pitch. It was a mistake. Two singles and a walk later, Buck took him out and Fonzie hit a grand slam to win it.

Arizona won the second game 7–1, but Rick Reed was terrific in Game 3, and we won handily 9–2.

Mike Piazza had been playing the past several weeks with an injured thumb. I felt Mike needed a day off and rested him in Game 4. I started Todd Pratt in his place. The Diamondbacks started a left-handed pitcher by the name of Brian Anderson. Al Leiter was on the mound for us. Before the game, I had to answer the question, "Why isn't Mike starting?" a dozen times. The writers felt that Mike in a wheelchair was more valuable in the lineup than a healthy Todd Pratt. But Todd was a spectacular teammate who would do anything for the team, who loved backing up Mike, who took pride in his role, and who made up for his lack of talent with great desire and heart.

The score was tied 3–3 when Todd came to bat in the bottom of the tenth to face Matt Mantei, Arizona's closer. Todd hit a ball deep to center. Arizona had a terrific center fielder by the name of Steve Finley, the master of the phenomenal catch, who routinely climbed the wall to bring balls down. Finley went up for it, and Todd was running and watching the ball. We were all standing on the top step of the dugout watching. Finley jumped for the ball, and came down to the ground in front of the fence with his glove beside his head. No one could tell whether he'd caught the ball or whether it had gone over the fence. Todd stopped running around first base. There was a groan of silence from the Shea Stadium crowd, and then Finley threw his hands up, as though he was saying, "How could I have not caught that ball?"

We realized it was a home run. We had advanced to the National League Championship Series against the hated Braves. It was one of those spectacular moments in Mets history. Had Mike Piazza hit that home run, it would have been on billboards across the country, because we had just slain the dragon. We did it with Todd Pratt, which, for me, made it even sweeter.

The NLCS, a best-of-seven series, opened in Atlanta, a place we hated to play. We lost the first two games to Maddux and Kevin Millwood, both on RBI singles by Eddie Pérez. The Braves had many offensive stars on their team. Eddie was not one of them, but somehow he was the offensive star of the first two games.

We returned to Shea Stadium down two games with a pitching matchup of Tom Glavine against Al Leiter. The Braves scored in the first inning on a throwing error by Mike Piazza. We scattered seven hits but never solved the puzzle that Glavine and closer John Rocker presented us that day. We lost 1–0. Leiter was terrific.

John Rocker, the Atlanta closer, was a lightning rod. During the season he mentioned something about all the homeless people in New York who travel on the subway and get off at Shea Stadium to watch a game. Our fans became pretty emotional, so much so that we had to cover the Braves' bullpen with tarpaulins down the left-field line so the fans couldn't throw things at Rocker in the bullpen.

When Rocker came in to pitch in the ninth inning of Game 3, all hell broke loose with the fans. The bad part: we couldn't touch him. Rocker had a really good fastball, a crazy windup, and a big overhand curve that gave us fits. I wanted to beat him so badly. It was the seventh time he shut us down that season. But we were down three games to none, and each loss was hard to take. In each game there were moments when, if things had broken a little differently, we could have won. But when we lost Game 3, we were left for dead.

In Game 4, we were down 2–1 after seven innings. In the eighth, John Rocker appeared again. This time John Olerud greeted him with a single that scored two runs. We went on to win 3–2 to keep the series alive.

Game 5 was the most amazing game I ever managed. It was action-packed every inning and seemed to last forever. Both teams had very good relief pitching and some spectacular defense. After giving up a two-run lead in the fourth inning, the game remained tied through the top of the fifteenth. The Braves scored one run in the top of the inning to take a 3–2 lead. But somehow, we never quit.

In the bottom of the inning, Shawon Dunston and Matt Franco led off with singles. Edgardo Alfonzo bunted them to second and third. Cox elected to walk Olerud. Robin Ventura, who had an uncanny habit of slugging based-loaded home runs, delivered once again in the clutch, hitting a long fly ball. There was one out, so when he hit it, I knew we had at least tied things up. Then the ball went over the fence, and most of our guys, instead of waiting for him at home plate, ran out between first and second. It was a mob scene. Todd Pratt tackled Robin after he rounded first base as two runners scored. With 55,000 people standing after a five-hour game, we lived to play another day. I tried to convince Red Foley, who was the scorekeeper, that Robin should get a home run. He was only credited with a single because he never touched second base. He had stopped between first and second when he was tackled. He did touch first, and that was the key, or he could have been called out on appeal.

We trailed Atlanta 3–2 in this best-of-seven series. Al Leiter was on the mound for Game 6. Kenny Rogers had been slated to start, but some of the coaches and players felt Al needed to get the ball. If we were going to be eliminated, let's have Al pitch. He had pitched very well in his last game. He had pitched really well in Cincinnati. He pitched well enough in Arizona. He was the man to pitch against John Smoltz, whom Atlanta pitched every chance it could.

Al said he felt good, but he had never pitched on three days' rest for me, and I normally was against that. I believed pitchers needed a certain minimal amount of time to recover. For Al, three days seemed one day short.

Al started and gave up five runs in the first. After that, it was pretty miraculous that we would take an 8–7 lead into the eighth, as Melvin Mora singled home Benny Agbayani. Pat Mahomes was really good again. Turk Wendell, Armando, and Johnny pitched well in relief, but the Braves tied us in the bottom of the eighth. The game went to extra innings, and we scored off Rocker in the top of the tenth, but then Atlanta tied it again 9–9 in the bottom of the inning.

Kenny Rogers entered to pitch the eleventh for us and gave up a double to Gerald Williams. The ball went over the bag at third and was fair by inches. He wound up on second, and now they had the middle of their order coming up. Kenny was rested. He had pitched a little in relief in the fifteen-inning game. I had Octavio Dotel, a rookie, in the bullpen, but the leadoff double was tough, and I was just rolling the dice, hoping and praying for a line drive at someone in the infield. I wasn't going to let Chipper Jones beat us, that's for sure, and I walked him intentionally. Brian Jordan, the next hitter, was really good, and with the count 2 and 0, I decided to put him on as well.

That brought Andruw Jones up with the bases loaded. Jones had maybe 700 at-bats that year and perhaps 50 walks. Jones was not a walker. He was a swinger. I really thought Kenny's changeup or sinker could get a ground ball, so we could miraculously get out of the jam. I had known Kenny since his Texas days, and he was a reliever for me and, at times, a stopper. I was confident. He was confident. But with the bases loaded and the count 3 and 2, he threw a pitch that wasn't good enough for Jones to swing at. If it had been a good sinker that had been close, I guarantee you Jones would have swung. Ball four. Take your base. The run scored. The game was over. Our season was over. We had put on a really great effort against a really good team. It was a tough loss, one of the toughest of my career.

Overall, we played with them. We might even have outplayed them. We just didn't score enough when we had to. We didn't quite have what it took to get to the World Series in 1999. Maybe we were overmatched in talent, but we sure had the heart to do it, and we had Mike Piazza—an amazing story, an amazing person, and an amazing player.

Mike had started out as a nothing baseball talent, and he became arguably the best offensive catcher ever to play the game. It came with a lot of hard work. He had a tremendous intellect. He could win *Jeopardy!* without rehearsal. He would sit in front of the TV and answer a question from the category Artwork for $1,000 and knock it out of the park. He had a lot of skills.

He also had idiosyncrasies that everyone had to understand. Mike had intense anger. He had an internal state that no one could get to at times. I'm not sure where the anger came from. Maybe because he was Italian. He had a chip on his shoulder. He was the sixty-second-round draft choice, and everyone thinks you're nothing, and every single time when you strike out, you're thinking, *Maybe they're right.* His anger was never at the other team. His anger was never at the umpires. It was always directed toward himself. Mike would punch concrete walls, really punch them. I have no idea how he didn't break his hands or fingers. I heard Lasorda once tell him, "Hit the wall with your head, because at least you can hit with a cracked head." There were dugouts with low ceilings, and I'm surprised his fist didn't go right through the top of the dugout.

We had what was called Back to the Future Day, and the Mets wore futuristic uniforms. The colors were not Mets colors, and the players' names were vertical rather than horizontal. On that day we were called the Mercury Mets, not the New York Mets, and Mike despised the whole idea. He didn't want to wear the uniform. He wanted nothing to do with it, and before you knew it, the game was over and he didn't get any hits. When he went to the clubhouse, he didn't take his one-button pullover uniform off over his head. He just grabbed the sides in front of the collar, pulled them apart, and tore the uniform right down the middle. He then flung it into the middle of the clubhouse and exclaimed that he would never be caught dead in that uniform again, not necessarily in those words. He left everyone spellbound.

I really loved that team. I loved them so much I can't even describe how much I loved them, except in the eighth inning of that final game Orel Hershiser came over to me and said, "You're not going to believe this one." Orel was one of the great competitors of all time. He was enjoying the hell out of this series. It was at the end of his career, and he'd become like a player/coach. I would bounce things off him because I still hadn't gotten to the point where I had a great relationship with my pitching coach. Not bad, but I didn't have full trust.

We were playing the game to determine whether this was it for the season. It was a close game, with 50,000 people in the stands. Every player was on the top step for every pitch thrown, except Ricky Henderson and Bobby Bonilla, who were in the clubhouse playing cards. I had thoughts that I should run into the clubhouse and demand their presence on the bench. My other thought was to pretend like it wasn't happening, make like I wished I didn't know it was happening. I did the latter, and after we lost, when we went into the clubhouse, I addressed the team and told the players how proud I was of them.

"Without a doubt," I said, "this was the best effort I had ever seen in all my years in baseball. You have nothing to be ashamed of and everything to be proud of."

The thing I was proud of in 1999, off the field, was initiating a charitable foundation. It came about at Mickey Lione's funeral and immediately was supported by his core group of friends. Driven by the inspiration that Mickey gave us all, we created the Mickey Lione Jr. Scholarship Fund for Youth Excellence. In 2003, we created the Bobby Valentine Food & Wine Extravaganza, an annual event that raised well over $1 million in its first ten years. I was able to become one of the city's best auctioneers, donating many of my treasured pieces of sports memorabilia to the event, while connecting with my hometown community of Stamford. To date, the foundation has awarded more than $1 million in scholarships to high-school-age boys and girls in Stamford, and is still going strong.

CHAPTER 25

My Big Mouth

I had been left out of a lot of the decision-making by the Mets in 1999, and in 2000 I was permitted even less access. It was a situation I had to deal with, because general managers around the league were becoming more authoritarian, creating a different model than the relationship I'd had with Tom Grieve in Texas. The new general managers wanted to make their decisions without collaboration, because by doing it that way, they became more important to the owners and started to make a lot more money. That the manager was making more money than the general manager didn't jibe well in the new world of baseball organizational charts.

It was well planned by the likes of Billy Beane. Beane and Steve Phillips had been in the minor leagues together, and now they were among the aspiring GMs who wanted to spread their wings and become the leaders of the pack. This was a real power play. It's the way it is today in most organizations. Theo Epstein became the emperor of all general managers, along with Billy Beane. It became the way of the world, which

I didn't like. Who likes change? No one. It was change for me, and not a good one.

During the winter after the 1999 season, John Olerud became a free agent. John wasn't playing the game for money. He was playing it because he could, and he was making money because he could. I knew that John intended to sign with Seattle, but I was sure that if I could corner John and talk to him, he would stay with us.

"Steve, listen," I said, "I got word that John's going to go to Seattle, because that's his home. He's from there. He played at the University of Washington, and he wants to settle." I told Steve I didn't want to accept that. I felt he could go home in three years. I knew his wife Kelly liked New York, liked John playing with the Mets. I also knew that John liked Tom Robson, and John really liked me. "I want to fly out and see him if he's at home, or I want to call him on the phone," I said.

"You can't do it," Steve said. "I'm dealing with this. You can't call him."

I was *not allowed*. I'd also been told that I wasn't going to be participating in the winter meetings. I was left to stew in a room by myself while Jim Duquette and Omar Minaya went out to talk to agents and other teams. Steve formed our team without Olerud. We gave Rey Ordonez, a spectacular-looking fielder who I didn't think was trustworthy, a three-year contract. We signed outfielder Derek Bell, whom I didn't think we needed. Two of my pet projects were outfielders Roger Cedeno and Benny Agbayani. Roger was fragile but talented. He was a switch-hitter, a very fast runner, and a good defensive outfielder with a strong arm. I thought if handled properly, he was on the verge of becoming a very, very good player. Benny came on strong the second half of '99, and I thought he should be a regular outfielder. Derek Bell precluded that. And we still had Rickey Henderson.

When I heard we had gotten Derek, I asked Steve, "What did we do that for?" All year I had to figure out how I was going to keep an eye on Derek. Derek had played in the Little League World Series, so he had a pedigree, but he was a little different—*really* different. I didn't know if he was good different or bad different. The first day of spring training, Derek walked into the coaches room while we were having a meeting. He was wearing an Adidas jumpsuit with some beautiful sneakers.

"Hey guys, how ya doing?" he said, before going around and introducing himself to everyone in the room. "I want you guys to take a look at me," he said. "Look at what I'm wearing, because if you ever see me wearing the same outfit twice, I'll buy everyone in this room a Brooks Brothers suit."

From then on, Derek never wore the same clothes. He never wore the same sneakers. Every single day—for 202 days—he came to the park in a different outfit. He wore them once and never wore them again. On every road trip, he had a different suit, with matching snakeskin shoes or boots. He spent an amazing amount of money on clothes. At the end of a home stand, he would pack up all his clothes and ship them to people he knew and to minor-leaguers. He was interesting and cool, but bizarre. Derek decided he wanted to live on a houseboat in a marina on the Hudson, and he lived with his mom, who became affectionately known as Ma Bell. She was a terrific part of our cheering section. But everything always seemed a little off with Derek. We couldn't quite put our finger on it. I played him a lot of the time, and he had some big hits for us. Late in the season he got hurt, and I was able to play Timo Pérez and Benny more often.

At the winter meetings we signed Todd Zeile. I recall Jim Duquette, Steve's assistant, calling me up in the room where we were doing research. We had our laptops out.

"We just signed Todd Zeile," he said.

"Yeah," I said, "but he doesn't play first base."

"He plays third, so of course he can play first," said Jim. It wasn't computing with me. In turmoil, I left the winter meetings a day early.

Steve had done well when he traded Roger Cedeno and Octavio Dotel for pitcher Mike Hampton. This was the deal that brought Derek Bell. Hampton was what we needed after losing Kenny Rogers, who had given us a lot of starts. We were trying to get pitchers who could supply some offense, and Mike could hit. He loved to hit and could run the bases. A really good fielder, Mike was very competitive on the mound.

We were going into the season with a starting staff of Hampton, Al Leiter, Rick Reed, Bobby Jones, and Glendon Rusch. I loved having Glendon on the team. He was a terrific guy who went out there with less than quality stuff but performed better than average more often than not. In the bullpen we were going to have Turk Wendell, Dennis Cook, and Johnny Franco, who had settled into his eighth-inning role. Armando Benítez was doing great as a closer. Life was pretty good in the bullpen. When the 2000 season began, we had a good team, on paper.

Early in the year, we traveled to Philadelphia to play the Phillies, and on April 13 I spoke at the Wharton School. In 1999 I had started an internet company, a bid-for-charity dot-com, and one of my investors was Glenn Fuhrman, a University of Pennsylvania and Wharton grad. He worked at Goldman Sachs along with another friend, Anthony Scaramucci, and when he left Goldman, he went to work for Michael Dell at MSD Capital. Glenn asked me to go and speak at Wharton, because of his affiliation. On April 13 I made a nice speech to the students about the business of baseball. As I was leaving the building and walking down the steps, a group of Penn students came running over to me. They had Mets t-shirts on.

"Hey, Bobby. How ya doing? Great to have you on campus. We pull for you every night. Love your team." They started throwing questions at me as I was walking. "Who's pitching tonight?" I told them. "Is Piazza going to play, or will he have a night off?" "I think he's in the lineup." "Why did we sign Derek Bell?"

Here was a chance to vent my frustration with the front office. I reverted to sarcasm and got in a few digs at Steve. My mother often said to me, "Bobby, please keep your mouth shut." I have to say she was not wrong.

"Because we didn't want to give Benny a chance to become a star," I told them.

"Why did you give Ordonez a multiyear contract?"

"Because we wanted to reward him for having the lowest on-base percentage and slugging percentage in the history of baseball."

"Why did you sign Todd Zeile? What happened to John Olerud?"

I said, "Because it would be too easy for us to win and have four Gold Glovers with him playing first base. We needed a challenge."

I wasn't thinking that, in the new era of social media, previously anonymous people could make names for themselves through blogging. I had no idea my smart-aleck remarks would appear on one of these students' blogs. The student's name was Brad Rosenberg. His blog name was Brad34. When I arrived at the ballpark, a reporter from the *New York Daily News* asked me, "Were you at the Wharton School today?"

"Yes," I said.

"Do you know who Brad34 is?"

"I have no idea who Brad34 is."

"He wrote some things in his blog about what you said at the Wharton School," he said.

"Really? I said all good stuff at the Wharton School."

And that was that, until that night when the story broke.

The next morning, Steve Phillips called me up and asked me if I said certain things about him in my speech at Wharton.

"No, Steve," I said. "I absolutely did not say those things in my speech."

"If you did," he said, "I'm going to come down and fire you. I want to meet with you before you go to the ballpark."

Oops.

Steve came to my room at the hotel and had me read the article from the *Daily News*. "I didn't say those things at my speech at the Wharton School of Business," I said, "and you should go and talk to the professor and find the tape. They will tell you I was talking about the business of baseball."

I got on the phone to Glenn Fuhrman, told him about the kids, and asked him to find out if there was a tape of my conversation with Brad34. "I think I'm going to get fired," I said.

"You're kidding," he said. He went, bought a newspaper, and called me back. "Oh shit," he said. "We'll find Brad before anyone else does."

I then heard from Dave Waldstein, a sports reporter at the *New York Times*. He informed me that the Mets had hired someone to find Brad34.

"Do you know who he is?" Dave asked.

"No, I don't know who he is," I said. "And for whatever it's worth, I didn't say those things in my speech."

"Sure you didn't, Bobby," he said.

The Mets hired investigators who went to the Wharton School to see if they had videotaped my speech. They had, but they debated whether to let anyone see it, so there was a delay. There was a frantic search for Brad34. That evening, the person Glenn hired found Brad, and he learned that Brad did not have a tape of our conversation. He said that I did not say those things, and he was just writing his own thoughts. Prompted by Glenn's guy, Brad told reporters, "Geez. I was just paraphrasing. I kind of made up some of the stuff I had said."

Brad was great. I never emailed him. I never talked to him again. I was sitting on pins and needles. A couple days later, the witch hunt for Brad ended, and I learned there wasn't going to be anything more to come from it. I stuck to my guns, which was that I didn't say those things in my speech. Thank God no one ever asked me, "Did you say those things walking out of the building?"

Fast-forward ten years. The craziest thing happened. I was having lunch with Marc Lisker, a corporate counsel for MSD Capital and a very good friend, and he said, "I want to introduce you to someone."

At lunch he introduced me to Brad Rosenberg, who had been hired by MSD. Amazing!

CHAPTER 26

World Series or Bust

Todd Zeile was a client of Seth and Sam Levinson. Steve Phillips seemed to have a special relationship with them. Maybe they represented the players the Mets needed. I never could figure out the attraction, but I had players whom they represented, and the Levinsons made my relationship with them much more difficult.

I remember one of my pitchers coming into my office to say, "Gee, I thought when I came here, I was going to be playing for the devil incarnate. It turns out you're more like an angel."

This was after I had put one of the Levinsons up against the wall and held him by the throat for trying to ruin my reputation. This was also after I had sarcastically referenced Todd to Brad34.

A month after we signed Todd, we were doing our winter caravan outreach to fans. The Mets were at the hospital greeting sick kids and making appearances to drum up season ticket sales. Todd flew in from California for the events. We went to a police station, then to a hospital, and then to the All Star Café in Times Square to have lunch and a live radio interview with *Mike and the Mad Dog*. When we played against Todd, I had an image of him being a blue-collar, right-handed hitter who was going to battle at the plate and be upset if he didn't do well, but he always kept on an even keel. I arrived at All Star Café and went around to all the fans saying, "Hello, how are you doing? Thanks for coming out. Hey, how ya doing?"

This guy who looked like a movie star was sitting on a high-top table. His hair had nice gel in it, and he had a cool shirt on and a real hip sport coat. I went over to him and said, "Hey, how are you doing? I'm Bobby Valentine. Thanks for being here."

"Oh hi," he said, "How are you doing? I'm Todd Zeile, and I'm going to be playing for you this year."

Oh, I thought to myself, *what a wonderful first step that was.* I am embarrassed about that to this day.

We had won a lot of games in 1999. We had made the playoffs and we had things going in the right direction, and my contract was going to run out at the end of 2000. My agent, Tony Attanasio, approached the Mets during the winter to try to get an extension, because if anyone outside of Walt Alston and Tommy Lasorda manages in the big leagues with a one-year contract, he is called a "lame duck." When that happens, you're just waiting for people to take shots at you.

The first day of spring training 2000, Fred Wilpon showed up and held a news conference, which he did periodically. But this press conference was different, because in it he said very emphatically that I was not going to get a new contract unless I took the Mets to the World Series. Fred loved the way I managed on the field, but he felt there was too much controversy surrounding the comments I made every now and then, and because Steve Phillips was his boy.

Steve and I had our situation, and during the winter meetings it didn't seem as though it was getting all that much better. Our job descriptions seemed more separate by the day. Most of my little guys who were a big part of the '99 team were gone, and so were my original coaches. I had to build another support staff around me. Hearing Wilpon's edict of having to reach the World Series to keep my job wasn't exactly what I expected. But I put my concerns aside and prioritized building a successful team.

Roster decisions were made throughout the spring. This spring training would be shorter than normal, because the Mets and Cubs would be playing an opening series for the first time in history outside of North America. The plan was to leave Florida nine days before the other teams broke. We would go to Japan for three exhibition games against Japanese major league teams, then open our regular season with two games against the Cubs in the Tokyo Dome.

There was a debate on who would be the twenty-fifth man on our roster. My vote went to Benny Agbayani. Steve wanted more pitching. Benny was saved by the bell when the commissioner allowed each team to take a twenty-seven-man roster to Japan.

We opened the regular season with a loss. In the second game, with the score tied at 1–1, I sent Benny to the plate as a pinch-hitter. The bases were loaded, and on a 3–2 count, he cleared them with a grand slam. We flew back to the U.S. with a .500 record for our home opener at Shea Stadium against the Padres.

Early in the season, I was not the only one unhappy about my contract situation: so was Rickey Henderson. He had not been given a raise after a fine season, and a controversial clubhouse card game to end it. Push came to shove with Rickey right after my birthday, which is May 13. For the third time in his short Met career, Rickey hit a ball that he thought was a home run but wasn't. Ricky had a stylish way of leaving the batter's box and slowly jogging toward the dugout on the first-base side, doing a little pick, grabbing his jersey, picking it a couple times as he jogged to first. That meant he had picked out a good pitch and hit a home run. The ball bounced off the wall, and Rickey was standing on first base when the left fielder threw the ball in to second. He had been warned in a game against Atlanta the year before. This time, I talked to him in the dugout and took him out of the game.

That's your third strike, I thought. *And we play with three strikes.* After the game, I talked with Steve about what we were going to do. "We've got to find him another home," I said. We had tried to trade him during spring training. I just felt we had too many outfielders.

"No," said Steve, "you've got to live with him. You've got to get him to play the way he played last year."

"If you had given him a raise," I said, "he'd probably be happier."

Rickey's last straw came soon thereafter, when he tried to intimidate a young Andrew Marchand of the *New York Post*. Marchand asked Rickey why he didn't run, and whether he would run harder the next time.

"I run at that speed when I hit a home run," Rickey said, "and that was a home run."

Well, it wasn't a home run. The wind had blown it back. When he hit it, I thought it was a home run, but we had crazy, swirling winds at Shea, so this supposed home run became a single. One of my managerial practices in a situation where reprimanding a player is necessary is to do it in private, the first time. When the second time occurs for the same breach, I do the reprimand in front of his peers. A third time and I do it publicly.

"It's just unacceptable behavior," I said at my press conference, "and because it's been repeated, I'm at a loss as to how to correct it."

Rickey had also said to Marchand, "If you weren't such a young punk, I'd kick your ass."

Marchand wrote about it, other reporters talked about it, and when Rickey got to the ballpark the next day, Steve decided to release him.

As for Rickey: I was the manager of possibly the greatest player to ever play the game. He had some ability left in the tank, but it was time for him to move on. I had a guy who would show glimpses of brilliance. He knew that age was fighting him and that he no longer had the desire he once had, and that made the decision to release him easy for me. It was tougher for the organization, because they had to eat his $1.9 million salary.

Moving past Rickey, it was smooth sailing until July, when we lost Rey Ordonez for the season to an injury. Kurt Abbott was our backup shortstop. We also had Melvin Mora, who was versatile and I felt could play an adequate shortstop. I committed publicly to play Melvin on a regular basis, but soon thereafter, Melvin was traded to Baltimore for Mike Bordick. I was fine with the trade. Mike was the opposite of Ordonez. He was consistent and reliable on defense, and his offense was much better than Rey's. We'd put together a very nice team. We remade our infield with Bordick and Zeile, who was learning the first-base position and getting big hits. Ventura and Fonzie were having solid seasons offensively and playing spectacular defense. And Leiter, Hampton, and Glendon Rusch were a trio of highly dependable left-handed starters, with Bobby Jones and Rick Reed adding quality from the right side. Our left-right combo in the bullpen—Johnny Franco and Dennis Cook from the left, and Armando Benítez and Turk Wendell from the right—gave us versatility and quality every day. Pat Mahomes was our swing man, after going 8–0 the previous year out of the bullpen. The guys in the outfield were major contributors, without having household names. We won 94 games, which was good enough to capture the wild-card spot, pitting us against the Giants, who led the league with a 97–65 record, in a best-of-five series, while the Cardinals played the Braves.

The powerful Giants featured Barry Bonds, Jeff Kent, and manager Dusty Baker. We lost the first game in San Francisco 5–1. Hampton was not as sharp as normal. We knew we needed to win Game 2 for a road split before heading home. We had a 4–1 lead in the ninth when their first baseman, J. T. Snow, hit a towering fly ball against Benítez down the right-field line that just scraped the foul pole for a three-run homer to tie the game. Armando had saved forty-one games during the regular season. When Snow hit it, I was sure it was foul, but it never hooked. Usually, the ball hooks and you say, "Damn, he just missed it." Instead, I said, "Oh damn, it's a three-run home run." We were one game down, and the Giants fans in Pacific Bell Park were going crazy. We were looking at being down two games to none, and a long plane ride home.

In the top of the tenth, Darryl Hamilton hit a double, and Jay Payton scored him with a single. With a one-run lead in the bottom of the inning, Johnny Franco, who had been our setup man most of the year, faced

Barry Bonds with two outs. Bonds represented the tying run, and Johnny ran the count to 3 and 2, and then threw him an off-speed pitch that caught the inside corner of the plate for a called strike three to end the game. We had a relaxing plane ride home. We had gone from "Oh God, Barry is coming up," to getting on the plane with smiles on our faces.

Barry Bonds was the best hitter I ever saw. He was the best hitter when he was small, the best hitter when he was medium, and the best hitter when he was large. Barry had the best pitch recognition of any hitter. My God, one year he walked 232 times! When you threw Barry a strike, he knew it was a strike. He choked up on a small bat, so he was only using about twenty-eight inches of wood, and he was able to center the ball whenever it was a strike, and do damage better than anybody I ever saw. And Barry was a joy to watch. Every time he came up, I enjoyed watching him hit, and it didn't matter what the outcome was. Some guys—George Brett was one—brought an entertainment value when they came up to the plate. Mike Piazza had it, though in a more subtle way. For us to get Barry out was incredible.

In Game 3 we had one of our most dependable starters, Rick Reed, on the mound. Their starter, Russ Ortiz, had a no-hitter going for six innings. Timo Pérez, starting in place of Derek Bell, who had pulled a hamstring, singled in Mike Bordick to make the score 2–1 Giants after seven innings. We tied it in the eighth on Fonzie's double. Then in the bottom of the thirteenth, with one out, Benny gave the standing-room-only crowd at Shea the memory of a lifetime with a walk-off home run that rocked that stadium. You could hear the roar in the entire tri-state area. You can imagine how happy I was. A guy who wasn't supposed to make the team gave us a 2–1 lead in the best-of-five series.

I had to make a decision before Game 4 as to who was going to be our starter. Hampton could come back on short rest, or I could go with Glendon Rusch or Bobby Jones. I was getting advice from everywhere—all the members of the front office, the fans, and the press. Bobby Jones wasn't getting many votes. The night before, I was asked to announce my starting pitcher.

"I'm not going to make that decision until tomorrow," I said. That was controversial, because everyone thought it was gamesmanship.

Bobby V isn't announcing his starting pitcher. What's up with that?

There were sly comments about it, but in truth I couldn't figure out whom to choose, and I wanted to sleep on it. As I walked into the ballpark, I still didn't know what I was going to do. I walked down the tunnel from the parking lot under the bowels of Shea, past the garbage dump, past the batting cage that was rat-infested, and around the corner to the clubhouse. As I got there, I ran into Bobby Jones and his wife Kristi. I knew she was going to say something to me about who was pitching, and I wasn't sure what I was going to say.

Before I got a word out of my mouth, Kristi said, emphatically, "Pitch Bobby today. He's going to pitch the game of his life." She looked me right in the eye, and I gave her a hug and a kiss on the cheek. I walked into the clubhouse, grabbed a game ball out of the ball bag, and went over to put the ball in Bobby's locker.

As Bobby was walking back with some food from the snack room, I said, "The ball's in your locker. Go get 'em. Have the game of your life."

Bobby Jones pitched a complete-game one-hitter. It may have been the best game any Mets pitcher ever pitched in postseason play. Kristi predicted it.

We had eliminated the Giants. I was with some friends in my office after the game when Bonds, dressed impeccably in a green suit and matching tie, came over and congratulated me. I'd always liked Barry, and now I knew why. Our strategy going into the series had been to keep the hitters in front of Barry off the bases. My philosophy was, Let's not waste a lot of time on how we're going to get the Hall of Famers out, because they don't get out that often. Let's get the guys hitting before him out, because it frustrates Barry to hit with no men on base. In this series, Barry even swung at some pitches out of the strike zone. I don't know if I ever saw him do that before. He did it because he was trying to do more than was humanly possible.

Our next opponent was the powerful St. Louis Cardinals, led by manager Tony La Russa, who were coming off a three-game sweep of the defending National League champion Braves. La Russa had been the manager of the White Sox when I managed my first game against him. I was thirty-five years old then, and I was fifty now. Tony and I had many battles over the years when he managed the A's during my Rangers tenure. Now we were meeting for the NL championship in a best-of-seven series. I was always trying to stay ahead of the curve, and Tony was always the smartest guy in the room, whom everyone bowed down to. I had a lot of desire to beat him any time I could. There wasn't a lot of love lost.

Cardinals star Mark McGwire was injured and was not going to be in the starting lineup. Tony was going to use him as the ultimate decoy. He was going to make sure I worried about Mark pinch-hitting. The only problem for him was that I had McGwire's kryptonite: Turk Wendell. It seemed like Turk could strike McGwire out at will. To our good fortune, McGwire never had an at-bat in the series.

We weren't very good against left-handed pitching during the season, and the Cardinals had a left-hander, Rick Ankiel, who had electric stuff. I was really concerned about him. The rest of their starting staff were righties, and we were really strong against right-handed pitching. We beat right-hander Darryl Kile 6–2 in the first game in St. Louis. Mike Hampton was sharp. Ankiel started Game 2 for the Cards, and to our surprise he was incredibly wild. He lasted two-thirds of an inning, giving up one hit, three walks, and two wild pitches. He left with the score 2–0 Mets. In a see-saw struggle, our right-handed hitters did plenty of damage, and we eventually won 6–5 on a Jay Payton RBI single in the ninth.

Ankiel wasn't the factor we thought we had to deal with, but there was still plenty of work to do. We went home for the next three games with a 2–0 lead in the series. Although the Cards won Game 3 by the score of 8–2, we scored ten runs to win in Game 4, and we clinched the pennant with a 7–0 rout in Game 5, behind Mike Hampton's shutout. Before the game, Mike was talking about "pitching the game of my life," and he did just that. He pitched a complete game, allowing just three hits and one walk, while striking out eight. Hampton was on a mission. He had a football mentality, showing his emotions. He didn't mind grunting when he threw one hard. He didn't mind swinging hard at the plate. When he got on a roll, it was not easy to get him off his horse. On that day, he wasn't getting off that horse. He was spectacular and for his great effort was named the MVP of the National League Championship Series.

Fonzie also continued to hit. Fonzie and Robin hit well in those playoffs, and Timo Pérez set a record for runs scored. It seemed like he was on base every time I looked up. Timo played great defense in right field and was the spark. From the time he got in the lineup, he was a difference-maker. Timo had moved to center field for Jay Payton, who had been beaned the inning before, and Timo caught a fly ball for the final out of the game. We were going to the World Series.

When the game ended, the whole Mets team, led by Mike Piazza, jogged slowly and joyfully all the way around the stadium. We wanted to make sure the people sitting in the bleachers got the same appreciation as the ones in the expensive seats. Our fans were tremendous, and we wanted to acknowledge them.

When we won, we didn't know whether we'd be playing the Yankees or the Mariners. The Yankees had won two straight World Series, sweeping each 4–0, but they had stumbled to the finish line at the end of the regular season. They seemed to be vulnerable.

CHAPTER 27

The World Series

The Mets were in the World Series for the first time since 1986. Everything I did was exciting. Everywhere I went it was exciting. There was a buzz, an aura. I was living on the Upper East Side in 1999 and 2000, on the corner of Second Avenue and Seventy-Third Street. My son Bobby was thinking of going to NYU, so we spent a couple of summers in the city walking the streets, so he could get a feel for the environment. Everybody was in Subway Series mode. It was like a ten-day Mardi Gras. Everyone—waiters, doormen, cab drivers, truck drivers, hostesses—was into the same thing, and it was really inspiring. There had not been a Subway World Series since the Yankees played the Brooklyn Dodgers in 1956.

In New York, a manager is always busy managing. Managing in New York for the World Series was something else entirely. There were more interviews than you can imagine. I hardly had the time to collect my thoughts, and before I knew it, we were doing battle with the New

York Yankees, a team that had won twelve straight World Series games over three of the past four years.

I had played for and against Joe Torre and managed against him, and before the first game, we met at home plate. I had never seen him so worried. They had won two consecutive World Series, and yet I felt he was worried that if he didn't win this Series, Steinbrenner might do something stupid like dismantle the team or fire him.

"It doesn't seem like you're enjoying this, Joe," I said.

"What the fuck is there to enjoy?" he said.

I got it. He was working for George Steinbrenner.

Interleague play started in 1997, so we were familiar with the circus environment that prevailed when we played each other. *But this was the World Series,* and the first two games were at Yankee Stadium.

Al Leiter started Game 1 against Andy Pettitte. We knew Pettitte inside out. Mookie Wilson, our first-base coach, dealt with base runners. He told the players that Pettitte had such a good pickoff move that we suggested base runners just stand on the base when he pitched. His move was that deceptive. Even so, Pettitte picked off Mike Piazza and, later in the game, Kurt Abbott. To give up two outs to the Yankees was ridiculous. Then there was a play where Todd Zeile hit a ball that looked like it was going foul. It rolled slowly down the third-base line. Scott Brosius stood over it and let it keep rolling. Todd never left the batter's box. Then the ball rolled fair, Brosius picked it up, and threw Todd out. That was a third out we gave them. Then, in the infamous sixth inning, Todd hit a ball that everyone thought was a home run. The Mets fans in Yankee Stadium started cheering. The Yankee fans stood in silence. Timo, who started the game because of his spectacular play in the previous two series, was on first base when Todd hit the ball. He slowed coming around second, because he was sure it was a home run, but then the ball hit smack dab at the top corner of the outfield fence. Everything seemed to stop for a second, as the ball rebounded into left field. David Justice, the left fielder, made a quick recovery and threw the ball to the infield. Derek Jeter was late getting to his relay spot because he thought it was a home run, but he caught the ball on a sprint going toward the third-base line and threw a strike to Jorge Posada at home plate. Timo slid in. Posada made a high tag. Out at the plate. I believe to this day if Timo had either stayed at third or scored, Joe Torre would have gone to his bullpen, where the Yankees were vulnerable. We thought we could get to the setup pitchers in front of Mariano Rivera.

The game was a scoreless tie in the bottom of the sixth when pesky José Vizcaíno led off with a single. After a walk to Chuck Knoblauch, left-handed-hitting David Justice drove in both runners with a double to left-center. Yankee Stadium erupted. We were down 2–0 with three innings to play.

We had a World Series-caliber team that was able to rise to the occasion the entire season. I went to the bench for the first time in the series, and Bubba Trammel drove in Agbayani and Payton to tie the game. Once again, we got up off the floor and scored three runs in the top of the seventh to take the lead. In the bottom of the ninth, our lead remained 3–2. Armando came in to face Paul O'Neill, a great battler and a great hitter. Armando threw some unhittable pitches that O'Neill somehow fouled off with weak swings. Several of those pitches should have been put in play for weak outs. Instead, O'Neill walked, and that started the rally that tied the game and gave the Yankees some life. We basically gave the Yankees four outs in the first World Series game. Nonetheless, the game was close. We lost 4–3 in the twelfth inning when, with the bases loaded, José Vizcaíno, on a first-pitch slider, got a single to left off of Turk.

The Yankees beat us 6–5 in the second game. This was the Roger Clemens game at Yankee Stadium. Roger was the best pitcher I ever saw up close and personal. He won seven Cy Young Awards. But the one batter Roger couldn't get out was Mike Piazza. Mike, who was also a great competitor, won a lot of the battles with Roger. Roger never could properly throw an inside fastball to Mike, and he'd get behind in the count and Mike would just crush him.

When we played the interleague series during the regular season, Roger got tired of not being able to throw the ball inside on Mike, and he hit him in the head with a fastball. It made a loud sound, and Mike went down. He probably was concussed. We didn't have a concussion protocol then. Several times the benches threatened to clear, but we never came to blows. There wasn't even any good name-calling. Roger settled down after that, and in part because we were worried, he was going to hit someone else in the head, he shut us down in that game.

Roger threw a two-hit shutout for the first eight innings in Game 2 of the World Series, striking out nine and walking no one. But the part of the game everyone still remembers was Piazza's at-bat in the first inning. It was his first at-bat against Roger since his regular-season beaning. Roger threw an inside fastball that was in between Mike and the plate, and Mike swung, and the bat broke in half. The top part of the bat went propelling toward the mound. The ball went into foul territory. Roger picked up the fat part of the bat as though it was a baseball, and flung it, trying to skip it, only to have it bounce in Mike's direction, about three strides up the line. It looked like Roger had thrown the bat at Mike. Everyone was in total disbelief. No one had ever seen anything like that. Everyone was waiting for a confrontation, but nothing of note occurred, other than everyone in our dugout screaming and yelling at everyone in their dugout.

Before the World Series. the commissioner, Bud Selig, had addressed both teams in their clubhouses. "This is New York against New York," Selig said. "This is the eyes of the baseball world upon us. This is our crown jewels, and we'd like to have everyone on their best behavior. We understand about the rivalry. We understand tempers can flare. Bobby V," he said to me in front of the team, "go easy on the umpires, and don't get thrown out. It's not a good look."

Everyone on the Mets chuckled a little. He was warning us about the Clemens situation. He didn't want the game between two of the premier franchises to wind up in a wrestling match. And here Clemens had thrown a bat at Mike, and everyone was wondering, *How do we react to that?*

I went out and soft-spoke to the umpires to try to get Clemens thrown out of the game. "It's a deadly weapon that Roger was throwing at Mike," I said. Personally, I didn't think it was any big deal. He was throwing a twenty-ounce piece of wood toward our dugout, but it landed in the grass in front of Mike. After we couldn't succeed in getting him ejected, Roger collected his thoughts and his energy before mowing us down.

The Yankees were leading 6–0 in the ninth inning of Game 2 when Mariano Rivera came into the game and gave up a three-run home run to Jay Payton. Before you knew it, we were one run behind and ready to steal one. We had Todd Pratt on third base and Bubba Trammell on second with one out. Timo was hitting, and we had the contact play on. As soon as the ball was hit, Pratt was supposed to run. Timo hit a high hopper over Rivera's head, but Pratt thought Rivera was going to field it and didn't run. Timo was thrown out at first, and with Piazza on deck with two outs, Mariano struck out Fonzie, and we were done.

It was another nail-biting game of high drama. Both games had gone down to the wire. There was no question we belonged in the arena with the champions.

We went back home for Game 3. What was weird was that before the game, not one reporter was talking about the game. The players weren't even talking about the game. They were talking about George Steinbrenner moving *all* of our furniture out of the visitor's locker room at Shea Stadium, including the chairs and couches used to watch TV, and substituting Yankees furniture. This was unheard of. It might even have been disallowed, if Steinbrenner had bothered to ask permission. It was *our* stadium. After George put in his furniture, the sprinklers went off in the visiting clubhouse. There were accusations that maybe I had done it. Maybe I did. I can't remember.

It was a great distraction and helped us relax. We were able to win 4–2 behind Rick Reed and Armando Benítez.

Down two games to one, I started Bobby Jones, who was coming off the best game of his life, in Game 4. He was feeling good about himself. The move of the Series came when Joe Torre led off Derek Jeter in Game

4. Jeter had batted second in the first three games. On the first pitch he saw, he hit the ball over the left-center-field fence. It was a momentum changer. It was demoralizing, even though the score was only 1–0. This was the thirteenth consecutive World Series game in which Derek Jeter had delivered a hit. It shook us.

The Yankees scored another run in the second and another in the third, and then we scored two in the bottom of the third. Denny Neagle held the lead for the Yankees, and with two outs and no one on in the bottom of the fifth, Mike Piazza was the batter. Neagle had pitched $4^2/_3$ innings and only needed one out to get credit for the win, but Torre didn't do what managers usually did: leave him in. Instead, Torre went to the bullpen and brought in David Cone. The move made sense. Mike had hit a home run off the left-handed Neagle earlier, and Neagle really didn't have the pitches to get him inside. Cone threw a pitch that wasn't that fast and wasn't that inside, but Mike popped out to the second baseman to end the threat. We had the men on base. We had our guy at the plate. It was the only batter Cone pitched to in the entire Series. He slayed the dragon. We were shut out the rest of the way and lost 3–2. Mariano Rivera pitched the eighth and ninth innings, giving up only one hit.

I had Bubba Trammell in right field and Kurt Abbott at shortstop in the fifth game, and neither at the beginning of the season was given a thought as a starter. Trammell did a great job as a pinch-hitter and was a competitive player. But if you asked a hundred Mets fans who the starting right fielder was in the fifth game of the World Series, I doubt if two would say it was Bubba.

We were down to our last game, and Al Leiter got the ball to carry us forward. Bernie Williams hit a home run in the second, and we scored two in the bottom on an error and single by Benny Agbayani. Then that damn Jeter homered to tie the score at 2. In the ninth, Leiter struck out Tino Martinez and Paul O'Neill, and then he walked Posada and gave up a single to Scott Brosius. Leiter was throwing incredibly well, and the next batter was Luis Sojo. Really? With the star players the New York

Yankees had, they were batting Luis Sojo? Vizcaíno had beaten us in Game 1. Luis Sojo now?

When we revisit history, I wonder, *Why was Kurt Abbott playing Luis Sojo to pull?* Sojo hit a weak ground ball to the shortstop side of second base that Kurt dove for but didn't get to. If he had been playing up the middle, it would have been an easy ball to catch. Al had a cutter, and we did play a lot of the right-handed hitters to pull. If I could do it over again, I'd have played him more straight up.

Soho's hit drove in two runs, and the Yankees took a 4–2 lead into the bottom of the ninth. Benny Agbayani drew a one-out walk against Mariano. With two outs, Piazza came to the plate as the tying run. The moment was electric: their best against our best. Two future Hall of Famers. Expectations were high. On an 0–1 count, Piazza crushed a ball to center field. The sound of it hitting the bat was convincing. Nearly everyone in the ballpark assumed it was a game-tying home run, but somehow the ball stayed in the park, and Bernie Williams made the catch for the final out.

That was how the World Series ended. I told the players how proud I was of them, that we'd had a great year. I think the players realized that. We were playing a team that got hot at the right time, who got the breaks. We probably didn't cash in as much as we could have, but there was nothing for us to hang our heads about.

The 2000 Mets were a *very good* team. There's nothing wrong with being the National League champions. But it sure would have been a whole different storybook if we had won the Series. For both sides. There isn't always justice. I suppose the Yankees were supposed to win it. I don't know.

CHAPTER 28

Embarrassment

F red Wilpon had said that the only way I was coming back to manage
the Mets was if I was able to lead them to the World Series. We did
that, and the last thing I wanted to do during the Series was answer
questions about my contract. Everyone knew it was time to get it done.

"This shouldn't be a tough thing to do," Tony Attanasio said to me.
"Why don't we get the contract done before the Series begins?"

"If you can do that," I said, "let's get it done."

Tony and I talked about how much money I wanted and what the
market was like. During the season we had emailed each other, and at
times he would say something derogatory about Wilpon or Phillips, because, quite frankly, we didn't feel I had been treated well, considering
the strides we had made.

The next day I held a practice, and at the end of practice Steve came
down on the field. "So," he said, "what do you want to do about your
contract?"

"Didn't you get Tony's offer?" I asked.

"No," Steve said. "I didn't get anything from Tony."

"You're kidding," I said. "Why don't you check. I'll go and do the press conference."

I met with the press, and they asked about the contract, and I said, "The contract is not going to be an issue by the time we get to the World Series. Let's talk about the players. Let's talk about the game."

Steve called again.

"I didn't get anything from Tony," he said.

I called Tony.

"Tony, what's going on? I thought you said you were sending out the contract offer."

"I did," he said. "Oh shit, I have an office temp working. Maybe she didn't get around to it. Brenda's not in today." Brenda was his secretary, who later became his wife.

We would have to wait until *after* the World Series to settle the contract. There were three days between the end of the Series and when my contract expired. Two other teams had contacted me about being their manager—the Dodgers and the Reds—but my heart was in New York, and I intended to get a long-term contract—perhaps as many as five years.

Shortly after the end of the World Series, I got a call from Fred Wilpon.

"Bobby, we received the offer from Tony," he said. "Why don't you come out to my house in the morning, and we'll work it out."

"That sounds great, Fred," I said, "but Tony won't be able to get there in time."

"We'll put him on speaker," Fred said. "It shouldn't be that hard."

Spectacular, I thought.

The next morning, I said to my buddy Doug Romano—one of the sons of my partner in the restaurant business, whom I had known since he was a six-year-old Pee Wee hockey player—"Why don't you come over, and we'll drive over to Fred's place and celebrate when it's over?"

"Great idea," he said.

He picked me up, and we drove to Fred's mansion on Long Island Sound. Doug stayed in the car, and I went to the front door. The manservant who answered the door said, "Mr. Wilpon will meet you down in the cabana." Fred had a beautiful poolside cabana overlooking the Sound. On the way, I passed his horses.

"Can I get you something to drink?" the manservant asked.

"I'll have whatever Fred's drinking," I said.

Fred hadn't arrived yet. The manservant returned with two glasses of white wine. There were chairs around a little glass table in the middle of the room, and there was a phone in the middle of the table. I sat down, and then Steve Phillips walked in, and then Fred arrived. We said hello, and Fred got right to it.

"This should be an interesting conversation," he said. "Why don't we get Tony on the phone?"

He dialed the number, and Tony, who lived in L.A., picked up and came across on the speaker.

"Tony," Fred said, "how's the weather? I hope you're well."

"Congratulations, Fred," said Tony. "Great job. This is going to be great. Why don't we get down to business?"

"Tony," Fred said, "I'd love to do that."

There was a stack of about thirty pieces of paper on the table. Fred grabbed them and held them in his hands. He said, "But before we get started, Steve received quite a few emails from you the other day."

I frowned, wondering what he was getting to.

"As a matter of fact, I have thirty-five pages here," he said.

I sat there totally confused.

"Before we get into the contract, Tony, on September eighteenth, can you tell me who you were referring to as 'the little prick you were going to get by the short hairs once the National League championship was won?'"

I couldn't breathe.

Then Fred said, "Or maybe you can tell me on September twenty-third, exactly what you meant by 'you were going to crush them and squeeze their balls till they screamed'? Whose balls were you going to crush, Tony?"

I now realized that Tony's temp secretary, when told to resend the contract proposal, had sent the hard-copy files, and Steve and Fred Wilpon had *all* the email correspondence between Tony and me for I don't know how long!

Red-faced, I got up and walked out of the cabana. I walked to the car, and Dougie said, "Holy shit, that was quick."

"Let's get the fuck out of here," I said.

As Doug drove away, I sat there shaking and feeling very pissed off. I had my window down, and yelled out every profanity I could think of. Doug pulled over.

"What happened? Didn't they make you an offer?"

I tried to collect myself and told him what happened. We got out of the car, and by the side of the road I picked up a rock and threw it as far as I could throw it. Doug screamed something, and it was the most horrible day I spent in my entire life. I got home and called Tony, who said he was on the phone with Steve and Fred trying to straighten it all out.

"Straighten it out?" I said. "How are you going to straighten it out? You know some of the things you and I said in those emails." I later called Tony again. "Tell me all the emails they have," I said. "Tell me what I said. Tell me what you said."

Tony went into total defense mode. Either he couldn't get it all together, or he didn't want me to know. When I saw Steve Phillips I said, "Hey, I hope you guys understand. I hope you can be fair with whatever's going to happen with the contract."

Some way, somehow, I did get a contract—but for three years, not five. It wasn't the numbers we were hoping for. I had zero leverage, and who knows what scars those emails left. I was really upset with Tony for quite a while. It was one of those *I wonder how it might have been* situations. We'd had leverage like I'd never had leverage before. Even the guys in the press who hated me felt that Fred was going to have to give me a long-term deal. Talk about a swing and a miss. Or maybe it was a swing and a foul ball. Either way, I was still swinging.

CHAPTER 29

9/11

D espite the horrendous screwup, I signed a three-year contract for decent money to return to the Mets. I never talked to Fred about the emails, and he never mentioned them again. We were riding high as National League champions, and my goal was to build the best team in the world. To do that, I begged Steve to sign Ichiro Suzuki, who had had a spectacular season in Japan and was going to become a free agent that winter.

When I managed the Marines in 1995, Hideo Nomo had gone from Japan's Pacific League to pitch for the Dodgers. The hierarchy of Japanese baseball was not pulling for Nomo. They felt he was a traitor. He was a renegade, the first Japanese player to be a free agent without abiding by the posting system. Since he'd broken the system, the Japanese hierarchy wanted him to fail. They wanted players to believe, or maybe they believed, that the Japanese players weren't good enough to play in America, so they would stay in Japan. Nomo proved them wrong. In his debut season in Major League Baseball, he was an MLB All-Star and National League Rookie of the Year, and he went on to win 123 games over his twelve-year career. The first modern-day Japanese player in the major leagues was a left-handed pitcher by the name of Masanori Murakami, for the San Francisco Giants in 1964. But Nomo was the first to make a splash.

I was managing in Japan when Ichiro won his first MVP award. I got to watch him and would tell reporters, "He's one of the five top talents in the world," based on his speed, his hitting ability, and his defensive ability. He ran faster and threw harder and farther than anyone else in uniform. We had just gone to the World Series. Why shouldn't the Mets take the next step?

I was sure the next step was to get creative and go outside the box and win the bid for Ichiro. It was a posting system, where each team made a single secret bid. Our commissioner would open the envelope and reveal the high bid, and that team would have seventy-two hours to come to an agreement with Ichiro. There was no history to figure out what that bid should be, and when Steve and I and the others in the front office got together, I had more of an emotional connection to and first-hand knowledge of Ichiro, since the Marines had played against him twenty-four times in 1995. His team, the Orix BlueWave, had won the championship. I felt his transition to MLB would be smooth, and I didn't think we'd have any problem signing him. I strongly recommended we overbid everyone else by a lot, because I was sure Ichiro was worth it. Steve Phillips was less convinced.

"We don't need a singles hitter playing in the outfield for us," he said.

We made a low bid, and the Seattle Mariners got Ichiro. The rumor was that Seattle's offer was only a million dollars more. Ichiro was the MVP of the American League in 2001.

We made other moves. We let Mike Hampton go but replaced him with Kevin Appier. We needed another left-hander, and we signed Bruce Chen, a serviceable pitcher. Alex Rodriguez was a free agent, and we contemplated making him an offer. Alex had starred with the Seattle Mariners. He may well have been the finest shortstop in the history of the game. He finished his career with 696 home runs, more than 3,000 hits, and more than 300 stolen bases. Only Barry Bonds was in his class.

Nelson Doubleday was talking about selling his share of the club, and he was getting his estate in order. The Mets had spent a lot of money for Mike Piazza, and I didn't know whether he would do it again, but I sure hoped so. Scott Boras, A-Rod's agent, made us a presentation. On the radio, A-Rod had made a comment about how he'd enjoy the chance to play for the Mets, and everything was heading down the road until Boras handed us a fifty-page proposal, which had A-Rod's history. The proposal included Boras's predictions about Alex's future with the Mets: when he'd break Babe Ruth's home-run record, when he'd break Hank Aaron's record, and how much money the Mets would make from having A-Rod on the team, which would increase the value of the franchise.

It was a well-thought-out, lengthy proposal. One of A-Rod's demands was that because of the configuration of the Mets locker room—meaning the shitty, unworkable locker room—he would need his own place to have press conferences, if needed, and for companies that would be pitching him, or just to have A-Rod's family and entourage be with him somewhere other than the decrepit runway bowels of Shea. We had a perfect place for him: the locker room used by the Jets, which was adjacent to the Mets locker room. I was all in on A-Rod.

What a splendid thing it would be to expand the Mets locker room, I thought, *not just for A-Rod, but for others as well when necessary.* But Fred, Steve, and the organization used it as the excuse not to sign him.

"We're about the team and not the individual," came the cry.

Ba-da-boom! A-Rod was no longer a part of our Team of Dreams. Alex signed with the Rangers and played there until 2004, when he joined the Yankees and played out his career on the other side of town. Because Jeter was the shortstop, Alex moved to third base, depriving himself of being named the greatest shortstop in baseball history. In today's metrics, which values WAR (Wins Above Replacement), Alex in 2001 would have been worth eight WAR over Rey Ordonez. That would have given us ninety wins and the NL East championship.

Unfortunately, teams that go to the World Series often suffer from a hangover, and we were no exception. It's magical to go to the World Series. When things work out, you rejoice. We had a couple of All-Stars, and we were a good group, and the group is always the key component to a team.

I took my team to the White House to visit with President George W. Bush. My friend Doug Romano got a private plane from Miami, where we were playing, and flew all my players who had been on an All-Star team, and all the Texas natives on the Mets, to the Oval Office on June 3, 2001. I enjoyed telling George how Zack Minasian and I had had a fight on the Capitol lawn with two protesters during his inauguration. Everyone seemed to enjoy the story. However, he ran over our allotted time, and we were ushered out by an angry Dick Cheney, who was worried that George was not going to be on time for a Rose Garden speech. This was a stark contrast to the time I was at the White House with Tommy Lasorda during the Reagan administration. At that time, Ronald Reagan joined us for lunch at the Roosevelt Room and told Larry Speakes, his press secretary, to cancel the rest of his afternoon appointments.

We had serious injuries in 2001. Edgardo Alfonzo was one of the leaders of the team. Everyone looked up to Fonzie. He could get a big hit against a good pitcher, but Fonzie was hurt a lot that season. Todd Zeile, another clutch hitter, had 62 RBIs. Except for Mike Piazza, who hit 36 home runs with 94 RBIs, we didn't have a lot of star quality, but we had a great many workmen grinding it out. Even though Robin Ventura was hurt, he hit 21 home runs and had 61 RBIs. Our outfield of Benny, Jay Payton, and Timo didn't produce much, though Tsuyoshi Shinjo did hit well enough to get us 10 home runs and 56 RBIs. Our record dropped to 82–80. There wasn't a lot of fun that year.

What should have been a highlight for me after we won the National League pennant in 2000 was that I was the manager of the National League All-Star team in 2001. I wanted to be the manager who was most fair in picking his team. I didn't want to get a bad rep for picking my own players over players on other teams who deserved it more. I did an in-depth statistical analysis and also got input from every other manager in the league. I asked them who should be selected from their team, and to my mind I came up with a darn good team.

The biggest problem for me was that I didn't pick many players from the Mets. Some of the guys felt that just because they were my guys, I should have put them on the team. To make matters worse, Joe Torre, the manager of the American League All-Stars, picked seven Yankees: Roger Clemens, Jorge Posada, Bernie Williams, Derek Jeter, Andy Pettitte, Mike Stanton, and Mariano Rivera. I had chosen only Mike Piazza and Rick Reed. And remember, Rick Reed was a scab. The sabermetricians of today, if they analyzed what I did, would agree with me on just about every pick, if not every pick. There were some close races, but I came out with the names on Sunday before the break, and on Monday there was an uproar that I had not selected Cliff Floyd of the Florida Marlins. Floyd's agent, Seth Levinson, my sworn enemy, told the press that I had told Floyd he was on the team, and as a result he bought $16,000 worth of airplane tickets for his parents, father, cousin, and three friends.

"The tickets are the smoking gun," said Levinson.

When the press told me what Levinson had to say, I said, "Cliff Floyd's agent is a liar. I talked to Floyd. He knows exactly what I said. I told him he was on the bubble. I love him as a player."

I was upset by the criticism of my choices. I knew I had done a great job.

I had to decide which pitcher to start. Going into the break, Randy Johnson and Curt Schilling, both of the Diamondbacks, were statistically even. I called Bob Brenly, Arizona's manager, and asked him to tell me who I should start. My choice would have been Johnson, but I wanted to do what their manager thought was right, so I went with Schilling. I announced the starting team at the All-Star dinner. The starting pitchers from each team got up to say a few words. Schilling gave a ten-minute soliloquy. "This is the greatest honor. This is one of the highlights of my career." I hadn't counted on how upset Johnson would be about not starting the game. He had starred for Seattle, and the game was being played in Seattle, and he owned Seattle. After the dinner was over, I got on the elevator to go up to my room, and Randy was on the elevator. He was standing in the back. He's six foot eleven, and I'm five foot nine and a half. He leaned down and he said in my ear, "If that prick can't go, don't look to me to start the game."

Randy went to his room, and I went to my room. I called Charlie Hough, my great friend and pitching coach on the All-Star team, and I said, "Charlie, did you hear anything about Schilling not starting tomorrow?"

"No, Skippy. I haven't heard anything. If I do, I'll let you know," Charlie said.

Five minutes later my phone rang.

"Hey, Skippy?'

"Yeah."

"Curt just called me, and he says he wants to go out in the morning and play catch and see how he feels."

"Isn't he feeling good?"

"He said he has to test his arm to see how it feels."

This is not good, I thought.

The next morning Schilling went out with Charlie and played catch. I was getting ready to go to the field to watch the Home Run Derby when Charlie came to my room. "Curt can't go," he said.

I gave a big gulp. I had already gone over with each pitcher when he was going to enter the game. I told those who had pitched on Sunday that they weren't going to pitch. Schilling was supposed to pitch the first three innings, then Randy Johnson, who said he would only pitch one inning, would come in and pitch the fourth. Josh Beckett would pitch the fifth, Mike Hampton the sixth, Jon Lieber the seventh, Matt Morris the eighth, and Jeff Shaw the ninth. I had Billy Wagner and Ben Sheets in reserve with Chan Ho Park. Park had been incredible the first half of the 2001 season, winning ten games, and when I told him he wasn't going to pitch, he was fine with that. But now, with Schilling not pitching, I had to make up three more innings.

In the last game of the first half of the season, one of the selected NL outfielders was injured. In such a situation, the next guy on the list was designated to make the team. I called Cliff Floyd to come and play.

We lost the game 4–1. Randy Johnson started and pitched the first two innings. I had to ask Chan Ho Park to pitch, and in true manly style he said, "Of course I will pitch in the game." His back was stiff in warmups, but he came in and pitched anyway, and he gave up Cal Ripken's final hit as an All-Star, a home run. Chan Ho hurt his back, and he didn't pitch well the whole second half, which was terrible.

The other terrible thing, in retrospect, was that I watched the Home Run Derby with Chris Quackenbush, who had donated $20,000 to my Mickey Lione foundation. He'd won an auction for his kids to be batboys at the game. Chris was a partner at Sandler O'Neill, high atop the World Trade Center. It was to be the last game he and his kids watched together.

During that Home Run Derby, I went over to Barry Bonds, and I said, "Barry, you're in there tomorrow. One thing I know about you, you have a lot of trophies, but you don't have an MVP trophy from an All-Star Game. I'd like you to play all nine innings, and I know if you play all nine innings, you'll be the MVP."

"Great idea, Bobby," Barry said. "I appreciate that."

Fast-forward to the sixth inning, and we were having a rally, and Joe Torre brought in Mike Stanton to pitch. Dusty Baker, one of my coaches, came to me and said, "Who do you want to hit?"

I wasn't making any switches.

"For whom?"

"For Barry," he said.

"Where's Barry?"

"His private plane arrived early, and he's taking off."

"Okay," I said, switching gears, "Why don't we have Vladimir Guerrero hit?"

That's how the All-Star Game was in those days. It was a picnic game, until later they gave the league that won the game home-field advantage in the World Series.

One other interesting event: I petitioned the league to allow me to bring in Tommy Lasorda as a coach. He had retired in 1996 after winning four pennants and two World Series championships with the Dodgers, and a gold medal in the 2000 Olympics. We had never been in a big-league uniform together, and for me it was a dream to come true. The commissioner gave special permission. In the sixth inning, Tommy asked me if he could go out and coach third.

"You haven't been out at third base in a long time," I said. "Shit happens really quickly out there. Why don't you stay in the dugout with me, and we'll enjoy the game?"

He asked again, and this time I caved. Tommy went out, and the fans gave him a standing ovation. Our first hitter was Guerrero, pinch-hitting for Bonds. Tommy was out there doing all these gyrations, clapping his hands, and yelling to Vlad to get a hit. Vlad swung at a low and away breaking ball, as he often did, with only one hand on the bat. He let go of the bat, and the bat became a helicopter without a cabin, propelling its way right toward Tommy's forehead. Tommy went flying backwards, and everyone, including me, held their breath. The bat missed him. He jumped up, put his hands above his head, and received a standing ovation. I almost had a heart attack.

The experience in Seattle was cool. Ralph Branca and Bobby Thomson were honorary captains on the fiftieth anniversary of their Shot Heard 'Round the World. It was a great spectacle. It's always a great spectacle, but what should have been one of the most enjoyable weekends of my life turned out to be pretty miserable.

In August 2001 we were plodding along, thinking the 2001 Mets would have to undergo another remake, taking a step back so we could take two steps forward. We had done that a couple times, and this was a definite step back.

Then came 9/11.

We were in Pittsburgh, staying downtown at the Marriott. It was one of our two family road trips, so Mary had accompanied me. I woke up early that morning, did my exercise routine, went back to the room, had a cup of coffee, and turned on CNN. The first plane had just hit the North Tower of the World Trade Center. The phone started ringing, and we were trying to figure out what was going on. I looked out the window, and I could see a string of black sedans blocking off the entrances and exits of the building's underground parking garages. I went downstairs and was advised not to leave through the door facing the building across the street, because it was the local FBI headquarters. I called Charlie Samuels, our traveling secretary and clubhouse man.

"I think we should get out of Dodge if all these places are being targeted. We need to leave."

Everyone packed up and got on the bus that was supposed to take us to the ballpark. We checked in at a Holiday Inn out by Robert Morris University, in the countryside of Pennsylvania. We were all confused and fearful of what might happen next. We watched the six o'clock news and decided we would leave for the safety of our homes early the next morning. There were no planes flying. We would take the bus from Pittsburgh to New York.

Everything was orderly. It wasn't chaotic or hectic. There was no panic or fear. I didn't sleep that night. We left at three in the morning. It was an eight-hour ride. Most everyone fell asleep, and we were waking up as we rode on the Jersey Turnpike on the west side of the Hudson River when we were first able to see Manhattan. Everyone was anxiously waiting to see what we could see, and as we came around a corner, all we could see was black smoke. You couldn't see the skyline. The entire island of Manhattan was covered in black smoke.

Then a little panic set in. There were tears and sighing and not much talking. The music in the bus was turned off. The ride from the George Washington Bridge to Shea Stadium was as solemn a drive as I can remember. My first thought was to enlist in the military. Maybe they needed an old man with leadership qualities. I felt there was service to give to my country. I was good friends with our commander in chief, George W. Bush, and I wanted to support him anyway I could.

When we arrived at Shea, I gave the players hugs and told them to stay close by the phone, but to stay safe and get to their families. I was doing the same, rushing back to Westchester, happy to find Ralph Branca, my father-in-law, safe. He had been incommunicado for several hours that morning, because he was with Mayor Rudy Giuliani dedicating a statue to Jackie Robinson. Ralph was seventy-five, and he walked across the Brooklyn Bridge from Lower Manhattan to get a cab home to Westchester.

In the immediate aftermath of the attack, the Chelsea Piers were the staging area for all those working in the recovery effort. After the second tower fell, the Chelsea Piers were deemed unsafe because the ground had shaken so much, and the Shea Stadium parking lot was chosen to be the new staging area.

Mary and I drove home to Connecticut. After realizing my family and friends were all safe, I got back in my car that night and returned to Shea. The parking lot was in chaos. The idea was to organize it in such a way that the things people needed in the rescue area could be piled up, inventoried, and delivered to the workers at Ground Zero. Kevin McCarthy, our stadium operations manager, and Sue Lutz, his assistant, did a really great job, and I did some of the lugging. Meanwhile, at Ground Zero, every able-bodied uniformed person plus thousands of others worked through the night sifting through the rubble, trying to rescue people.

The workers at Ground Zero who came looking for supplies were covered in soot and looked like coal miners. We had bandages, medical salve, t-shirts, eyewash, glasses, gloves, and flashlights. The second night of the rescue effort, they had run out of batteries for the flashlights, and the next morning an eighteen-wheeler from Atlantic City delivered hundreds of boxes of flashlights with batteries. We were totally fatigued and needed rest, but were disrupted by the roar of many motorcycles approaching the parking lot. We were so exhausted we were going to just let this motorcycle gang have anything they wanted. But to our delight and amazement, one of their members yelled to me, "I hear ya need some help." I waved them in. There were about forty guys and gals, all equipped with a sharp object or two that allowed them to open the packaging and assemble the much-needed flashlights and batteries within only about two hours. The work was done, and they were on their way. The flashlights and other supplies were transported to Ground Zero in about ten police cars, whose back seats had been removed to maximize storage space.

Baseball was not my major concern. The only thing going on that mattered was loved ones trying to find their lost ones. I spent a good amount of time at Ground Zero. I rode down there in a police car. Lower Manhattan was still smoldering. It actually looked like a war zone. By the time I got there, the National Guard had pitched their tents along the roads. Cars had four inches of soot on them.

By the fourth day, there were funerals to attend. After that I had battle fatigue, and I drove back to Shea Stadium and went to see Steve Phillips, who had news that we were going to try to start playing again in Pittsburgh in two days.

We called the players and had practice, and after practice all the players went into the parking lot to help out with the supplies. About eight of us got in police cruisers and went to Ground Zero, where we handed out Mets hats to cheer people up. A couple of first responders gave Robin Ventura and Todd Zeile NYPD and NYFD hats, and asked if they'd wear them on the field in memory of the lost first responders. We couldn't wear them during the game because Major League Baseball had a license with the New Era hat company.

"I know what everyone's dealing with," I said. "No one has ever dealt with a situation like this before."

"So, Bobby, how are you handling this?" Al Leiter wanted to know. "How are you dealing with the fear?"

"I'm trying to make sure my family is as safe and secure as they can be, so I can be as brave as I can be, but every moment I look at the sky, I think of a plane flying over and I'm going to have fear. You have to deal with fear on an individual basis. But if we have strength in numbers, we can have courage in numbers. If we all decide to do this together, it might help us all out."

Steve Phillips and Fred Wilpon were there, and Fred decided to give the players a pep talk about winning, how they should put everything aside and get their act back together, and get back to the World Series, where we belonged. *That was weird*, I thought. While we were in Pittsburgh, we were contemplating going to Atlanta, even though our games were scheduled as home games, when we got a message: "The commander in chief thinks it important that we play the games in New York."

During a phone call with Atlanta manager Bobby Cox, we determined that before the game I would walk over to him and we would embrace, that our players would embrace their players. Even though we were heated rivals and hated each other, we embraced before the game.

The first game back was on September 21. We lined up for the national anthem. Our entire right-field scoreboard had been transformed into an American flag. It was lit up with the words "We will never forget." It was the most emotional day I ever experienced on a ballfield, because we were in New York playing baseball after ten days of horror. I still have trouble describing how emotional it was.

The audio system at Shea played "New York, New York" during the seventh-inning stretch. As Liza Minelli was singing, members of first responder units were in uniform, and they were doing a chorus-line kick, crying as they were kicking.

The game itself was melodramatic. We were behind, and when we scored a run, there was excitement but the reaction was muted. The crowd was huge. Everyone wanted to be a part of it, but no one knew how to participate. Cheering seemed wrong in light of the three thousand deaths from the attacks.

Trailing 2–1 in the bottom of the eighth, Mike Piazza hit one of the most memorable home runs in baseball history to take the lead from the hated Braves. Every frown was turned upside down. For a brief moment, every tear of fear and sorrow became a tear of joy. It was a monster blast that landed in the television booth in left-center field. It had been quiet in the stadium, but the cheers that resulted from that hit were resounding. They echo still in my heart and brain.

It would have been incredible if we could have won every game and gotten back into the playoffs and met the Yankees again in the World Series, but we didn't.

One other note: On September 6, I opened a restaurant in a hotel across the parking lot from Shea Stadium. We were contracted to serve airline pilots and flight crews and provide room service at the hotel. Instead, for a month we opened up for all first responders' families. And then we provided Christmas dinner for those affected by 9/11.

I tried to do things for kids. A friend of Ralph Branca had hired a fellow who was in his office when the towers fell. The man had four kids and had lived in Brooklyn. Ralph asked if I would go over and say hello to his kids. The victim's name was Kevin Conroy. His wife, Jet Conroy, was one of those amazing Irish women who'd become a widow and did amazing things with her four children—a boy and three younger daughters—who all became part of my family. All four went to college. Matty was the captain and pitcher on his club team at Northwestern. They won the club world championship, which I got to announce on ESPN. Matty lived with me in Japan for all six years. This wonderful family entering my life became one of the silver linings to come out of 9/11.

Mets PR director Jay Horwitz started Tuesday's Children, and every Tuesday for the rest of the season the Mets invited children of those who were killed on 9/11 to be guests of the Mets. The charity still goes on.

CHAPTER 30

Discord

After the 2001 season ended in mediocrity, Steve organized a think tank. The objective was to try to come up with more offense without spending any more money. That didn't bother me. The Mets had always been fiscally responsible. We were given a budget, and we had to deal with it. At a meeting, we asked ourselves, "What can we do?"

"We have to find a high-priced player on our team," I said, "and trade him for a high-priced hitter on another team. Let's trade a pitcher for offense." Kevin Appier, who was making $10 million, was suggested.

"How about Mo Vaughn?" I said. Mo had grown up in Norwalk, Connecticut. His mom and dad were both educators. His dad was the principal of Norwalk's Ponus Ridge Middle School.

If Mo can still hit, I thought, *this will be a natural.* In 1995, Mo had been the AL MVP. He had signed a six-year contract with the Red Sox for $80 million, then played two years with the Angels. In 2000, he hit .272 with 36 home runs and 117 RBIs, and then in 2001 he suffered a ruptured tendon in his left arm and missed the entire season. At this point in his career, he had a lifetime average of .298 with 299 home runs and 977 RBIs. Steve arranged for the front office staff to drive up to Mo's home in Massachusetts to see him hit.

We met Mo at a batting cage near his home. With him was his private batting coach, Mike Easler, who had played with the Pirates and Red Sox and had also been a batting coach with the Red Sox. Mo was wearing one of those rubber suits that guys would put on when they were a little overweight. He swung a weighted bat, and he hit with a great amount of effort and power. After five swings, he'd rest, and then he'd hit again. He was sweating profusely, and after we saw him hit about thirty balls, we adjourned. Steve and Carm Fusco went to talk with Mo while the rest of us were segregated in a different room. After an hour, Mo came out and waved to us, and we got into the two cars that we'd driven up from Shea. Steve was in the other car. Jim Duquette and I talked about what we had seen. I said Mo seemed much too heavy and out of shape, and that I didn't think signing him was going to cut it.

"We don't have a DH," I said. "How is he going to play first?"

After an hour and a half, we stopped for gas, and Steve came to me and said, "It looks like we came to terms."

Shortly after that, we traded our best pitcher, Kevin Appier, for Mo's money. We traded Appier to Kansas City for someone who wasn't making much money. If Bobby Bonilla was Disaster 1.0, then Mo Vaughn was Disaster 2.0. He provided us with left-handed power and drove in some runs—he had 26 home runs and 72 RBIs—but in the field he was a washout. He couldn't move, and it was hard for him to get around the bases. The good pitchers didn't have much trouble with him, and he just wasn't a very good influence on the team. He had plenty of money, and very little commitment to the team. With every distraction known to man, New York City was calling Mo's name. It wasn't a good look, and it wasn't a good fit. Mo came back the next year, hit .190 in 27 games, and we released him.

Steve and I also disagreed about whether to keep Robin Ventura. I was all for keeping him. He may have been the guy least likely to be seen in the weight room, but he was skilled at third base. He was a spectacular fielder, and, even though he had hurt his ankle before coming over and playing for us, he made the play coming in on the ball as well as anyone, except maybe Brooks Robinson. He slumped, but he had hot streaks and he got clutch hits for us. After the 2001 season, there was a question as to whether Robin was going to get in a little better shape by working hard during the winter. We had a strength and conditioning coach who gave him a program, and Steve wanted to see if he was fulfilling it. During the winter, Steve and I had breakfast in Greenwich. Steve wanted to see what Robin looked like.

"I've been talking to Robin," I said. "He's been working hard. You don't have to worry about anything. It's all fine and good."

We went to see Robin, and we asked him how his workout program was going.

"It's going really well," he said. "I'm really enjoying the kickboxing classes."

I thought it would make his ankle stronger. "That's cool," I said. "That's a great way to go."

Robin got in his car and left, and I said to Steve, "That's good to learn. He's doing kickboxing. It's a rigorous workout."

"That's not the kind of workout I was expecting him to say he was doing," said Steve.

Two days later, Robin was traded. It was right after I told Robin, "Steve and I talked, and we liked the fact you were getting in shape."

The one addition to the Mets in 2002 that excited me was Roberto Alomar. When Steve told me about the trade, I was thrilled.

"Great job, whoever we gave up," I said.

Cleveland got Matt Lawton and Alex Escobar. But the same thing happened with Roberto that happened when we got Carlos Baerga several years earlier. They were both tremendous American League players. Both were switch-hitters who could hit with power, and they were bookend terrific guys. Carlos was more outgoing. Everyone loved him. Roberto was quiet but well liked and respected. When I played for the Angels, his father was my double-play combination, and Roberto was just a baby. But besides being great people, they were total washouts in New York. With Roberto, like with Carlos, there were weeks when he didn't hit a home run in batting practice. Not days. Weeks. It was hard for me to comprehend.

They're going to find whatever it is that's missing, I kept thinking, *and tomorrow is going to be the day.*

They had both been so good before coming to New York. It was baffling. I loved Carlos, and Carlos loved me, and every time Roberto met with futility, it hurt me as much as it did him. I died with his at-bats. We had gotten each of them at a time in their career when the motor must have run out of oil, and they could never get it running again.

There were also off-field distractions.

Steve Isenberg was a former publisher of the *Stamford Advocate* and went on to be the publisher of *Newsday* and later the executive VP of the *L.A. Times.* We were friends from his Stamford days. When I was the manager of the Rangers, he came to spring training with his young son Christopher, whom I let be our batboy for a few games. Dash forward to the year 2002: Christopher had graduated from journalism school at NYU, and he landed a job with a little weekly newspaper in the Village in New York City.

Steve called me up and said, "Hey, would you mind if Christopher did a Q and A with you?"

"I'd be delighted," I said.

Christopher came to Shea Stadium, and we sat in the dugout. No one was around, and we did a little Q and A. "What do you think of the DH?" "What are your chances of winning the pennant?" "How are the crowds at Shea Stadium?" In the middle of all these questions came, "Do you think it's time for an openly gay player to play in the major leagues?"

I didn't think this was such a big deal to answer, and so I said, "Of course it's time for baseball to have an openly gay player. Why not? The entire society understands that it's perfectly acceptable." End of answer.

A week later, the magazine came out. The conjecture in the press was that I had said about it being okay to be gay because I was trying to expose Mike Piazza for being gay. Why that was what was conjectured, I have no idea. There was a rumor blowing around, which I ignored, so I was not defensive about the rumor. Quite frankly, I don't know how I could have answered the question any other way. But the commentary was that I had made the statement because Mike was on the team, so Steve Phillips and Dr. Allan Lans decided they had to hold a pregame press conference to address the issue.

Meanwhile, Danny Lozano, Mike's agent, was complaining to the Mets that Mike wasn't getting some endorsements because of this accusation. He suggested a possible lawsuit. Lozano flew in for a press conference, and Mike had to sit up there and announce, "I'm not gay."

My jaw dropped. I couldn't believe what was happening around me. Yet again, a lot of fingers were pointing at me. I didn't appreciate it, but I didn't want to add fuel the fire, so I tried to let it rest. But I couldn't put the genie back in the bottle. It left scars. And it was ridiculous. These are the things that get managers fired. The manager's job is to try to keep distraction *away* from the players, and often in New York when you try to do that, the players become distracted because of the circle-back rule.

I would submit to an interview, and the writer would then circle back to the player, and too often misquote on purpose what I'd said, to get a reaction. The writer then would circle back to me to give me the player's reaction. It was a great way to stir up stories, and often my writer friends would come over and tell me what other writers were plotting. There was always a situation when a player didn't play. It was always a "benching," never a "rest." Anytime Mike Pizza didn't play, it was reported as a crisis, because neither the writers nor the fans seemed to understand that *rest* is one of the formulas for success. Some managers put their starting lineups out there every single day. Leo Durocher did that in 1969, and he cost the Cubs the pennant when the starters all at once got tired and stopped performing.

Not many catchers play every day, and I always tried to protect Mike. Many day games that followed a night game were the perfect opportunity to give Mike a rest. Even though this may not have been accepted by the press or the fans, it was best for Mike. Often, that day game was a Sunday, and on that Sunday a father would bring his son to see his son's favorite player, and his favorite player wouldn't be in the game. On the way home, that father would dial up WFAN and he'd say, "How the heck can I bring my son and spend all that money to see Mike Piazza, and that idiot Valentine doesn't have him in the lineup?" "Yeah, he's an idiot," the talk radio guy would say. "Why wasn't he in the lineup?"

We finished the 2002 season with a 75–86 record. Mike Piazza was his usual terrific self, with 33 home runs and 98 RBIs, and Mo Vaughn added 72 RBIs. But the rest of the lineup was mediocre, and without Kevin Appier, so was the pitching. Al Leiter was our ace with a 13–13 record. Armando saved 33 games.

In August 2002, Nelson Doubleday sold his half-interest in the Mets to Fred Wilpon for $135 million. This came after a bitter dispute, during which Doubleday insisted he was being cheated by a low appraisal of the team. Commissioner Bud Selig had to intervene to get the dispute resolved. At the end of the 2002 season, after twenty-two years of Doubleday at the helm, ownership shifted to Wilpon. In 2002 we limped to the finish, losing twelve games in a row at home in September. Nevertheless, Fred stated that I would be coming back to fulfill the final year of my contract.

About a week before the end of the season, Wilpon, Steve Phillips, and I had a meeting to discuss what we should do to right the ship. During the conversation, I said that we ought to explore trading Piazza to get prospects to rebuild. I was on thin ice, because Mike was Mike, and the face of the team. But I had grown up in the Dodger organization under Al Campanis and Tommy Lasorda, who quoted Branch Rickey, who said you should always trade a superstar a year or two early rather than a year or two late. I mentioned that we might get some real value for Mike, and we should explore AL teams first, because Mike could DH there. Somehow, my suggestion got out of the room and made its way to Mike. More importantly, it got back to Mike's father, Vince, who always stopped in to my office before games to talk about his son. During that final home stand, Vince came to see me, and during our conversation, he discussed the possibility of Johnny Franco replacing me as manager.

"He would be loyal to Michael," Vince said.

I said I didn't think that was a bad idea, except that I would be the guy he was replacing. *Why would Vince say such a thing?* I wondered. Before this, Vince had always treated me like family. I tried to find out who'd told Vince, but I ran out of time.

Tom Robson and Fred's son Jeff had attended the meeting in which I had discussed trading Mike. Fred had asked me if it was okay for Jeff to attend.

"All he wants to do is sit with you and learn from you," Fred said. "He isn't going to open his mouth for two years."

I told Fred I had no problem with Jeff sitting in. During the meeting, Tom Robson was discussing hitting. For the umpteenth time, Tom was explaining to the executives in the room the physics of the swing. This was at a time when it was debated whether to swing up at the ball to hit home runs, or to swing down to make contact. Tom was being explicit so everyone understood. We wanted this to be what we taught all through the organization. From the corner of the room where he was sitting, Jeff Wilpon piped up that he disagreed with Tom's theory because he takes golf lessons all around the country, and every golf pro teaches a different swing.

"Why wouldn't it be the same for baseball?" he wanted to know.

"We're not talking about the stance and the look," Tom said. "We're just talking about the physics of the actual swing."

"Jeez, Jeff," I said. "I thought you weren't going to say anything for two years."

There was silence in the room, and soon thereafter the meeting adjourned. There is no doubt in my mind that that was the impetus for

Fred changing his mind and firing me. The next day, October 1, I got a surprise call from Fred to come see him, and that's when I learned I was not coming back to manage the Mets for the 2003 season. That was that.

It had been a tough stretch. I had had Fred and Steve Phillips read the scathing emails between my agent and me while I was trying to get a new contract. There was the World Series loss. We had 9/11, where I was just in a different place. The 9/11 catastrophe, I felt, was my biggest failure, because I really thought when I was out in the Shea Stadium parking lot for that week, and when I was going to the funerals and meeting the families, like I was going to help cure the world and that the Mets would be appreciative. Apparently, the wound was so deep that, regardless of what I did, it wasn't going to be enough. When the decision to fire me came down the way it did, I was dejected, but I also felt that I had kind of had enough.

I went home and isolated myself for several months while my father and I built a deck on the back side of my property. My dad, a gifted carpenter, had lost most of his skills and wasn't as sharp as he once was, but I got to work with him for three months. No one else but me drilled or assembled anything, and that was the way I reset myself.

I was told that when Art Howe walked into the room, Fred had said he knew he had his man, my replacement. *Well, we'll see*, was my reaction. I knew Fred wasn't right when he said that Art Howe was "the perfect guy for the job." Art had been one of my coaches, and I knew him well. He was a good baseball man and loved being in uniform, but New York was not going to be a good fit for him. In New York, the workload is so much greater. There are more press conferences, more questions, more criticism. It just keeps coming at you. Of course, there's also more joy. Each win is more. Each loss is more. Each young player you try to develop is more. Each veteran whose style you don't like is more. Every general manager is more. And often the pay is more. If you want to manage in New York, you better have a thick, thick skin.

I finished my tenure as manager of the Mets with a 536–467 record. It seemed there were many more good times than bad, the joy of being with so many great players, coaches, and front office staff, as well as the other employees of the Mets, and of course the great fans and media. New York was really good to me, and I like to think I left Shea Stadium in a better place than when I arrived.

CHAPTER 31

A Return to Japan

spent 2003 working for ESPN as an analyst and commentator on *Baseball Tonight*. Norby Williamson and the whole upper management staff were great. John Walsh, my executive director, gave me a first-class schedule, and I did a good job for them—other than being a little argumentative and confrontational at times, because I didn't like people talking incorrectly about baseball. Whenever someone started talking about why batters should swing down on the ball, or why a pitcher should stay on top of the ball, I went crazy.

I also spent much of 2003 doing charity work and conducting charity auctions. Chris Quackenbush, who worked for Sandler O'Neill and was with me at the All-Star Game in Seattle, died on 9/11. In November, the firm was relocating to a space provided by the Bank of America Building on Third Avenue, and Chris's partner, Jimmy Dunne, asked if I would drop by and try to lift their spirits as they were connecting computers and putting up partitions. I was scheduled to have lunch with another friend, Bobby Castrignano, and we first went to the new offices and brought coffee and some smiles. Bobby said he wanted to buy me lunch at the posh Four Seasons in Manhattan. I had never been there. We went and had a great lunch together, and as we were finishing, a man came over and said, "What a coincidence that we are having lunch in the same restaurant."

The man was Akio Shigemitzu, the son of the owner of the Lotte Corporation, a $40 billion company that owned the Chiba Lotte Marines, which I had managed a decade earlier.

"I heard the news, and I was going to contact you," Akio said. "Would you consider coming back and managing the Marines again?"

"I'd love to do that," I said. "How about a handshake?"

We shook hands. A month later, I was on a plane to Japan, and on November 3, 2003, I was introduced as the new manager.

Returning to Japan was one of the most exciting things ever to happen to me. I was met at the airport by thousands of Chiba Lotte fans, and it was a great welcome back. I was able to bring some coaches with me—Frank Ramppen, Tom Robson, and Paul Pupo—as well as some players: pitcher Dan Serafini, and outfielders Benny Agbayani and Matt Franco.

Serafini was interesting. He had a lot of tattoos, and the challenge for him was that most people in Japan associate tattoos with the *yakuza*, the Japanese mafia. If you have tattoos, there are places in Japan you're not allowed to enter, including the *onsen*, the hot spring baths that are so good for you. Dan tried going there a couple times, and it wasn't a good scene. Nothing physical happened, but it was upsetting for him when they wouldn't let him in.

I got to play Benny every day, something I couldn't do in New York, and he turned out to be the kind of everyday player I thought he would be. Franco had played for me in the minor and major leagues, and he was a welcome sight every day at the ballpark.

Many were my young players from nine years before. It was great to be reunited with guys who had been inexperienced but terrific players, who now had some seasoning and were welcoming me back with open arms. One of them was Kazuya Fukuura, a sweet-swinging first baseman.

I had a second baseman named Koichi Hori, a young guy who adopted Tom Robson's and my philosophy nine years earlier and had become a very solid baseball player. Satoru Komiyama came back. He had been my opening-day pitcher in 1995. When the Mets had signed him in 2001, I knew he wasn't the pitcher he once was, but I was never consulted, and at the press conference, Steve Phillips talked as though Komiyama was still in his prime and how he was going to be a reliever. He talked about all the games he had saved. But Steve had read the stat sheet wrong. GS wasn't games saved. It was games started. Satoru had relieved perhaps two or three times, and this was to be the guy who was going to help our bullpen?

In 2003, Komiyama was playing in the Central League and became a free agent, and I got to sign him back as my protégé signing, a fine player but also a steadying influence. I signed Seung Yuop Lee, who was Korean. He had very good power but had to adapt himself to Japanese pitching.

At the start of the season, I brought up four players from the minors, led by Toshiaki Imae. Veterans were always tough to deal with when young guys are coming up to take their positions. Imae was a third baseman, and Kiyoshi Hatsushiba, who played third, had basically been the captain of the team when I managed them in '95. He was now a veteran, disciplined and skilled, but his defensive skills were slipping, and he didn't love the idea of being replaced, so I broke Imae in slowly.

The same thing happened with our shortstop, Makoto Kosaka, a spectacular fielder and leadoff hitter. I had my sights on making the youngster Tsuyoshi Nishioka the starting shortstop, and it was a little uncomfortable for a while, but we worked as a team, and the players trusted me. Good teamwork and good team play were the result.

When I arrived for fall camp, there was a marketing position open, and I brought over sportswriter Larry Rocca to fill it. Larry, the brother of humorist and journalist Mo Rocca, had worked at *Newsday* and the *Newark Star-Ledger*. I was told the team wanted to market differently and do things American-style. I got Larry the job, and he sank his teeth into it. He went head over heels, selling sponsorships to companies like The Hartford and other multinational companies. He was also our mascot, who came out and did footraces with the fans during the seventh inning stretch. Larry organized the cheerleaders. He named them the M Splash—M for Marines and Splash because the stadium is on the water. His nickname was M Crash, because he did bizarre things in his rainbow-colored wig and gold suit.

I put in an analytic system, one that is used today by many major league teams. I hired Data Stadium, a data collection company. We devised ways of putting every pitch into the program, so a computer could tell when pitches were thrown and at what velocity, what location, and we designed programs that showed where balls were hit and how fast the ball went off the bat, how far it went, and in what direction.

Paul Pupo, who had run my restaurants for about twenty-five years, was very good at data interfacing. He connected the dots. We always talked baseball, and he became head of the data processing department. When scouts came to see what we were doing, I let them hang around with Paul. A lot of general managers came back to the States and started duplicating what Paul and I were doing.

The baseball community in Japan was really challenging, because the first time I came to Japan, I'd done that Compaq computer TV ad where I said I was going to change the world and I was going to change the game. I was bringing in new ideas to show Japan the American way of doing things. My ideas were met with stubborn resistance.

One thing I learned when I was there in 1995 was that what they were doing before I arrived was damn good. What I needed to figure out was how to fine-tune it, how to bring an individual approach that might enhance it. So when I came back in 2004, that was the entire challenge: not to tell anyone what to do but to try to figure out how everyone should be doing what was best for success.

A couple of my Japanese coaches were challenging and weren't loyal. But that was nothing in comparison to the Japanese baseball world and Japanese society itself—the last thing in the world they wanted was for me to succeed. Japan has always been a closed society. Baseball and sumo wrestling are their sacred sports. I was entering their world. I was the minority. I was the one who stuck out in a society in which no one stuck out. Back in 1995, there were a lot of things I wanted to force-feed. I wanted to make sure everyone knew what I knew, until I realized they didn't care what I knew, didn't give a damn what I knew—until they first knew that I had come to Japan to do something for the team, the baseball community, and maybe even Japanese society.

In 2004, that's what I set out to do. I tried to educate the two coaches, who weren't loyal, why I was doing things. When the season was over, I took the coaches on my dime to the States, and we spent ten days in New York and went to a casino. Some stayed in my house. Some stayed in a hotel. I tried to let them know that everything we were doing was for the "we," not for the "me." Over time it resonated, but it wasn't easy.

That first year, we were 65–65. It was an improvement, and then in 2005 we were really excellent. The owner handed the organization over to me, and it was smooth sailing.

The fans came back. We set attendance records. I changed the look of our uniforms a little, adding some color to the black and white pinstripe, and we got creative with our hats. I wanted to do this for our fans, because when I left in 1995, there was a petition signed by 20,000 fans for me to stay. It was initiated by the *ōendon,* the organized cheering section in the right-field stands. They carry signs. They have songs they sing. The organized cheering starts at the beginning of the game and continues right to the end. They have a song for every Marine hitter. They will sing the song and chant the name of the hitter during his entire at-bat, regardless of the score, and if someone does something good. When the team takes the field, the right-field stands will call out each position, and that player will tip his hat. The Yankees used to do that. When the fans would chant, "Derek Jeter," he would tip his hat. That came from the *ōendon.* The Japanese fans are so much a part of the game, and they were so much a part of my coming back, because I was so inspired by their enthusiasm and commitment to me during the ten years I was away. There were signs in the stands, "Bring Bobby Back." I'm sure the owner saw them.

In addition to changing the uniforms, with the help of the PR department I retired uniform number 26, saying that it meant that the fans were the twenty-sixth player.

In 2004, I got more familiar with the international scouts, the major league scouts who came to our games, and became friendly with John Deeble, who lived in Australia. I explored the idea of holding spring training in Australia. Deeble and Isao O'Jimi, one of my scouts, found a fabulous facility with multiple fields in Geelong, Australia. I convinced the ownership to rent a 747 and take everyone there, which is right across Lake Victoria from Melbourne, a beautiful area in the southeastern part of the country. I thought it was a great way to show the players that they were special.

The mentality of the baseball community in Japan dictates that being a baseball player is a job. The players are there to *go to work*. You had to put in a lot of hours in the day working hard, and after you put in a lot of hours and years, maybe you become a star player. I wanted my players to feel a little better about themselves, to expand their horizons, and to understand how there are other parts of the world that exist. I thought the ten-hour flight to Australia was going to be worth it. We stayed at a four-star Sheraton Hotel. We brought all our balls and protective netting for practice, and tons of rice and water. I didn't know it, but Australia was in the middle of a drought, and water was at a premium.

The first game of the season was against the Rakutan Golden Eagles on March 26. We lost a close Game 3–1 to Hisashi Iwakuma, who would go on to play in Major League Baseball. For Game 2, we broke out our newly designed uniforms. It was the first year for the Golden Eagles in their beautiful ballpark. They were all excited about winning their season opener, but then we won the second game 26–0. The uniform number 26 that was now hanging in our dugout as a symbol of the fans took on a new meaning. Our final game was played on October 26—important in this very symbol-conscious country. Our fans now knew: *We are in it to win it.* After losing the opener, we went on to win ten games in a row.

I wanted to do more for the fans. We had a little 30,000-seat stadium in the suburbs. We didn't have foot traffic like most of the stadiums in the big cities. We were a destination location with a stand-alone stadium, so we started doing things for the fans before and after the games. We had the kids run the bases on the field, which had never been done before. The parents came down on the field to get their pictures taken with the players, and they were able to get autographs. That had never happened before. We set up food courts outside the stadium, something that had just started in the United States, after teams saw how well it worked. Before and after games, we set up a karaoke stage outside the stadium, where players would make special appearances and sing their favorite songs with fans. They also did what was called the Hero's Interview. At the end of the game, the star would rush to the sideline so he could be interviewed on television by the sideline reporter. The fans at the game could watch the interview on the big screen in center field.

In Japan the entire stadium was screened, but I took down some of the screening so the fans and players wouldn't feel so isolated. I was also developing the talented young players at the major league level, which was not the Japanese way. Tsuyoshi Nishioka was only twenty-one years old. He was a switch-hitting shortstop, who with Toshiaki Imae, the third baseman, became synonymous with our team's always-smiling, hard-working young players. Nishioka didn't drink, but he was social and was seen at a lot of the right places at the right time. A lot of TV shows wanted him. In Japan, the parking lot of a major league team looks like a convention of Wall Streeters—high-end Mercedes, the best BMWs, the sleekest Lexus. Nishioka decided to get a gray Hummer with his name sewn on the seats, and flashing red lights. If anything in Japan was ostentatious, it was a Hummer, which took up both lanes of most streets in the country.

Imae was cool. He was at the other end of the spectrum. He married a beautiful TV commentator who was six years older. He was always on time, said and did the right thing at all times. That benefited him when, during the pennant drive, his pregnant wife was ready to have her baby.

Imae came into my office and said his wife wanted him there when she delivered the baby. Could he leave the team for a day and be with her? My interpreter, when Imae said that in Japanese, couldn't get the words out. Never before had a Japanese player missed a game, not for the birth of a child, not for a funeral. I brought my coaches in and asked them what they thought, and the Japanese coaches turned seven shades of gray. Wouldn't it destroy the *wa* of the team? How could we possibly permit this? There was uproar. I thought it was beautiful for Imae to want to be with his wife, so I let him do it, and he went home, and he came back happy and wound up becoming the MVP of the Japan Series. We lived happily ever after.

The Japanese press, of course, had a field day at my expense. I was learning to speak the language, but I never did learn to read Japanese, which was a good thing, because if the commentary was bad, I didn't want to know about it. I was scrutinized for just about anything, including my preference to bunt for a base hit rather than sacrifice. The Japanese press felt that a hitter bunting for a base hit was selfish. I was pushing the envelope, and there were many times when I might have gotten the result of a sacrifice bunt but didn't call for it.

During the 2005 playoffs, I had runners on first and second. We were down a run in the eighth inning. My right-hand-hitting catcher, Tomoya Satozaki, was at bat, and their pitcher was being talked to by their pitching coach. Katsuya Nomura was one of the greatest players who ever played and for twenty-six years starred for the Nankai Hawks, getting 2,901 hits. He later became a very successful manager and now was a TV commentator, and he was going on and on about how the sacrifice bunt was a necessary weapon, and if I didn't sacrifice in this situation, I might be sacrificing my job. I ignored the pressure to bunt. Satozaki hit a double off the wall, both runs scored, and we won 3–2 in what was the last game that Sadaharu Oh ever managed.

In 2005 we finished the season with an 84–49 record. We finished first in the division for the first time in the history of the Chiba Lotte Marines. The number of fans grew immensely. In 2004, we might have doubled our fans from 600,000 to 1.2 million. In 2005, we went up to 1.5 million.

Our ace that year was Shunsuke Watanabe, a submariner to the nth degree. His fingers were about two inches from hitting the ground. He threw about 82 miles an hour. He also had a big, sweeping slider/change-up, so his 82-mile-an-hour pitch looked a lot faster when it was delivered in his submarine fashion. Shunsuke pitched in some of our biggest games, finishing with a 15–4 record and an ERA of 2.17 in 2005.

He paired with Naoyuki Shimizu, who was a little older and a little more of a leader. Shimizu was terrific the entire time, finishing with a record of 10–11. Our closer was Masahide Kobayashi, who had one of those magical seasons. He came in, and twenty-nine times shut out the other team in the ninth, to give us the win.

Another of our stars, Saburo Omura, was the number-one draft choice in 1995. He was now a veteran outfielder with a great arm. He played very good defense and, most of the year, batted fourth. He was also one of the first players in the league to wear his first name on the back of his uniform. It's what Ichiro also did. Using his first name was kind of different, and it lent itself to me. Saburo hit .313 with 14 home runs and 50 RBIs, even though he didn't play every day. He was a very solid player.

Tsuyoshi Nishioka had become the starting shortstop, and he finished the 2005 season with 48 RBIs and 42 stolen bases. With Nishioka playing full time, Makoto Kosaka, the player whose job he shared, also had an excellent year. He stole 26 bases and was a terrific defensive player at short.

Koichi Hori, our second baseman, should have been the first position player to go to the States. I came to Japan in 1998, when I was managing the Mets, to try to convince Hori to sign with the Mets. He was a terrific Bobby Grich-type second baseman, steady, and he could hit the tough pitchers. His kids were young, and his wife wasn't sold on the idea of his going to the States by himself, of his not being with his kids when they were growing up, so he turned down a pretty good offer. That was before Ichiro. In 2005, Hori was thirty-six years old. He could still hit the tough pitchers, but his back wasn't good, so he played sporadically. Kosaka and Nishioka played regularly at second and short.

Good depth makes a good team. Some guys didn't get into a game until mid-May, but I always wanted my players buying into the idea that we needed all twenty-five players to win. And with this team, everyone was buying into it. You didn't have to play every inning of every game, and so we had a lot of parts that were interchangeable and complemented each other. We had the kid Akira Otsuka, who was a superb defensive center fielder. He hit .293. He didn't hit against right-handed pitching often, but he did well against lefties, and he was the right-left combination with Matty Franco.

Satozaki, our catcher, who batted right-handed, caught more often than not. Tasuku Hashimoto, our other catcher, was like Geno Petralli on my Rangers team, a guy they tried to get rid of every year. I kept trying to find a place for Hashimoto to play, and he wound up making a pretty good living and contributing that championship year. Dan Serafini made about 20 starts and finished the year 11–4 with a 2.91 ERA. He had a great pickoff move and a really good curveball. Matt Franco and Benny Agbayani had great years. Matt had 21 home runs, 78 RBIs, and hit .300. He was always a good hitter. He was that tweener guy in the States, because his defense was below average at third base, and at first base he was adequate if not stellar. Those positions are tough to crack in the big leagues. I had a very good first baseman in Fukuura, but I was able to play Matt at DH and in left field, and a little at first when Fukuura needed a rest. Matt was almost a regular. He never had the opportunity to get at-bats in the majors, but when he came to Japan, Matt made the best of it, and a lot of his hits were big hits.

All year I went with a six-man rotation. We had Monday off, and I wanted to make sure our pitchers were healthy, and I kept telling them, "We're going to make the playoffs, and I want to see everyone strong at the end of the year." We had six pitchers who pitched once a week. All were healthy. No one missed a start because of injury. I had a left then right setup combination with Yasuhiko Yabuta and Soichi Fujita, who pitched in front of our closer, Masa Kobayashi. They were fantastic. Yabuta had a better-than-average changeup to go along with his 93-mile-an-hour fastball, and Soichi had a really good cutter from the left side, a good curveball, and he threw about 91 miles an hour. Kobayashi had a 93-mile-an-hour sinker and an 88-mile-an-hour split-fingered fastball that were really tough to put in play. He broke a lot of bats and didn't give up many home runs. They were always there for me.

We finished the season 84–49, four and a half games behind Sadaharu Oh's Fukuoka SoftBank Hawks.

CHAPTER 32

Bobby Magic

Japan's Pacific League had established a new playoff system the previous year, and our second-place finish gave us home-field advantage for the first playoff round in 2005 against the league's third-place finisher, the Seibu Lions. All games would be played at our stadium. Seibu had a spectacular pitching staff led by Daisuke Matsuzaka, who was in his fifth year of professional ball after being a legendary high school pitcher. In the Koshien high school tournament final he pitched twelve innings, only to have to replay the game the next day, and he started the next day and pitched nine innings to win. Now we had to beat him in Game 1.

Seibu also had Kuzuhiro Wada, one of the real fine veteran hitters. In 2005, Wada led the Pacific League with a .322 batting average. He hit 27 home runs. In Game 1, Seibu scored in the first inning to take a 1–0 lead, and then in the sixth we had men on first and second with my young shortstop, Nishioka, up at the plate. In this situation in Japan, the conservative move was to sacrifice bunt. I hated giving up an out, so I gave him the sign to bunt for a base hit. He got down a good bunt that Matsuzaka bobbled, and with no outs we had the bases loaded.

Hori—who could have been the first Japanese position player to go to the majors, a terrific hitter who was now thirty-six years old—hit a ball that should have been a grand slam. But our ballpark was on Tokyo Bay, and much like Wrigley Field, there was always a prevailing wind. On this day it was blowing straight in from left, and the ball was caught in front of the fence for a sacrifice fly. We were tied 1–1.

In the eighth, with a runner on second, manager Tsutomu Itō brought in his star left-hander, Koji Mitsui, to pitch to Fukuura, my veteran number-three hitter—a left-handed hitter who always hit .300 and had a perfect swing. Fukuura drove in the run to give us the lead. Leading 2–1 in the ninth, I brought in Masa Kobayashi, who, like most closers, was much maligned. Masa always made the game exciting. He reminded me of Armando Benítez, who had had two forty-save seasons in a row with me on the Mets, but every time he came into the game, Mets fans bit their fingernails and worried about what might happen. Masa came in, and with runners on first and second and one out, induced a ground ball to the shortstop for a double play to end the game.

We only needed to win one more game to move on. In Game 2, Seibu started Kazuyuki Hoashi, their other ace, and I started my other Kobayashi, Hiroyuki Kobayashi. He was a young right-hander who had come into his own with a 92-mile-an-hour fastball and an excellent breaking ball. He pitched very well, holding Seibu to one run. I started Kosaka, our veteran, excellent-fielding shortstop who had lost his job to Nishioka, and he responded with a leadoff triple in the bottom of the first. He then scored on a sacrifice fly to make the score 1–0.

Benny Agbayani was having back problems at the end of the year and was not in the starting lineup. I had sent him to the minors so he could work out his swing, then brought him back for the playoffs. In this game, Benny got up in the sixth with a runner on second and drove him in to make it 2–0. Benny then took off on a hit-and-run, and our power hitter, Seung Yuop Lee, executed perfectly with a base hit to left field—the shortstop had vacated the spot to take the throw from the catcher—and Imae drove in our third run with a single.

Hiroyuki Kobayashi looked like he was going to pitch a complete game, but their young power hitter, Michael Nakamura, hit a home run and I decided once again to bring in Masa to close out the game. He got the first two batters and then had to face Wada. We all took a deep breath, and then Masa got him to ground out to shortstop.

Seibu was out. Lotte was in, to the elation of the 40,000 standing Marines fans. At the end of the game, I looked across to the Seibu bench, and I could see manager Ito looking at me. I walked toward home plate, he met me there, and we shook hands. He wished me good luck going forward. I thanked him for a great series and season. As we were on the field celebrating, the entire Seibu team stayed in the dugout respectfully applauding us. I was moved by that.

After the game, both Kobayashis—the starter and the closer—did the Hero's Interview, and then they honored me by asking me to speak. I mentioned that we had retired uniform number 26 at the start of the season to honor the fans, because they were the twenty-sixth man on the team. And in a loud voice at the end, I shouted, "Let's all go to Fukuoka!"—which was about 2,000 miles to the south, at the extreme southern part of the islands of Japan—where we had a five-game series against the Fukuoka SoftBank Hawks to see who would go to the Japan Series.

We had such wonderful fans. The cheering section—the *ōendon*—cheered all game long, regardless of the score. Many of these fans would take the summer off from work to travel with the team. They and I had a real bond, and I wanted to recognize them. They were my strength and my spirit and, of course, the strength and spirit of the team. We knew they all couldn't go, because the visiting team only got 5,000 tickets, so for the first time in Japanese history, we opened our ballpark to our fans, so they could watch the game on the big screen in the outfield. It was free, and the stadium was packed. I would have loved to have been with them, because it seemed like a five-day party.

It's a five-hour ride on the bullet train from Tokyo to Fukuoka. Instead of playing in Marine Stadium, which was built very much like Riverfront Stadium in Cincinnati and Three Rivers Stadium in Pittsburgh, the Fukuoka ballpark had a retractable dome and seated 50,000 fans. All the games of this best-of-five series would be played in their stadium, since they had finished in first place.

The team was led by the greatest home run hitter of all time, Sadaharu Oh, who hit 868 home runs playing for the Yomiuri Giants in Tokyo. He had managed the Giants but was now managing the Hawks, who were owned by one of the richest men in the world, Masayoshi Son, who owned SoftBank, a communications network, and properties all over the world. We knew we were in for a battle. Their foreign players, Jolbert Cabrera, Tony Batista, and Julio Zuleta, were something to deal with. Cabrera was a Colombian who had played seven years in the majors with Cleveland, the Dodgers, and Seattle; but with Fukuoka in 2005 he hit close to .300 and was a dangerous hitter. Batista in 2004 with Montreal hit 32 home runs, drove in 110 runs, and stole 14 bases, and in 2005 with Fukuoka, he hit 27 home runs and drove in 90 runs. Zuleta had amazing power and hit in the middle of the lineup. They also had two left-hand-hitting superheroes, a fleet shortstop named Kawasaki, and a first baseman/DH named Matsunaka—the closest thing to Barry Bonds that the Japanese had seen, other than Hideki Matsui, who played for the Yankees. In 2005, Matsunaka hit 46 home runs and drove in 121 runs while hitting .315.

The stadium was packed with 50,000 Fukuoka fans. There wasn't another media credential to be had or another ticket to be sold. Benny Agbayani and Matt Franco were there to give the team some stability, as they had been during the 2000 World Series with me. Even so, the power and strength of the Japanese teams came from the talent of the Japanese players and the spirit of their fans.

I started my *gaijin* pitcher, Dan Sarafini, in Game 1. Dan had bounced around from major league team to team. He was looking for a new start in Japan, and I gave it to him. He had pitched well. In the second inning, Cabrera hit a 91-mile-an-hour cutter for a home run, and they led 1–0. But in the fourth, my platoon outfielder, Akira Otsuka, got a base hit off Toshiya Sugiuchi, their ace left-hander; and after Hori advanced him to second on a hit-and-run, Saburo Omura hit a double to right-center to drive in Otsuka and tie up the game.

We went up 2–1 when Satozaki, my star catcher, who didn't play against Seibu because he was injured, came back and hit a home run in the top of the seventh. I went to my bullpen and brought in Shingo Ono to pitch to Cabrera. Shingo was a sinkerballer, and it didn't work out the way I wanted, because Cabrera doubled to left-center. I then brought in my left-handed specialist, Fujita, to pitch to the next two hitters, who were both left-handed. The first one bunted the runner over to third. Sadaharu Oh then pinch-hit Naoki Matoba, a right-hander, who singled against Fujita to tie the score at 2.

Hori led off the eighth inning for us and singled. Fukuura was next, and this was another one of those situations where everybody in Japan wanted me to sacrifice. I let Fuki hit away, and on the first pitch he took a slider for a strike. I put on the bunt, and he took a high fastball. Sadaharu Oh had his pitcher throw over to first a few times to try to pick off Hori, knowing I liked to hit-and-run. Then the pitcher threw a high fastball, almost a pitchout, and Fuki took it. With the count 2 and 1, I took off the bunt. Fuji showed bunt, pulled back his bat, and hit a high fastball into the gap in right-center. Hori stopped at third. I thought he should have scored, but my third-base coach Norifumi Nishimura, my center fielder when I first went to Japan, held him up.

Benny Agbayani came to bat, and Benny hit the first pitch on a line off the left-field wall, scoring two runs. The ball bounced right to the left fielder, and Benny was held to a single. We led 4–2, and in the eighth, Yabuta pitched a perfect inning and I brought in Masa for the last three outs. Matsunaka led off—either he or Kawasaki always seemed to come up in key situations—and Matsunaka put on a great at-bat, fouling off a couple of tough pitches before striking out on a nasty sinker for the first out of the inning. We let out a sigh of relief.

Then came the two *gaijins*. Batista hit a ball that looked like it was going to leave the park, but Benny went back and caught the high, towering fly right in front of the left-field fence. Cabrera was hitting with two outs, and Masa got him on a ground ball to third, and the Marines were ahead of the Hawks one game to none.

All of Japan was in shock. Fukuoka was supposed to win. They had spent the most money. They had the best stadium. They had Sadaharu Oh as their manager. They had two of the best foreign players. Their starting staff, their bullpen, their lineup were the best in the country. It was easy for the betters to pick Fukuoka to win the series, but now we led one game to none.

I started Shimizu, the ace of our staff, in Game 2. During our pre-game meetings, our main concentration was how to keep Kawasaki off the bases and how to get Matsunaka out, because they were the heart and spirt of their team.

Takahashi, a hard-throwing right-hander whom we had difficulty hitting during the season, started for Fukuoka. Shimizu gave up a run in the fifth inning, and in the top of the sixth, Nishioka, my young shortstop, doubled over the first-base bag. They brought in their star left-handed reliever, Kazumi Saito. He walked Hori.

I didn't have the next hitter, Fukuura, bunt, and he popped out. Saburo then walked to load the bases. Saito hadn't walked two hitters in an inning the entire season, and now we had the bases loaded with Matt Franco coming to bat. Matty was DHing this day, and with two strikes, he hit a split-fingered fastball to right-center for a double that drove in two runs. It was as incredible a hit as Matty ever got since an interleague game that the Mets played against the Yankees, when he got a ninth-inning, game-winning base hit off Mariano Rivera.

We scored a third run on a high hopper to the infield, and after six innings we were ahead 3–1. Shimizu was still pitching a strong game, when that little pest Kawasaki led off the sixth and hit a home run into the first row of the right-field stands. That wasn't easy. The first row is thirty feet off the ground, behind a high wall that went around the entire field. When this little guy hit that home run, we were starting to think that maybe the Fukuoka gods were going to come down and haunt us. The score now was 3–2, and it stayed that way into the ninth.

I brought Masa Kobayashi in again, and with two outs, the slugger Matsunaka came up again. On a 3–2 count, Masa threw a 90-mile-an-hour sinker, and Matsunaka hit a towering fly ball to left-center. We held our collective breath until it came down and landed in our center fielder's glove. We won 3–2, and now led two games to none.

Just before the start of Game 3, our fans rose as one to hold up banners that were three feet high by five feet wide and read, "I BELIEVE!!" The entire left-field stands were filled with thousands of these signs. At this time, our fans were really believing. It was in our hearts and minds. We really did believe. The fans had heard that I told my players to "Believe in yourself, believe in your teammates, believe that the outcome will be what you want it to be. Be prepared to do what you have to do and give your best effort…and BELIEVE!"

We went into Game 3 with great confidence. Our players were loose. Batting practice was extremely relaxed. The press wasn't as confrontational as it usually was. All of a sudden, they weren't doubting. They were saying Lotte had a chance.

For Game 3 I started Shunsuke Watanabe, my submarine pitcher. He had the guts of a burglar, and everyone loved him. We got two runs in the third and two in the eighth, and we led 4–0. Shunsuke was cruising. If we won this game, we would go on to the Japan Series.

Before the series began, I had told my ace reliever, Masa, "I can't wait until the last out of this series is made and you are standing on the mound."

Now it was the ninth inning, and Masa had a chance to do just that. The first batter, Cabrera, singled, which wasn't a concern, because Masa always made it a little exciting. The next batter popped out to second, and as I looked down our dugout, it was full to capacity. Every pitcher, all our staff, and our auxiliary staff were in the dugout, getting ready to run onto the field and celebrate.

310

The next hitter got jammed and hit a weak grounder back to Masa, who ran toward the third-base line to bare-hand the ball. He threw off-balance to first, and the ball went down the right-field line. Now, with one out, they had runners on first and third. The crowd was roaring as the infielders went to settle down Masa. Everyone in the dugout was still confident. We had a four-run lead.

The next batter singled to make the score 4–1, with men on first and second. Their pesky leadoff hitter, Kawasaki, was the hitter. Whenever he came up, something bad happened, and this was bad to the nth degree. He hit a high hopper to Imae's left at third. Imae leapt to glove it, but the ball eluded him, and his momentum caused him to brush against the runner coming to third. The umpire pointed to the play. The runner stopped at third. The bases were loaded.

What happened next was pure Hollywood, because from the Fukuoka dugout slowly came Sadaharu Oh, the most respected man in Japanese baseball, to argue with the umpires. The third-base coach and the runner stopped yelling, and the umpire acknowledged Sadaharu Oh's presence and walked over to talk to him. After a couple minutes' conversation, and with the other umpires in consultation, the umpire awarded the runner home plate. When he did, it was like a bomb went off, as the place erupted in jubilation. It was time for me to make an entrance. I slowly walked out to the umpire the same way Sadaharu Oh had done. I called all the umpires together and explained to them through my interpreter that I had seen the umpire point to the play, which indicated that there had been an obstruction. Then I told them what the rulebook stated: after the umpire acknowledges a play like that, the play must continue. After the play is completed, the umpire then determines whether the obstruction impeded the runner enough that he should be awarded an extra base.

"The runner, after he touched my third baseman, stopped at third base instead of trying to score. He did not continue running to home plate," I said. "You should not have allowed him to score."

As is customary in Japan, the home-plate umpire went to the microphone behind home plate to tell the fans what was being discussed.

This is unlike the U.S., where the fans have no idea what the umpires are talking about. He explained that though he initially had awarded the runner home plate, upon further consideration of the rules, the runner had to return to third. Sadaharu Oh just sat in the dugout and nodded his head yes. The fans met the decision with displeasure, and about fifty fans started throwing debris onto the outfield. We had to wait another five minutes for the cleanup crew to come out and collect everything.

Masa stood on the mound the entire time. In 1977, Mike Torrez stood on the mound and did nothing, waiting for Bucky Dent to walk off a foul ball that had hit him on the shin in a famous Yankees-Red Sox playoff game. On the next pitch, Dent hit the home run that cost the Red Sox the pennant. It was in my playbook that the pitcher must warm up during a timeout. Since that game, I always told my pitchers to warm up during delays. When I got back to the dugout, I asked my coaches whether Masa had thrown any warmup pitches. No one seemed to be sure, and on the first pitch, with the bases loaded, Masa threw wildly. Only a diving stab by Hashimoto kept the ball from going to the backstop. On the next pitch, the batter singled in two runs. Our lead was down to 4–3. The elation that had swept our dugout was gone, and in its place were the most solemn looks imaginable. I didn't even want to look at my players. The next batter grounded out. That left runners on second and third with Matsunaka, their Barry Bonds, coming to the plate.

Matsunaka hadn't gotten a hit in the series, but I was not going to let him get the game-winning hit that would uplift his team and its fans. I ordered Masa to walk him intentionally to reload the bases. Julio Zuleta was next. Masa threw four pitches, and not one was in the strike zone. Zuleta's walk tied the game at 4.

We went to the tenth. Their closer, Takahiro Mahara, who had 22 saves, held us. In the bottom of the tenth, I brought in Shingo Ono, who gave up a couple of hits and a walk. I took him out and brought in Fujita to pitch to their leadoff hitter, Kawasaki, and sure enough, he got a base hit to win the game 5–4. It was a disastrous loss, just as we were about to win the series. We were now in a different place.

Wada pitched for Fukuoka in Game 4, and Julio Zuleta hit two home runs to put them ahead 3–2 in the ninth inning. What happened next was amazing. My entire *ōendon*, the Chiba Lotte contingent of fans, stood and displayed their "I Believe" signs. *Everyone* was standing. We were down by a run with one out and Toshiaki Imae at the plate. With the count at 3 and 2, Imae checked his swing, and the umpire called it a ball.

Sadaharu Oh once again made his presence felt, as he slowly walked out to talk with the home-plate umpire. He demanded the umpire check with the first-base umpire to ask whether or not Imae had swung at the pitch. The first-base umpire raised his arm to signal he had swung. The game was over!

We now could feel that the tide had turned. We knew we were in the home of the Hawks, the home of Sadaharu Oh, and it appeared that maybe Bobby Magic had run out. The Fukuoka crowd was going crazy. No manager wants to see the look our players had in their eyes. I asked my players not to leave the dugout. Right there, while the Hawks fans and players were going crazy, I called a meeting and had everyone gather around in a circle.

"*Domo, domo, domo* [Thank you, thank you, thank you]," I said. "This is the most exciting time I have ever had in my lifetime, and because we lost this game, it gives us an opportunity to play Game 5, the game I've been looking forward to this entire season, the one that will determine who the Pacific champions are going to be. We are lucky enough to have *this* opportunity tomorrow, right here in the Fukuoka Dome, so I thank you guys for giving me the opportunity, and you should feel that you are the luckiest people in the world to be enjoying this moment with me."

My talk was rendered in Japanese by my translator. I saw some smiles, and I knew my guys were with me. I don't know if anyone slept that night, because I didn't. I couldn't wait until the next day. I was full of anxiety.

I started young Masa Kobayashi on the mound.

SoftBank went ahead 2–0 on a home run in the second inning and an RBI single in the third. In the fourth inning, we had men on first and second and no outs, with Saburo, my cleanup hitter, at bat. I chose not to have him bunt, and he hit into a double play. The doubters were second-guessing: *Why wouldn't you bunt him in that situation? The double play is the worst thing you want.* And that's exactly what happened. Sugiuchi, their ace left-hander, was cruising. Nishioka led off the sixth with a single. With a left-hander on the mound, I did what I wasn't supposed to do: I gave Nishioka the steal sign, and he stole second. I could feel the mood in the dugout lighten. Nishioka arose from the base shaking his fists, and our next batter, Fukuura, laced a double to right-center to cut the lead to 2–1. Saburo Omura once again popped out, and with a runner on second, Satozaki stranded him. We went into the eighth down 2–1.

Hori, my star second baseman, couldn't play in this game because his back was bothering him, so I played a rookie named Hayasaka and batted him second. He was scheduled to lead off the inning. I decided to pinch-hit for him. I asked Hatsushiba, who had been my third-place hitter—the heart and soul of the team in 1995 but who was now on the bench at the end of his very fine career—to bat. Hatsushiba hit a magical ground ball, a high hopper between third and shortstop. Both fielders went for it, and there was a slight collision, an off-balance throw to first, and a bang-bang play in which Hatsushiba was called safe. The tying run was now on base. Fukuura, who went on to get 2,000 hits in his career, then hit a line drive to right field for a single.

Saburo was now at bat. This was another sacrifice-bunt situation, and I gave him the sign to bunt for a base hit. He took that pitch, and on the next pitch he popped out. Satozaki was at the plate with Koji Mise, their closer, on the mound. We had hardly scored against Mise the entire year. Satozaki hit a fastball off the left-center-field wall. Fukuura, running on the crack of the bat, slid home safely on a bang-bang play. We were up 3–2, and our dugout went absolutely crazy.

The Hawks did nothing in the eighth, and we didn't score in the top of the ninth. One more time it was Masa time! Masa Kobayashi came in to close out the game.

In the left-field stands, our *ōendon* displayed the thousands of white "I Believe" signs. They were holding and jumping, holding and jumping, as Masa took what seemed like a ten-minute walk from the dugout to the mound. I can only imagine what was going through his mind, the minds of all our fans, and the minds of all our players.

I really believed in Masa, and as he walked out, I yelled to him: "I believe!"

Their seventh-place hitter led off the ninth, and he was in the middle of a nine-pitch at-bat, fouling off pitches, as I was having a flashback to Armando Benítez pitching to Paul O'Neill in the 2000 World Series, when O'Neill led off the ninth and fouled off five pitches before walking. On the tenth pitch of this at-bat, he walked. I was sure the next hitter was going to bunt, and he popped the ball up behind home plate. Satozaki, our catcher, broke forward then back and made a leaping dive for the ball, which hit the edge of his glove and rolled into foul territory. On the next pitch, the batter sacrifice bunted successfully to move the runner to second.

Sadaharu Oh called time-out and, in his slow fashion, walked out to get the umpire's attention to signal for a pinch-hitter, a left-handed veteran who Masa jammed and got to pop up to second. We were up by a run, and they had a runner on second with two outs. The 50,000 fans were on their feet yelling and screaming, and coming to the plate was their leadoff hitter, Kawasaki.

I had it in my mind that I should walk him, but I didn't want to put the winning run on base, even though I truly wondered whether Masa could get him out. I looked at my coach Frank Ramppen, and he looked at me quizzically, as if to say, "Is this going to happen again?"

The count went to 3 and 2. Masa threw a fastball down the middle that Kawasaki just missed hitting out of the park. The deep fly ball was caught by Jun Inoue, my left fielder, and the Chiba Lotte Marines were the Pacific League champions.

Before I knew it, I was running out onto the field as the entire team was jumping up and down and hugging each other behind the mound.

Then, without my realizing what was happening, about ten of my players grabbed my legs and shoulders and lifted me up. In the traditional fashion after winning a championship in Japan, they threw me in the air, then caught me. Threw me in the air, then caught me. Threw me in the air, then caught me.

In this symbol-conscious country, this ritual showed that in order to win a championship, you need two things: trust and teamwork. During the season, the team needs to trust the manager. And after the victory, the manager knew the players had the teamwork to throw him into the air, and he had the trust that they would catch him. While I was in the air, I was in the most relaxed state I had ever been in in my life. I was smiling so broadly. Inoue had given me the game ball, and I was holding it in my hand as I was being tossed up and down. My feet were together. My hands were in the air, and it was as fine a feeling as I had ever experienced in or out of a uniform.

We then grabbed uniform 26 from the dugout, and the entire team ran across the field to the *ōendon*. We held up uniform number 26 to show our fans, who were delirious. What was amazing, not a single Fukuoka Hawks fan left. They were respectfully standing and applauding as our fans were hugging and crying and jumping and cheering.

It was an amazing evening to experience. I will cherish it forever.

CHAPTER 33

Japan League Champions

The Hanshin Tigers had not won a Japan Series championship since 1985. When they won that year, the joy was so extreme in the Osaka area that many of their fans celebrated by jumping in the river adjacent to Koshien Stadium, their home stadium. In their excitement, some of the fans ran to the nearby Kentucky Fried Chicken restaurant and took the statue of Colonel Sanders off its moorings and brought the Colonel with them into the river. The Colonel was never seen again. The folklore was that Hanshin would never win another title until the Colonel was rescued from the river. In the United States, the Chicago Cubs were facing a similar curse. When William Sianis, the owner of the Billy Goat Tavern, was forbidden from taking his goat into Wrigley Field for the 1945 World Series, Sianis declared that the Cubs would be cursed and never win another World Series. The Billy Goat Curse lasted seventy-one years, until the Cubs finally won it in 2016.

Ever since 1985, each time the Tigers had a chance to win the Central League, their fans would dive into the river and try to find the Colonel

Sanders statue. Right before our series was to begin, there was a rumor that pieces of the statue had been found, but it was just a rumor.

Hanshin was like the Cubs in another way. They had the oldest, most traditional stadium in Japan, with ivy on the walls like Wrigley. Hanshin is Osaka's team, and their fans are incredibly loyal and boisterous. They were representing the Central League against the Pacific League in the Japan Series. We opened the best-of-seven series at home, which was a real treat for our fans. We were away the night we won the Pacific League championship. Thousands of fans attended a pregame pep rally, and when we opened at our home stadium, it was standing room only, with nearly 30,000 Marine fans. In the left-field stands were 5,000 of the other team's *ōendon*, all wearing Hanshin's yellow jerseys. It was quite a spectacle.

The last time a Lotte team had won the Japan Series was in 1974. Known then as the Lotte Orions, they played in the cities of Sendai and Kawasaki until the team moved to Chiba in 1992 and was renamed the Marines. It had been thirty-one years of frustration for Lotte fans. Until now. In the prefecture of Chiba, the world had turned upside down because we were finally in the Japan Series. For this game, we handed out white towels for everyone, and everyone stood and waved their towels throughout most of the game.

I had my two young stars, Nishioka and Imae, batting one-two, and when Imae homered in the first inning to put us up 1–0, the fans absolutely erupted. We scored three in the fourth when Seung Yuop Lee, my young Korean slugger, homered, and after my veteran catcher Satozaki homered in the sixth, we led 7–1. Our starter, Shimizu, pitched a great game. He had a four-pitch mix and was a great competitor. He held Hanshin to one run, so I didn't have to go to the bullpen.

The Tigers had very good veteran hitters, including Tomoaki Kanemoto, a perennial All-Star, and Norihiro Akahoshi, their center fielder, who also was an All-Star. In the first inning they had runners on first and second, but Kanemoto hit into a double play, a sign of things to come. Shimizu held them at bay.

Marine Stadium is right on Tokyo Bay, directly across the water from Yokohama. And on this night, for the first and only time it ever happened during a game, around the sixth inning an incredibly dense fog came off the water and engulfed the stadium. When Benny hit a two-run home run in the seventh to make the score 10–1, the ball disappeared as it ascended into the fog. The outfielders went back toward the stands, but we didn't know it was a home run until we heard the crowd in the stands singing Benny's song. Right after that, the umpires called the game. We had won the game in the fog.

In the second game, Watanabe, the submariner who came into his own that year, pitched a complete game at home, and we won 10–0. We didn't know it was going to be our last game at home. It was best-of-seven, and everyone thought the series would be quick if Hanshin won, and long if we won.

Ahead two games to none, our fans were ecstatic, and we left town on a high. But now we had to go to the hallowed grounds of Koshien, an ivy-covered brick structure that seats 55,000 of the most amazing fans in the world. Koshien is where they play the Japanese high school tournament in the summer. Four thousand high school teams play single elimination, and the last twelve teams play at Koshien before a packed crowd. It's a great spectacle that rivals college basketball's March Madness.

During Hanshin's games in this stadium, the seventh inning is amazing! Fifty thousand hometown fans stand and sing the team theme song. While standing, they inflate elongated yellow balloons. When the song ends, they release the balloons, which soar fifty, sixty, sometimes seventy feet in the air. They fill the entire sky above the stadium, and then they release the air and make a whistling noise and fall onto the field.

Remarkably, before the pitcher finishes his eighth warm-up pitch, a hundred groundskeepers race around the field picking up the 50,000 spent balloons, and without delay play is resumed.

In this game, we were winning 10–1 when the balloons were released. In their minds, the Hanshin fans didn't think 10–1 was an insurmountable lead. They believed in their team, and they were still cheering loudly, as loud as you could imagine.

Young Kobayashi was our starting pitcher and starred, and Fukuura was our hitting star. We were ahead 4–1 in the seventh when Fuki hit a grand slam to open the floodgates. We were up 3–0 in the best-of-seven series.

We went into Game 4 with Dan Serafini on the mound. We were leading 3–2 when I brought in Shingo Ono, who got a double play. Yabuta had a 1-2-3 eighth, and when Masa Kobayashi finished in the ninth with a strikeout, all hell broke loose, and we were diving on each other in the middle of the diamond in Koshien, the baseball shrine of Japan.

While we were deliriously celebrating, the players all surrounded me and lifted me in their hands and tossed me high in the air. After I came down, I went into our dugout and grabbed uniform number 26, referencing our fans, and the entire Chiba Lotte team followed me as we went out to the left-field stands where our fans were seated. We acknowledged them and stood as they threw banners and confetti down onto the field. The Hanshin fans stood and acknowledged us as we walked around the stadium. Most of them cheered politely as we went by.

The Chiba Lotte Marines were the surprise champions of Japanese baseball.

The team celebration was back at the hotel, rather than in the clubhouse. A ballroom completely protected by plastic was prepared for a two-hour party. There were 260 bottles of champagne and 2,600 bottles of beer that were drunk and poured and sprayed until we could hardly stand. Oh what a night!!!

We had a couple days off, and then we competed in the Asia Series for the Konami Cup, named after the game maker. We played Korea, Taiwan, and China, which was coached by Jimmy Lefebvre and Bruce Hurst. We had no trouble winning that championship. The entire time we were in a daze—in a dream—and nothing went wrong.

Even before the season began, I boasted we would become the champions of Japan. The newly elected governor of Chiba had invited me to come to the governor's office and meet her. She welcomed me and said she appreciated the year we had had in 2004, and she asked if there was anything she could do for us in the upcoming season.

"Yes," I said, "you could create a parade route for us." There had been none. None was ever needed. There were reporters in the room, and she chuckled, and the reporters all laughed, and as I was leaving, through my interpreter, I said, "Please understand that you have to have a parade route ready by the end of the season for our championship team."

When we won the championship, the governor sent me a note that the parade route was set. It started at City Hall, miles from Marine Stadium, and went to the stadium. The streets were lined with 270,000 fans, and the players were in open-air buses behind the coaches in convertibles. Five blocks from the stadium, the street was lined with five-story apartments on both sides. Fans lined the rooftops of the buildings, and after ripping up 26,000 newspapers, they covered the sky and street with confetti.

I was riding with Akio Shigemitsu, the owner of our team. Two weeks before, his retail business in Korea had gone public, and he became the third-richest person in Korea. As we were riding down the street in Bay Town, sitting atop the back seat of a convertible, he looked at me and said, "This is the greatest day of my life."

"Did you forget what happened two weeks ago?" I asked.

He laughed and said, "No, this is truly the greatest day of my life."

It was a great day for me, too!

The fruits of victory were distributed to all the members of our organization in the form of a specially designed, hand-crafted, eighteen-carat gold ring, with black onyx inlay and twenty-six diamonds, with each person's name and the number 26 engraved on the side. While common in America for championship teams, this was the first time a ring had been given to professional athletes in Japan to commemorate a championship. Nippon Professional Baseball bestowed upon me their highest honor: the Matsutaro Shoriki Award, given to the person who contributed the most in 2005 to Japanese professional baseball. Being the first non-Japanese recipient made this honor even more special. I will always cherish that I was also made an honorary citizen of Chiba. A year later, the city council of Bay Town made a proclamation naming a street that we rode down during the victory parade Valentine's Way. It stated in the proclamation that the name would never be changed.

Frank Ramppen was a coach with me all six years I managed in Japan, and he had run my restaurants for twenty years after his professional playing career. He was living on that street in one of the apartment buildings. When asked about what it meant to him to have a street named after me, he said, "Well, it's amazing that I worked for him the last twenty-five years, and we always did things Valentine's way. And now I live on Valentine's Way."

The first World Baseball Classic was held in March 2006. After winning the Japan Series championship the prior season, the Chiba Lotte Marines were hot. The Japanese baseball federation selected nine of my players to play in this world championship. I was so excited to see so many of my players selected. They flew to San Diego with the Japanese team and won the tournament, becoming champions of the first World Baseball Classic. This was exciting, but also very challenging. Our season in Japan began the day the players returned from the States, still drenched in champagne from the victory. *Wa,* or team togetherness, is paramount to a team's success. Our *wa* was fractured and took much of the season to repair.

In 2005, one of our competitors, the Hokaido Nippon-Ham Fighters, won the draft lottery and signed Yu Darvish. In 2007, the Rakuten Golden Eagles drafted Masahiro Tanaka in the first round. We tried to get both players but failed, and the next few years they kept us from winning the championship, with Darvish beating us in championship games in 2007 and 2008.

In 2007, ESPN decided to test their market by airing a documentary for the first time. The subject was me and the Chiba Lotte Marines. The film crew consisted of three NYU film school seniors, Andrew Muscato, Andrew Jenks, and Jonah Pettigrew. We were together for the entire season. We skied in the northern part of Japan as the season began and did everything imaginable, including climbing Mount Fuji, to allow these three spectacular young men to make *The Zen of Bobby V*. There was enough footage for five films, but they succeeded in condensing it to ninety minutes. It debuted on my birthday, May 13, 2008, at the Tribeca Film Festival. Incredibly, NYU graduation for the three young filmmakers was the next day at Yankee Stadium. Since that first experiment in sport documentaries, ESPN has gone on to notable success with its *30 for 30* series.

By 2009, I had learned to speak Japanese. When I first came to manage in 1995, I had an interpreter by my side at all times. Isao O'Jimi, who later became an MLB scout, was a baseball guy who knew the game, but his translation skills were limited. In 2004, I hired Shu Nakasone, a professional language interpreter, who was with me at every practice, every game, and every social occasion. Shu was able to translate my words and ideas. We had so many fabulous dinners together, eating some of the best food in the world. I made so many new friends, and I was able to share my experience with many of my friends and family from the States. Included in my contract were twenty business-class round-trip tickets per year from the U.S., and I gave every one of them out to friends and family.

I continued to learn to speak Japanese, and after the last game in 2009, I gave a twenty-minute speech in Japanese, without an interpreter, in the middle of the stadium from the pitcher's mound, to the 40,000 fans in attendance. They laughed when they were supposed to laugh, and cried when they were supposed to cry.

After the 2009 season, my contract with the Marines ran out and I had to make a decision. Would I stay away from home for another few years, or, given that I was turning sixty, should I go back to America and start another chapter of my life? I was either going to sign a new contract or go home.

I was always pushing to change the system in Japan. I had done that from the day I was hired. I was someone who came in from the outside and created change. When Toshiaki Imae's wife was giving birth, I allowed Imae to go home for the birth of his child. I gave him the day off, which was unheard of. We created a fan-friendly atmosphere and proved a small franchise could become a champion. I drafted a player from an independent league, which had never been done before, who later became a batting champion. If a player didn't get drafted, he played in an independent league and spent the rest of his career there. There was no entry into Nippon Professional Baseball for players who weren't drafted. I wanted Chiba Lotte to buy an independent team so we could create a minor league farm system. I wanted it to be easier for minor leaguers to come up to the major leagues. Our general manager wasn't interested. Ten years later, many teams added minor league teams. One of the primary reasons I was stonewalled was that our acting owner, Ryuzo Setoyama, and some of his cohorts didn't want me running the organization anymore. They wanted to take over because they wanted to go back to doing things the Japanese way. It had become something of a struggle.

Tokyo's Yomiuri Giants were owned by the *Yomiuri Shimbun*, the largest-circulated newspaper in the world. Tsuneo Watanabe, their president, ran the league. The *Yomiuri Shimbun* started baseball in Japan, and the Yomiuri Giants were the New York Yankees of Japan. Watanabe-san ran Japanese baseball much the way Walter O'Malley used to run Major League Baseball, and most everything I wanted to do, he frowned upon. I wanted to stop the great Japanese players from going to the States. I argued that if the Japanese teams offered them better contracts, they would stay in Japan.

Shigeo Nagashima—the greatest Japanese-born player, who also managed the Giants—and Sadaharu Oh agreed with me. We were hoping Watanabe-san would step down, or someone would take over from him as supreme commander. But it never happened, and it didn't look like it was going to happen. I got tired of banging my head against the wall. I felt it was time for me to leave.

The players wanted me to stay, and so did the fans, 100,000 of whom signed a petition to that effect. They not only wrote their names but their addresses as well. Leaving wasn't easy. During my time in Japan, my teams compiled a record of 494 wins, 450 losses, and 23 ties. I am thankful for the opportunity and experience of a lifetime—the players, the people, the food, and the fun. Boy, I'm a lucky guy!

CHAPTER 34

Fenway at 100

When I came home from Japan, ESPN had an opening for an analyst for *Baseball Tonight,* and I was offered the job. It was as stimulating, challenging, glorious, and enjoyable a time as I have ever had. I got to travel around and announce and comment on the All-Star Game, the World Series, and even the Little League World Series. The drive to Bristol, Connecticut, was only an hour and thirty minutes, and I enjoyed sharing the studio with Harold Reynolds, Karl Ravech, and the ESPN team.

I also accepted the position as director of public safety in Mayor Mike Pavia's administration in my hometown of Stamford. I was the director of the police, fire, EMS, and Board of Health, with a total budget of $275 million. It was an amazing learning experience. I worked for minimum salary as the job was meant to co-exist with my ESPN duties and donated the salary to the Stamford Boys and Girls Club. I had my wife, friends, and family with me. My first restaurant in town was still going strong, I was in city government, and I had a three-day-per-week gig on TV that suited me just fine.

At the end of my first year of service, I was the recipient of the sixty-sixth annual City of Stamford Citizen of the Year Award, sponsored by the local Jewish War Veterans. My Little League teammate Frank Abbott, along with Rick Redniss, made an amusing video presentation documenting my life, starting with my lead performance in the high school production of *The Teahouse of the August Moon,* and ending with my "lead" as safety commissioner in Stamford city government.

I was really enjoying life when I got a call from Jeffrey Loria, the owner of the Florida Marlins. It was June 24, 2011. Jeffrey and I knew each other because he had owned the Texas Rangers' Triple-A farm club at Oklahoma City during my tenure as manager of the Rangers. He then became the owner of the Montreal Expos, and swapped franchises to became the owner of the Marlins in 2002. Loria called right after he fired his manager Fredi González, and said he wanted to talk to me about replacing him. Would I meet him in New York City and sit down with him and other members of the organization?

We met at his Upper West Side brownstone. We talked for a couple of hours about his situation. He said he wanted me to manage. Before he hired me, Loria said, he wanted me to talk with his baseball guys, including David Samson, who was the son of one of his ex-wives. They were waiting in his art gallery, which was on the first floor of his brownstone. We talked, and I went home.

Loria called me the evening of the next day and offered me the job. We agreed over the phone that I'd get a contract for three years at $2 million a year. The plan was that I would meet him at Teterboro Airport near Woodbridge, New Jersey. I was to fly down to Miami with him in his private jet, watch Saturday's and Sunday's game with him and his baseball guys, learning everything I could, and after the Sunday game, I would replace the interim manager and go on the road with the team as its manager. I packed my bags and went to dinner with my buddy Bobby Castrignano, to tell him the news and share a glass or two of wine.

Around ten that night, I received a phone call from David Samson. When I met him, I hadn't gotten a warm and fuzzy reception, but he didn't seem like anyone I had to worry about.

Samson was upset. Buster Olney, whom I worked with at ESPN, had broken the story that I was going to be the Marlins' manager. It was Thursday night, and he was accusing me of doing something I hadn't done: leak the news to Olney. I stopped him in his tracks.

"Hey listen," I said. "You don't know me very well, but one thing you need to know for sure is that I'm not a liar, and I'm telling you right now that I did not tell Buster Olney, nor did I tell anyone else about this job, other than my good friend and immediate family, and they didn't talk to anybody."

"Bullshit," he said.

I hung up on him. Later that evening, Jeffrey Loria called, and he said, "Listen, we have a problem."

"I guess I'm not coming down to manage your team," I said.

"No, you're the manager of the team," he said. "Don't worry about that. But the commissioner is upset because there's a rule that if you fire the manager, you're supposed to interview minority candidates before you announce the replacement, and we didn't do that."

"What does that mean?" I asked.

"It will work out perfectly," he said. "We're going to go to Puerto Rico to play a three-game series versus the Mets, and we'll do some interviews, and by the time the next series in Atlanta begins, you're going to take over the team."

That was Friday night, and on Sunday afternoon I was working in Bristol. The ESPN talent and staff would gather in a large room with multiple TVs and watch all the games of the day. If anyone saw something to discuss on our show, we would tell the producers what we wanted recorded and edited for the show. After the show, I was going to tell my bosses that I wasn't going to be around anymore, that I was going to manage Florida.

The Marlins were playing the Mets in Puerto Rico. One of the TVs was focused on the Miami dugout before the game, and as I watched, I could see Jeffrey Loria in the dugout. The players were coming in, and they were hugging and shaking hands with the Marlins' interim manager, Edwin Rodriguez. There was no sound on, but I could read the words scrolling across the bottom of the screen, that the Marlins had hired the first Puerto Rican manager in baseball history, *to be their manager.* When I read that, I thought, *How in the hell are they going to be able to fire him to give me the job?*

Before the game started, my phone rang. It was Jeffrey Loria. "Well," he said, "we had a change of plans. It will be impossible to fire the first Puerto Rican manager in major league history as soon as he leaves Puerto Rico, so I have decided we will keep him for the rest of the year."

"Thank you," I replied, "but don't ever pull my chain again."

I hung up, called Mary and told her the change of plans, and went back to work. I did the show that night wondering what had just happened. Then I went home and unpacked. I was determined to find out how Buster Olney had gotten the story that I had been hired by the Marlins. Buster is not the most communicative person. He doesn't share well.

After years of investigation, I think this is what happened, though I can't prove it: Tony Pérez was on the staff of the Marlins. His son is Eduardo Pérez, who worked at ESPN. My suspicion is that Tony told Eduardo, who was friends with Buster, who ran the story, which cost me my job. I don't think anyone was trying to do harm, but remember, I got blamed for Tony Pérez's firing in Cincinnati. The good news is I stayed with ESPN and the next year got the most prestigious job of their baseball telecasts: *Sunday Night Baseball.* On May 2, while televising a game in Philadelphia, I got a text from Matt Conroy, the boy who had lost his father on 9/11, informing me that Osama bin Laden had been killed. I notified our producer, and as the fans were cheering "U.S.A." in the stadium, we announced the event to our viewing audience. It was very emotional.

In November 2011, I scheduled a trip to Japan to film a Christmas show for a charity I had started in Tokyo. My agent, Tony Attanasio, called me the day before my departure.

"Larry Lucchino wants to talk to you about the Boston manager's job," he said. Terry Francona had left the team at the end of September, and Larry, the Red Sox president, wanted to set up an interview with me.

I had spoken to Larry once before, in 2003, right after Grady Little had left pitcher Pedro Martínez in too long, costing the Red Sox a chance to go to the World Series. Larry and I had a phone interview, but I had already agreed to manage Chiba Lotte, and I was not going to leave them hanging again. I saw Larry again in 2007, when he came to Japan to scout Daisuke Matsuzaka, who was pitching in the Pacific League. Theo Epstein, Larry, and a couple others from the Red Sox asked me to meet them at the Grand Hyatt hotel in Tokyo.

I brought my analytics guy, Paul Pupo, and scouting director, Shun Kakazu. Paul was my friend for many years, and Shun was a Harvard graduate that I'd hired the year before. We gave them all the information we had on Dice-K. I told them he was a very good pitcher, but there would be some loud sounds when he hung his slider. On the way out, Larry asked me what the Sox could do to be sure they got him.

"Pay the team a lot more than anyone else with your bid," I said. It's what I had told the Mets when I wanted them to sign Ichiro. "And tell the Lions ahead of time you're going to do that." They could work a side deal to get some of the money returned to them. The Red Sox got him. I hadn't heard from Larry since.

Larry called to ask if I was interested in the Boston job. "Of course," I said. "Let's talk."

The Sox set up a meeting in an obscure real estate office in Hartford. They came down from Boston. I drove up from Stamford. It was the day before I was leaving for Japan. I talked with Larry for about forty-five minutes. During the interview, Larry said, "We have to do something about the beer in the clubhouse. Can you do something about that?" There had been a situation in the clubhouse the past season with some of the pitchers drinking beer and eating fried chicken during a game. Someone had blown the whistle on them, and it was one reason manager Terry Francona was no longer the manager.

"Larry," I said, "why don't you just take the beer out of the clubhouse? It's your liability if they're drinking too much. I had this situation in New York, and ownership just said, 'We'll take out the beer.'"

"No, no, no," Larry said. "It has to be the manager's decision."

"There is no one who likes a cold beer or two after a game more than me," I said. But being the team player I was, I finally said, "If you really need me to do it, I'll do it, but it really should be an ownership decision."

I also mentioned to Larry that my film company, Makuhari Media, was releasing a documentary, *Pelotero*, about a young Dominican baseball player who at sixteen years of age was signed by the Minnesota Twins. I told him it was not very flattering to MLB, and he should be aware of it. He said it would not be a problem.

I then had an interview with Ben Cherington, the brand-new general manager. Theo Epstein had left in the middle of the night to take a job with the Cubs. I didn't know Ben. It was the first time I had ever heard of him. He said he wanted to ask me about my in-game process. He had some ball games recorded on his laptop.

"I'm going to show you video of three games," Ben said. "I will stop the video, and I want you to tell me what you would do next if you were the manager."

It so happened that I had seen all of the games that he had taped. When he stopped the video and asked, "What would you do?" I knew exactly what to do. For the first one I said, "I would guard the line here, because I don't think we should allow doubles." Terry hadn't done that. On the video, the ball then went down the line, the batter got a double, and the Red Sox lost the game. For the next game I said, "I would definitely bring in the left-hander." I knew the pitcher that Francona had not taken out was right-handed, and he surrendered a home run. I almost wanted to say, "Hey, I've seen all these games," but fuck it, this was *his* interview, and after it was over, I drove back to Connecticut, got some sleep, and left for Japan the next day.

I was in Japan for three days, and I was out to dinner with twelve of the guys from my championship Chiba Lotte team. We were almost through dinner. We had quite a few beers and a lot of laughter. We were enjoying the night when my cell phone rang. It was Ben Cherington, who said he wanted to talk about my contract.

"When do you want to do that?" I asked.

"How about in an hour?" he asked.

I returned to my hotel, took a quick shower, and called Tony Attanasio, who wasn't home. Ben sent me an offer by fax. I received it in the little office center of the hotel in Tokyo. I wanted three years, but Cherington kept sticking to the notion that he could only give me two. It was about four in the morning when my lawyer, Phil Hersh, approved of the language, and I accepted a two-year contract.

"When can you get home?" Cherington asked.

"I'm in Japan," I said.

"We'd like to have a press conference as soon as possible."

"I can fly back and get to Boston the next day," I said.

"Okay, done. Let's do it," he said.

Cherington had warned me that if the news got out before the press conference, the deal was off. I called home and told Mary the news, and also let Tommy Lasorda and Lou Lamoriello know. I told them to keep it a secret. As I was boarding the flight, my good friend Doug Romano called to congratulate me. I asked how he knew, and he said Tommy Lasorda had done a radio interview and spilled the beans. I had told Tommy Lasorda, and he told the world. As I entered the plane, my phone died. I didn't have my charger with me. I spent the entire flight thinking they would cancel the offer. I got my luggage and waited for Doug to pick me up. When I got in his car, he didn't have a charger for my phone. We sat around the JFK airport trying to find a way to charge my phone and eventually wound up at a Tire Kingdom store. I ran inside and borrowed a charger, charged my phone, and called Ben Cherington while holding my breath.

"Don't worry about it," he said. "It leaked out in Boston."

It was a crazy way to start a relationship.

The press conference was on November 29, 2011. One Red Sox executive I was pleased to meet was Bill James, the high poobah of sabermetrics. I had been a Bill James reader since the '80s and was excited to meet him, but at the press conference I talked about my affinity for another sabermetrician, Craig Wright, whom I had worked with in Texas. Craig turned out to be a competitor of Bill's. When I mentioned Craig's name, he gave me a weird look, and even though I worked for the Red Sox for a year, I never met or talked with Bill James again.

I announced at the press conference that I had requested the number 25, in memory of Tony Conigliaro. My normal number was 2, but that was Jacoby Ellsbury's. Tony C was a beloved Red Sox slugger whose career was cut short by a horrific beaning. He died at age forty-five from complications following a stroke. Tony C and I had been roommates on one of his comeback attempts. I have a vivid memory of lying on separate beds one night and comparing both of us having been beaned in the head. This is not a conversation you have with just anyone. It's a private place you don't want to go. We shared the same sensation of the ball seeming to slow down and thinking you can avoid it, but then the impact and incredible noise inside your head. I am happy our paths crossed, briefly, and was proud to wear Tony C's number.

After the press conference, the traveling secretary, Jack McCormick, said to me, "The organization thinks it would be a good idea if you went to David Ortiz's golf tournament." Terry Francona was scheduled to attend, but he wasn't going.

"That would be great," I said. "When is it?"

"It starts *tomorrow* in the Dominican Republic, in Punta Gorda."

I wanted to be a good soldier.

"Can you arrange a ticket?" I asked. "I'll go down there."

I brushed my teeth somewhere, bought a pair of shorts and a t-shirt, left my car at the airport, and flew to the Dominican. I loved the Dominican and was happy to be there, but I was taken aback that David was surprised to see me. Not happy—surprised—almost like I was crashing the party.

The highlight of the trip was getting to sit with Boston Celtic legend Bill Russell, who talked about his remarkable career in Boston, and how when he became a coach, it was different from what he'd expected. Though he had won more championships than anyone who ever lived, the players didn't give him the respect he thought he deserved.

"I get it," I said, and I told him about the day I was managing the Mets and we were playing San Francisco in the late '90s and Willie Mays was in the clubhouse. I gave Willie a big hug, and I asked him if he would come out and meet some of my players. There were players on my team who didn't know who Willie Mays was. "It was mind-blowing," I said to Russell. "We were in San Francisco! In San Francisco you walk past Willie's statue on the way to the ballpark. You *should* have a clue." Russell laughed when I told him that.

When I got back home, there were articles in the Boston papers saying there was to be no beer in the clubhouse. The Boston press had writers who were insiders who got all the information and played the organization's game. Boston, I would soon learn, also had writers who never asked questions, because they didn't want to be hampered by the facts. Some of these writers were making it out that Old Drug Czar Bobby V once again was putting his stamp on a team by becoming the beer gestapo. Again, I tried to make it perfectly clear it was anything but who I was, but after Steve Howe and my taking away the beer from the Mets and now the Red Sox, the blame landed squarely on me. The resentment from some of the veteran players lingered throughout the season.

I was also told there had been some players whose feathers I had ruffled during the previous season when I was talking about them on ESPN.

"It's important," said Ben Cherington, "that you go out and meet with these players before the season starts."

"Why don't I wait until spring training?" I asked. "We'll have plenty of time to talk."

"Oh no," he said, and he gave me a list of players he wanted me to go see. There was Josh Beckett in Cotulla, Texas, Carl Crawford in Houston, and Jacoby Ellsbury, Clay Buchholz, Dustin Pedroia, and Darnell McDonald in Arizona.

I was a commentator on *Game of the Week* during one of the games Beckett was pitching, and Beckett was taking a long time between pitches. As a commentator, I said, "This is ridiculous, and there are actual rules against it. Why don't they enforce the rules so I don't have to figure out what to say in between all this dead time? It's driving me crazy."

Josh heard about it and was upset, so I had to go and talk to him before spring training. I called and said to him, "Josh, I want to come out and speak to you face-to-face. I hear we have a situation we should clear up before spring training, and I'm willing to meet you any place, any time."

I tried to set a date, but he kept saying, "I can't do it. I can't do it. I can't do it," until he finally said, "You can meet me at my home on New Year's Day morning."

After two or three weeks of helter-skelter, interviewing coaches and catching up on sleep and finding a Boston apartment, I wound up flying out on New Year's Eve to San Antonio and staying in a hotel at the airport, then waking up in the morning on New Year's Day to drive out to Josh Beckett's ranch. When I got there, someone who was preparing food for a gathering of Josh's friends, coming to watch important college football games, invited me to come and sit by the pool. Josh had a spectacular, large, Texas-style ranch home on an enormous property. I was given a bottle of water, and I waited by myself out by the pool until Josh finally came out. We sat and talked. He wanted to explain why he took so much time between pitches, especially against the Yankees. He said it was his way of breaking their timing. It made some sense, and then Josh talked about how upset he was about somebody going to the press to talk about the pitchers eating chicken and drinking beer during a game, how deplorable that person was. He made it sound like the culprit was a player on the team. I listened, and after about an hour and a half, he said, "Well, it's almost time for the football game to start. I'm going inside. Bye." And then he said, "If I was making only $5 million from this game, I'd walk away from this game." He was making $17 million.

I walked through the house, through the beautiful kitchen that was full of food and merriment, to the den where his family members were sitting in front of the television, and exited through the front door. It was a rude encounter, to say the least. I went back to the airport, watched one of the bowl games, got on a plane, and flew back to Boston.

I had a pleasant dinner in Arizona with Dustin Pedroia, Darnell McDonald, Jacoby Ellsbury, and Clay Buchholz. They said I should stress fundamentals during spring training. They said that fundamentals had gotten away from the team. They said they wanted to work and get back to being a championship team.

I returned home and made numerous calls to Carl Crawford, who didn't answer the phone. I left a lot of messages, and finally I was able to see Carl in Houston where he was working out. I had a half-hour talk with him. Most of the time he was frowning, telling me how different it was playing in Boston compared to Tampa Bay. He said he hadn't gotten used to it but wouldn't elaborate. I had made a comment on TV about his not catching a ball in left field that cost the Red Sox a playoff berth in 2011, but he never brought it up. I asked if he had any problems with anything I had said, and he said no.

I met John Lester and his wife at one of the pre-spring training functions at Fenway. John was kind of cold. I was excited to see him, and I mentioned to him that I was going to make an early announcement that he would be the opening-day starter, because everyone including myself felt that he deserved it. John is a very placid guy who doesn't get excited often. He's a man's man. I thought he would be pleased, but he displayed very little excitement.

One of the most important decisions I had to make was over which coaches to keep and which ones to let go. When I'd interviewed with

Larry Lucchino, I mentioned what Tom Landry had said to me years earlier, about making sure the coaches spoke my language, and how important that was for the culture of the team.

"That's cool," said Larry, "but we're paying you, and we are paying Francona. We're in a little bit of a crunch. I have coaches under contract until next year, and I was hoping you would interview them and do what you can to keep as many of the guys as possible."

I felt Larry was reaching out to me to see what kind of a team player I was. And I am a team player, even when it's not in my best interest to do so.

"I get it," I said.

I didn't know these coaches, except Tim Bogar. I should have known, but the world was spinning pretty quickly. I figured I'd keep a few and add a few. It was late in the off-season, and most coaches who were worth their salt were already hired. The coaches I put on my short list were quality people, but there weren't many whom I knew personally.

I wanted David Cone to be my pitching coach. He was knowledgeable, and I knew I could work with him. I offered him the job without an interview. He said he was having a child and didn't want to leave home. I then decided to invite my friends. *Shoot, they know as much baseball as anyone*, I thought.

My first choice was Billy Buckner. I thought, *Oh boy, how is that going to go over?* Billy had let that ball go through his legs to lose a World Series game in 1986. That didn't mean anything to me. I brought in Buck to interview with Ben Cherington and his staff. I should have hired him. Not doing so was one of the biggest mistakes I ever made. I wanted Buck to be my bench coach, but what Billy Buck lived, slept, and breathed was hitting. He had been a hitting coach with a great credential at Chicago, but one of the coaches I had been bequeathed was Dave Magadan, who I interviewed. I was hoping I wasn't going to like the interview, but I was told all the guys loved Dave, and I did, too. Dave turned out to be a really good person on the staff. One of the caveats to hiring Dave Magadan was that since he was the hitting coach, he was the *only one* to talk hitting.

337

He didn't want the players to be distracted from his ideology, and I understood that. And since Billy Buck was all about hitting, I didn't think Dave and Buck on the staff together would be compatible.

"Let's do it next year," I told Buck.

"What is most important to me," Larry Lucchino had said to me, "is that we just get through this year. Don't worry about anything. Just figure out who can play, who can't play, and who we should move forward with. Next year you can have your own coaches."

I didn't take Buck, and I didn't hire Tom Paciorek, either. Looking back, I needed both of them. It would have been a life-enriching experience to have two of my closest friends in uniform with me at the major league level. I will always regret not doing so.

Allard Baird, one of the older executives in the front office, recommended Alex Ochoa, who I brought in because I wasn't going to have a staff void of a Spanish-speaking coach. In those days, if a Japanese player came over, he was given a translator. But if a Latin player came from the Dominican Republic or Cuba or Venezuela, he'd have to fend for himself, and I always thought that was a bad situation. Alex was working in the Red Sox front office in the scouting department, and I was asked to interview him. I had had Alex in the minors with the Mets, and I loved him as a player and as a person.

I also brought in Jerry Royster. I needed a third-base coach and an infield instructor, and I had hired Jerry to manage the Lotte team in the Korean League. Jerry and I had played winter ball together, and he was a friend of mine. I liked everything about Jerry.

I figured the holdovers and a pitching coach I hired—Tim Bogar, Gary Tuck, and Bob McClure—would work with me, work hard, and pull on the same side of the rope, and if all worked out after a year, they'd stay on. I didn't want to put guys on the unemployment line, because the other teams had already signed their coaches. *Why do it if you don't have to?* I felt. I always believed I could make chicken salad out of what came out of the chicken's rear end. As it turned out, these three just happened to be the worst coaches I could have imagined having on my staff. I don't like to badmouth, but they deserve it. They were *never* a help. They never cared to be a help, and they were blatant about demonstrating their unwillingness to help. It got to be an almost unbearable situation.

One person I wanted as my bench coach was Frank Ramppen. He would have been perfect, but I didn't want to disrupt his life again if I didn't think this was going to be a long-term situation, so I took a pass on him, which was a *big* mistake. I agreed to let Tim Bogar remain on the staff, a truly stupid move on my part. I knew Bogar hated me. It was blatantly obviously from past experience. When I first took over as manager of the Mets, Tim was vying to be the shortstop, but I favored Rey Ordonez, and so he was traded to Houston. Also, Tim was best friends with Todd Hundley. I knew Tim felt I had inflicted a bad scar on his life, and so right up front I said to him, "Hey, Tim, they tell me you're a good coach and know what you're doing. I know the situation, and if you can bury the hatchet, I'd like to give you the opportunity of being the bench coach on this team."

It was between Billy Buck, Torey Lovullo, and Tim. Torey had shone in his interview, and everyone loved him, and in my interview, I loved Torey. But I had this stupid idea in the back of my mind that maybe I had done Tim wrong, and I was going to show him I was a bigger man than that, and I was going to do him right. Tim and I had a miserable coexistence. It wasn't even coexistence. It was just misery. Luckily for me, Boston has the famous North End where I spent many a night eating great Italian food and spending time with friends.

As a manager, you need to build a foundation with your coaches, and the foundation was terribly formed because I didn't stick to my guns and listen to Tom Landry, who had told me to get rid of all the old coaches and bring in my own people. Part of the biggest mistake of my life was thinking I could just handle anything and everything. *Shit, if I can't handle this, what's wrong with me?* But it turned out I *couldn't* handle it.

There were games when Bogar wouldn't even acknowledge my existence in the dugout. If I asked him a question, he turned deaf and dumb. It was ridiculous. Incredibly, he wasn't the worst of the coaches.

That honor belonged to Gary Tuck, the bullpen coach. Tuck was described to me as the greatest catching coach of all time. Gary Tuck was fired by the Yankees, twice. Somehow, they hired him back after he left Boston. When he was around me or the coaches, he took a vow of silence. He would never participate in any conversations or have any dealings with the other coaches about the team.

Ben Cherington had told me that Daniel Bard, who had been a fine reliever the year before, had to be a starter this year because he was marrying the daughter of the second-richest man in Kentucky, and to stay in baseball and have her be his wife, he couldn't make the money he needed to make as a reliever. It was the most ridiculous thing I'd ever heard, but Cherington told me this with a straight face and told me I didn't have a choice.

"He was a starter at UNC," he said. "He has a three-pitch repertoire, and he throws ninety-seven."

I started him. A day after Bard stunk it up, I was walking into my office, and Gary Tuck said to me, "This experiment has got to end. Bard's got to be a reliever."

"No," I said, "we're going to stick with him as a starter."

I knew Bard should be a reliever, but it wasn't debatable. Ben had laid down the law when I took the job. I figured, *What the fuck? He throws ninety-seven. He's had success in the past. I'll develop him into a good starter.* That didn't happen, and Gary Tuck decided that because I didn't take his advice, he would never talk to me again. So he didn't talk to me *ever again.* It was crazy. I'd talk to Tuck, and I wouldn't even get a grunt. And then about halfway through the season, Gary didn't show up at the ballpark, and I was told his wife had been rushed to the hospital and Gary was taking a leave of absence.

Gary lived near Fenway Park, and after one game I was riding my bike home and met him and his wife walking through the park. When I asked Cherington about Gary not being at the game, and his wife looking fine to me, I'd get a cockamamie story that his wife was waiting for tests. It was just as well that Tuck stayed away.

Tom Robson, my spring training guru and organizer, had retired. Robbie was my filing cabinet, the guy who always made sure that batting practice ran on time, that if things were moved, he would make sure everyone was on board so I wouldn't be distracted. If anyone needed a day off, they knew they could go to Robbie, and that message would get to me. But Robbie didn't want to go back to Japan in 2010. He was a bigger, older guy, and he was having health problems, and he retired, and I was missing him. Without Tom, I brought in Randy Niemann as an unofficial coach. He got in uniform when Tuck and later Bob McClure went missing.

The big thing was to find a pitching coach. After David Cone turned me down, I asked Orel Hershiser, who also said no. I interviewed Neil Allen, who was with the Mets, but I didn't feel Neil had enough experience. Charlie Hough, my good friend, had landed back with the Dodgers, and I didn't think uprooting him from California was the right thing to do. Allard Baird, who had recommended Alex Ochoa, also recommended Bob McClure. Knowing the front office favored McClure, I again thought I'd be a team player and hired him after a couple of interviews. Bob was super nice, a good guy, and laid-back. Everything was going just fine when one day he said to me, "There are only two things I hate about being the pitching coach. I don't like going to the mound to talk to pitchers, because every time I go out, it seems they do poorly; and I don't like to talk to Gary Tuck on the telephone calling down to the bullpen."

These were perhaps two of the more important duties of the pitching coach. And so I wound up going out to the mound, and when I asked Tim Bogar to call the bullpen, Tim said he didn't think doing that should be part of his responsibilities.

No one liked to talk to Tuck. If you called and told him to get someone up, all he said was, "Okay."

"Is he ready?"

"Yep."

There was no conversation from him. Bob McClure's wife had twins during the season, and he took five weeks off to be with them. Whenever I complained about coaches to Larry Lucchino, I was told, "Just stick it out and next year you'll have your own staff. Please, just stick it out."

I hardly talked to the other Red Sox owners. John Henry came down once during a Yankee game. There was a new rule where you could ask for a replay on a home run. Mark Teixeira hit a ball off the top edge of the Green Monster that bounced back onto the field. The umpire called it a home run. I was figuring out how to make a pitching change. No one on the field or in the dugout was objecting to the call, but on the replay, which wasn't asked for, it should have been a double, not a home run. And so John Henry came down to me after the game and said, "Why didn't you ask for a replay?"

I looked at him and said, "I should have, John."

He also stopped by my office after a game and asked if Jon Lester had thrown too many pitches in the previous game.

As for the players, I was getting along with some of them, but for others, there was no chance of our getting along. Why was that? Perhaps because I had taken the beer out of the clubhouse. Perhaps a couple had the Levinsons as agents bad-mouthing me. Perhaps because they were a weird, spoiled group of guys. Perhaps I wasn't the right guy to manage them.

During spring training, we were doing pop-up drills. I was asking them for the proper protocol for calling pop-ups. When the infielder goes out and the outfielder comes in, the outfielder makes the call and the infielder is silent. It's called pop-up priority. It's the same with the infielder coming in and catcher going out. If the infielder can catch it, the catcher gets out of the way. Mike Aviles, who was going to play shortstop, a nice little hard-nosed player, kept calling for the ball during the drill.

"Let's do it again," I said, "but it's pop-up priority. The shortstop says nothing. The outfielder makes the call."

After the third time Aviles ran toward the outfield and called for the ball, in a loud voice I said to him, "What are you, fucking deaf? This isn't a tough drill. The shortstop says nothing. The outfielder makes the call. What is your problem?"

I hit another pop-up, and this time Aviles didn't say anything and the outfielder caught the ball, so okay, good, now we've got it. Let's move on to the next drill. The next morning before the 7:30 workout, a few of the players came into my office saying that Mike Aviles was crying in his locker after practice the day before, and I had to apologize to him. Wow! This place was different.

Before one spring practice, I called Bill Belichick, who was staying on the East Coast of Florida, and asked him to come talk to the team. I had known Bill from the time he had a short stint with the Jets in 1998, when I was managing the Mets. He would come out to Shea Stadium and take batting practice with the team. He loved baseball. One morning at 4:00 a.m. Bill got in his car and drove across Alligator Alley to Fort Myers. Dressed in cutoff shorts and a t-shirt, he spoke to the team in his casual way.

"When I took over up in New England," he said, "there were a lot of photographs of the past and a lot of discussion of things they did in the past, but I told my players it was time to do things a new way. You should have an open mind to do things in a fresh and exciting manner. It will lead to success."

"That was really spot-on," I said to him. Because I hadn't prepped him as to what to say, and I thought his talk was exceptional. But it was met with a kind of thumbs-down by some of the players.

"That was really cool," I said to them.

"Eh. I guess," was the general response.

After the first week of spring training, Cherington kept asking me, "Hey, how is Kevin Youkilis doing?" It was his daily concern.

Finally, after he asked me again, I asked Ben, "What is it about Yuke?"

Ben told me what the problem was. A couple of the older pitchers had been told by a couple of reporters that Yuke was rumored to be the guy who had told the press about the pitchers drinking beer and eating chicken in the clubhouse.

"Wow," I said. "Why did he do that?"

"I don't know if it was Yuke," Ben said. "I don't know who did it, but they are pointing fingers at Yuke."

Halfway through spring training, I learned how unhealthy the environment was in the clubhouse when a few of the older pitchers came into my office to ask me to rearrange the seating. They didn't want to sit next to Youkilis. It was as ugly a situation as I ever experienced. I changed the seating and called Kevin into my office to let him know I was in on it. I apologized to him for not understanding what was happening from the first day I was in uniform.

"I'm here to help and figure out any way I can to straighten out the situation," I told him.

"You don't have to worry," he said. "I'll play hard whenever I'm out on the field, but I'm not going out to dinner with them, because they all suck."

During batting practice, while walking around the outfield I would take a poll to see how serious the situation was, and I was finding out it was pretty serious. I got together with Josh Beckett and John Lackey, who was rehabbing, and received an obstinate answer.

"Screw him. We know he did it, and that's the end of the story."

A few days later, the clubhouse emptied out earlier than usual. I asked the clubhouse guy where everyone was going. He said to the hotel for the meeting.

"What meeting is that?"

"Tewksbury called a meeting of the pitchers and Yuke," he said.

I found out that Bob Tewksbury, a retired pitcher who had been hired by the Sox to be our shrink and help players with mental adjustments, had rented a conference room to help straighten things out by letting everyone clear the air. The next day, when I arrived at the clubhouse, I called Yuke in. He had been in my office a couple times to complain about the situation.

"So, Yuke," I said, "how did it go last night?"

"It fucking sucks," he said.

I asked Beckett and he said, "It just made matters worse."

As spring training went on, it was evident that some of the things that were being asked of me and the team were not going to work. One was Daniel Bard. The other was Andrew Miller. Larry Lucchino told me he thought Miller was a really fine pitcher, that he had been with several organizations, but that no one had cracked the secret of his talents.

"I want to find a place for him on this team so we don't lose him," Larry said. If Miller wasn't on the opening-day roster, we were going to lose him. Miller's success became one of my priorities. Every session I'd go over and watch him to try to figure out the formula for success. The front office was suggesting things to him. Bob McClure was making suggestions. Our shrink coach, Bob Tewksbury, was also giving him advice.

About halfway through spring training, I didn't think Miller was making any progress. After talking with Andrew, I determined that one of the reasons was that he was getting too much advice. One guy wanted him to go over his head with his windup. Someone else wanted him to stand on the left side of the rubber. He seemed really confused. After one practice, I made an open forum with all the coaches to meet in the video room to get out in the open what everyone thought. I thought it strange that Tewksbury was there. I just listened to what everyone was saying, and there was a lot. When my team psychiatrist started talking mechanics, I got a little frustrated. It was late in the day, and we were in the middle of a debate that wasn't going to get solved, so I just said, "Here's what we're going to do. Andrew is never going to throw another pitch out of the windup. He's only going to throw from the stretch. We're going to get him on the comfortable side of the rubber. I'm going to eliminate the leg kick, and he's going to throw the ball forward to the best of his ability and try to make our team."

There was silence in the room when Tewksbury said, "Oh, you can't do that. You can't tell him what to do."

"That's good," I said, "but *you* can't tell *me* what to do."

It was the last time I met with Tewksbury, and it was the last time Andrew Miller threw out of a windup. I tried to simplify everything. I told him how much I respected his ability to advance the ball forward, with his arm and his six-foot-seven-inch body and long legs seeming to get in the way of progress. Andrew bought into it, he made the team and had a pretty good season. He signed a darn good contract after that. I was happy the meeting turned out the way it did.

I decided we should do something together out of uniform to try to bond a bit. My assistant, Zack Minasian, rented out a big, brand-new Bass Pro Shop. It had a lake in the back, a shooting range, bows and arrows, and a party room. A number of the players, especially Josh Beckett and John Lester, were great outdoorsmen. I thought it would be cool to get groups together, the rookies against the veterans, the pitchers against the infielders, and have a fishing competition and, at the end, a karaoke competition. The wives would be there, and it would be a family event. Clay Buchholz was a gamer. He wanted to win at the all the games, and he did. It was a spectacular event, a fun night, and it only cost me $15k. Jose Iglesias surprised everyone with his ability to hit the high note in karaoke. It was the first year of the new JetBlue Park. It had a replica Green Monster in left field, and I think every friend I have got a free ticket to one of the games. The time passed quickly, and we were ready to start the season.

We opened the season on the road, lost three in Detroit and two in Toronto, and started with a 1–5 record—not the start I was hoping for. We won our home opener against the Rays 12–2 on April 12, then had a three-game winning streak stopped when Daniel Bard lost 1–0 on an unearned run.

Prior to that Sunday game, I did an interview with Tom Caron. He had a Sunday night show on NESN that would recap the prior week's games. Tom came down and taped the show before the Sunday game. One of the questions was, "What is it about Youkilis that he is having such a tough start? It's not Yuke. He's not walking. He's striking out. He's not driving the ball."

At the time, Yuke was dealing with a back situation. And, of course, he was dealing with the enmity of the pitchers, though this was being kept from the press and the public.

"He's struggling a little, physically and mentally," I said. "He's not able to give his best effort."

The show aired on Sunday night. I didn't watch it. The next game was an 11:00 a.m. game. On Patriot's Day, I was riding my bike along the Charles River as the sun was coming up. I rode my bike for about an hour every day we had a home game, to think in a peaceful manner about my lineup and the other things I had to worry about. When I was pulling into Fenway Park, my phone rang. It was Ben Cherington.

"Whatever you said last night didn't sit too well with Yuke," he said. "His agent is in an uproar."

I do a lot of interviews, and when I'm done, I forget them.

"Ben," I said, "I don't know what you're talking about. I didn't talk to anyone last night. Come down and we'll talk about it."

I got off the bike and went into my little 12 X 12 converted closet they called my office, and I took a shower. As I was coming out of the shower, Yuke was standing in my office.

"Hey, Yuke," I said, "Ben just told me I said something last night that you didn't appreciate. I'm sorry, but I didn't do any interviews last night."

"Fuck," he said. "Of course you did an interview. My agent texted me what you said."

"What did I say?"

Yuke told me what I'd said. *Oh,* I thought, *I get it.* "Hey, Kev," I said. "I didn't mean anything offensive by it."

"Well," he said, "it's the worst thing that anybody has ever said about me in my professional career."

"I apologize," I said. "I was trying to protect you."

Meanwhile, as I was getting dressed, one of the reporters went over to Dustin Pedroia's locker. Dustin hadn't seen the show, and the reporter ambushed him in his locker by asking him, "What did you think about Valentine criticizing Yuke's physical and mental ability?"

"He must think he's in Japan," Dustin said. "We don't do that around here."

It became a BIG situation, with Pedroia criticizing the manager and Yuke being upset with the manager. Cherington and the organization used the incident to trade Yuke. It's what *they* had planned. Youkilis had a clause in his contract that guaranteed him another year, and according to everyone I talked to, they didn't want to have to sign him again. Furthermore, Cherington and the front office knew what had transpired between Yuke and the pitchers, but that situation was never going to be made public. If it was, the person who really spilled the beans would have had to be revealed. The front office and the press conveniently were laying it all on Youkilis.

I got all this in bits and pieces. Not that I cared, but I always wanted to know who did tell the press, and from what I had heard, it wasn't Youkilis.

Yuke got traded on June 24, and I took the blame. On July 5, at the All-Star break, our record was 43–43. I went to the ownership during the break to alert them that my documentary was scheduled to preview on July 11 in one of the oldest movie houses in New England, the Coolidge Corner Theater in Brookline, Massachusetts. Larry again said, "No problem." The film's release date had been planned prior to my accepting the job, and I had made Larry aware of it in my interview. Nevertheless, on the day of the film's preview, I was told by Tom Werner, one of the team owners, that I could attend the screening but could not grant any interviews, nor ever make a comment about the documentary. I was executive producer of the film, but I was asked to not speak. Really?

The season was being challenged in many ways. On August 2, we were 53–53, at .500 for the last time. On August 14, a group of players led by Kelly Shoppach sent a text to team owner John Henry that was very critical of me. The text was sent from Adrián González's cell phone, but Adrián said Shoppach had used his phone to do it. The Red Sox had traded Shoppach away in a prior season because their star catcher, Jason Varitek, couldn't stand him, but after Varitek retired they brought him back. Shoppach was a real bad actor. Kelly Fucking Shoppach was a clubhouse lawyer, and he had friends on Podunk Radio, and he would leak what was going on in the clubhouse to them, adding to the craziness. Usually, it stays in the clubhouse and you try to make it be less than crazy. Once it gets out, it becomes more crazy. Shoppach was just a bad dude, and he certainly had it in for me. Something went on there, and I was blindsided.

It was great getting to know some of the guys on the team. Adrián González was easy to get to know because he talked all the time. During games he liked to talk strategy. He talked about whether a pitcher should add a new pitch, whether the manager of the other team was using the right strategy, whether the music at the ballpark was being played at the right volume. He was hyperaware of everything that was going on around him. A lot of guys didn't want to hear him and got tired of him talking, but I always liked it.

I got along extremely well with Jacoby Ellsbury, whom I felt bad for. I thought he was always out of his element and was trying to keep up with the Joneses. The year before, when he had his spectacular MVP-type season, I heard that he always had his personal trainer with him. His personal trainer gave him massages, and he'd whisper in his ear like the Dog Whisperer. Ben told me that he was banning Jacoby's trainer from the clubhouse. Other players were going to him, and the Red Sox trainers didn't like them going to someone else. They felt it was an insult. So the trainer wasn't allowed in spring training, and Jacoby didn't perform very well. He went from MVP to a platoon player. In batting practice, he no longer hit home runs. He was a shell of what I had seen of him the year before.

I loved him anyway, and I took him under my wing. I tried to do the same with Carl Crawford, who was another ostracized guy on the team. Carl never quite fit in.

I always felt that David Ortiz and I were on the same page. David always had my back. If someone hit a home run off our pitcher, he would say, "Don't worry about it. We'll get it back." At the start of the season, there was talk in the front office about not bringing David back the next year, but halfway through July his numbers were as good as anyone in the league. He was having an MVP season when he hurt his Achilles tendon running the bases on July 20 and went on the disabled list.

Dustin Pedroia was the most incredible player I was ever in uniform with. He played hurt most of the year and had to be told to go on the disabled list. He was the first one in the clubhouse, and he treated me with great respect. I knew he had a special relationship with Francona, but we bonded when his dad told him I'd played in a Babe Ruth League championship in the same stadium he played his high school games.

We were holding our own until Big Papi got hurt in late July. It was obvious how much we needed him and missed him, but I kept saying, "David, come back when you're ready. Your career is too important. If you injure yourself further at your age, you won't get a contract from anyone. Make sure you're a hundred percent when you come back."

David finally came back on August 24 and went 2 for 4. He was missed every day he wasn't in the lineup. The next day, I was watching ESPN on the flat-screen TV in my office, and I saw something about a possible trade between the Dodgers and the Red Sox. It was time for the national anthem, so I left the office and entered the clubhouse. Adrián González was standing there.

"What are you doing?" he said to me.

"Just going out, ready to win a game," I said.

"No," he said, "what are you doing putting my name in the lineup? I just got traded."

I had seen the name scrolling at the bottom of the screen, but I figured it had to be another González.

"Oh no," I said, "that has to be a rumor."

"No," Adrián said, "my agent called me and said the Dodger plane was coming to pick up me and Carl and Josh and Punto."

I had them in the lineup, too. "Come on, Adrián," I said. "Enough of this talk." I didn't want to be the only guy not in on a joke, so I said, "Let's go! We'll talk later."

The national anthem was playing, and after "the rocket's red glare," I was standing on the top step of the dugout. One of Cherington's assistants, Brian O'Halloran, pulled on my uniform to get my attention. I went down the runway, and he said to me, "You have to take González, Crawford, and Punto out of the lineup. We just traded them."

I wanted to say, "You've got to be shitting me." I sprinted back into the clubhouse. I needed a new lineup card to take to the umpires at home plate. Four players got undressed and were taken to the airport to board the Dodger plane. David Ortiz, rightfully so, decided not to risk injury, since we were no longer playing to win.

After the game, Ben came into my office and said: "It isn't about winning anymore, it's about the process."

We were left with one of the worst lineups to ever be called a major league lineup. Our record at the time of the trade was 60–67. For the rest of the season we went 9–26. We lost 12 of our final 13 games to finish at 69–93.

The 100th-year celebration of Fenway Park was over. There were memorable moments before games, when so many great players from the past returned to the ovations of the Sox fans. The fans were great. It was an honor to be there for this special season, but the games were hard to take. Sam Kennedy, CEO of the Red Sox, and his staff were phenomenal to work with. Having Luis Tiant befriend me and stand beside me made it a special and valued experience. I wish I could have done more.

On October 4, 2012, I was officially fired. So much for doing what I could this year so I could have my own coaching staff next year.

After the Red Sox and I parted ways, I didn't manage again.

CHAPTER 35

After Baseball

I returned to Stamford and settled in for what I decided would be life after baseball. Within weeks of my arrival, while working at my restaurant and helping to build a film company and sports academy, I got a phone call from Mike Larobina, legal counsel for Sacred Heart University. Michael had been legal counsel for the City of Stamford when I worked in the Pavia administration. He said the president of the school wanted to talk to me. Having no idea what he wanted, I put the meeting off for about a week.

Finally, the president and I met, and he asked if I would be interested in being the executive director of athletics at Sacred Heart. I told him he had the wrong man, that my college education was never finished, and that my film company was about to debut a documentary criticizing the NCAA. His response was that he wanted Sacred Heart to be the first place to show the film, since higher education was the place for dissenting opinions. That got my attention. Within a week and without a contract, I accepted the offer to help create a Division I model for athletics. He truly gave me a blank canvas, and I set out to do the best job I could.

The results over the past eight years, as the executive director of athletics at Sacred Heart University, include the expansion of the athletic department personnel. The women's coaches' pay has been increased to equal the men's. The number of student-athletes has increased by 40 percent. We have added many D-I teams, and built new facilities with scoreboards for football, lacrosse, soccer, and track. Now, with over a thousand student-athletes, I am confident that, with our newly established academic center and our strength and conditioning center and program, along with our expanded medical training facility, our students are prepared properly, with their health protected. I also fulfilled the wishes of the president by helping to build a $23 million Bobby Valentine Health & Recreation Center, with the balcony to be named after my mother Grace. Fundraising was needed for all of these projects, and the SHU community has teamed with many of my personal friends to make the experience for the student-athletes one to enjoy and remember.

When the Sacred Heart opportunity materialized, my Stamford restaurant was in its thirty-third year of business in the same location. I was exploring an opportunity to expand my brand into a larger venue. I was also considering expanding my sports academy, and planning to spend the summer with a youth baseball team that would play fifty-five games in sixty days throughout the southern United States.

When I returned home from Japan in 2010, I added the title of "movie producer" to my long and varied résumé. One of the young filmmakers from *The Zen of Bobby V,* Andrew Muscato, approached me about starting a documentary production company together. We decided to call the venture Makuhari Media, after the hometown of the Chiba Lotte Marines. Andrew and I have produced numerous critically acclaimed short and feature-length documentaries that have been seen all over the world. I am proud of all the work Makuhari Media has done over the past decade-plus, but a handful of projects are particularly close to my heart.

Branca's Pitch is a profile of my late father-in-law and Brooklyn Dodgers great Ralph Branca. *Ballplayer: Pelotero* is a gritty and honest look into the lives of teenage baseball players from the Dominican Republic with big-league dreams. One of those ballplayers, Miguel Sanó, would go on to become an All-Star third baseman for the Minnesota Twins. When it premiered in 2013, *Schooled: The Price of College Sports* was in the vanguard of reframing the conversation about amateurism and the business of college sports. And as of this writing, Academy Award-winner Peter Farrelly is working on a movie adaptation of *The Greatest Beer Run Ever*, which began as a short documentary Makuhari Media produced with Pabst Blue Ribbon for Veterans Day 2015.

My sports academy, with the help of a dear friend and partner, Pablo Stalman, and Frank Ramppen, has moved into a new 40,000-square-foot facility.

My restaurant has moved into a 30,000-square-foot facility. And to think, in 1980, the 2,200-square-foot building that housed the original Bobby V's, which opened with one television at the bar (against the wishes of my banker, who thought there would be no essential turnover of tables if customers had access to TV), has expanded to an operation with over two hundred TVs, two of them eighteen feet diagonal.

I have been lucky to partner with Sportech Venues in two restaurant locations, one in downtown Stamford and one in Windsor Locks, Connecticut. It amazes me when I think that the expansion goal in 1980 was limited to finding room for a Pac-Man and Ms. Pac-Man table. Over the years, we've expanded to seven different locations in four different states and continued to be referred to as the pioneer in the sports bar industry. It not only gives me great pride to have a very difficult business sustain itself through decades of economic and social turmoil, but it also gives me great satisfaction in the friendships that I have kept over all these years.

EPILOGUE

I have had the good health to continue to ride my bike, walk my dogs, and ski with some of the best people on some of the greatest mountains around the world.

I reference Tommy Lasorda often in this book, and with his passing on January 7, 2021, my life has concluded a wonderful chapter. Alongside Tommy in heaven are my mom and dad; my father-in-law and mother-in-law, Ralph and Ann Branca; and many other family members and friends who not only got to share this lucky life of mine, but who also understood that none of this could have happened without them.

Here on earth, my wife Mary, son Bobby, my big brother Joe and his wife Pat, and so many other family members and friends hopefully still enjoy sharing the experience.

I am so grateful to all of you.

THE TEAHOUSE OF
THE AUGUST MOON

ACKNOWLEDGMENTS

I'd like to thank Brian Balluff, Tom Chiappetta, and Andrew McAleer for their help on this book.

—Bobby Valentine

I would like to thank Sebastian Sorrentino for hooking up Bobby and me. Also, thanks to those who were instrumental in my career: Nick D'Incecco, Marty Appel, Roger Kahn, and especially Jim Bouton, who was like a brother to me. Finally, thanks to my agent of thirty-five years, Frank Weimann, and my expert editor, Jacob Hoye, and Robert Bidinotto, who crossed the t's and dotted the i's. I'm a lucky guy.

—Peter Golenbock

THE CAST

in order of appearance

Sakini	Bob Valentine
Sargeant Gregovich	Bob Kuchta
Colonel Wainright Purdy III	Marty Coleman
Captain Fisby	Jack Crisp
Old Woman	Betsy Bennett
Old Woman's Daughter	Nancee Hwa
Lady Astor	???
Ancient Man	Danny Rapp
Mr. Hokaida	Tim O'Brien
Mr. Omura	Melvin Dixon
Mr. Sumata	Dave Greenblum
Mr. Sumata's Father	Ricky Sprague
Mr. Seiko	Steve Messenger
Miss Higa-Jiga	Kathy Johnson
Mr. Keora	Jim Wirth
Mr. Oshira	Dave Wohl

Villagers: Jim Federici, Marc Crapsey, Tenny Flowers, Doug Babington, Mike Bartholomew, Linda Levey, Linda Manaly, Elaine Anderson, Judy Kahn, Robin Nathan, Kane Cadwell, Jave Covner, Karen Rubenstein, Linda Burdette.

Geisha Girls: Leslie Coleman, Lynn Jenkins, Gerri Henretty, Lisa Kline, Florry Weitzner, Becky Weimer, Roxy Sisson, Barbara Bullen.

Lotus Blossom	Joyce Manger
Captain McLean	Andy Cassel

ABOUT THE AUTHORS

Bobby Valentine was the fifth player chosen in the 1968 draft by the Los Angeles Dodgers, but his major league playing career was cut short by a broken leg several years later. He began his managerial career in 1985 with the Texas Rangers, before going on to manage the Chiba Lotte Marines; the New York Mets, whom he took to the 2000 World Series; and the Boston Red Sox. A second stint with the Marines resulted in the team winning the Japan Series and Asia Series in 2005. In 2002, he was awarded the Branch Rickey Award for his donations to and personal work with survivors of the 9/11 attacks. In 2018, the Emporor of Japan bestowed upon him the Order of the Rising Sun. He has also worked as an analyst for ESPN. Currently, he is the executive director of athletics at Sacred Heart University, the proprietor of the Bobby Valentine Sports Academy, and an owner of Makuhari Media, a company that produces sports documentaries. He was raised and resides in Stamford, Connecticut.

Peter Golenbock, who also grew up in Stamford, is one of the nation's best-known sports authors. He has written ten *New York Times* bestsellers, including *The Bronx Zoo* (with Sparky Lyle), *Number 1* (with Billy Martin), *Balls* (with Graig Nettles), *George: The Poor Little Rich Man Who Built the Yankee Empire,* and *House of Nails* (with Lenny Dykstra). He lives in St. Petersburg, Florida.